The New Deal in South Florida

The Florida History and Culture series

Florida A&M University, Tallahassee
Florida Atlantic University, Boca Raton
Florida Gulf Coast University, Ft. Myers
Florida International University, Miami
Florida State University, Tallahassee
New College of Florida, Sarasota
University of Central Florida, Orlando
University of Florida, Gainesville
University of North Florida, Jacksonville
University of South Florida, Tampa
University of West Florida, Pensacola

THE NEW DEAL
IN SOUTH FLORIDA

Design, Policy, and Community Building, 1933–1940

EDITED BY JOHN A. STUART AND JOHN F. STACK JR.

Foreword by Raymond O. Arsenault and Gary R. Mormino, series editors

UNIVERSITY PRESS OF FLORIDA

Gainesville   Tallahassee   Tampa   Boca Raton   Pensacola
Orlando   Miami   Jacksonville   Ft. Myers   Sarasota

13 12 11 10 09 08 6 5 4 3 2 1

Library of Congress Cataloging-in-Publication Data

The New Deal in south Florida : design, policy, and community

building, 1933-1940 / edited by John A. Stuart and John F. Stack Jr. ;

foreword by Raymond O. Arsenault, Gary R. Mormino, series editors.

p. cm. — (The Florida history and culture series)

Includes bibliographical references and index.

ISBN 978-0-8130-3191-0 (alk. paper)

1. New Deal, 1933-1939—Florida. 2. Florida—Politics and

government—20th century. 3. Florida—Social conditions—20th

century. 4. Florida—Social policy. 5. Florida—Economic policy.

6. Public works—Florida—History—20th century.

7. Architecture—Political aspects—Florida—History—20th century.

8. Housing—Florida—History—20th century. 9. Community life—

Florida—History—20th century. 10. Landscape changes—Florida—

History—20th century. I. Stuart, John A. II. Stack, John F.

F316.N49 2008

975.9'062—dc22   2007027920

The University Press of Florida is the scholarly publishing

agency for the State University System of Florida, comprising

Florida A&M University, Florida Atlantic University, Florida

Gulf Coast University, Florida International University, Florida

State University, New College of Florida, University of Central

Florida, University of Florida, University of North Florida,

University of South Florida, and University of West Florida.

University Press of Florida

15 Northwest 15th Street

Gainesville, FL 32611–2079

www.upf.com

TO OUR PARENTS

The late John F. Stack

The late Margaret Mahoney Stack

Wayne A. Stuart

Joanne M. Stuart

Contents

Illustrations

Sources (Abbreviations)

Farm Security Administration/Office of War Information Collection,
    Prints and Photographs Division, Library of Congress (FSA/OWI)
Federal Emergency Relief Administration (FERA)
Florida Photographic Collection, State Library and Archives of Florida,
    Tallahassee (FPC)
Historical Museum of Southern Florida (HMSF)
National Archives and Records Administration, College Park, Md.
    (NARA)
Public Works Administration (PWA)
Works Progress Administration (WPA)

Color Plates (follow page 140)

1. Coral Gables Women's Club and Library, WPA, 1937
2. Postcard of the Overseas Highway to Key West, PWA, 1939
3. "Negro migratory workers by a juke joint," photo by
    Marion Post Wolcott, 1941
4. Postcard from the early twentieth century
5. Detail of central scene in Denman Fink's *Law Guides Florida
    Progress*, 1941

Figures

Foreword

The New Deal in South Florida: Design, Policy, and Community Building, 1933–1940 is the latest volume of a series devoted to the study of Florida history and culture. During the past half-century, the burgeoning population and increased national and international visibility of Florida have sparked a great deal of popular interest in the state's past, present, and future. As a favorite destination of countless tourists and as the new home for millions of retirees and other migrants, modern Florida has become a demographic, political, and cultural bellwether. Unfortunately, the quantity and quality of the literature on Florida's distinctive heritage and character have not kept pace with the Sunshine State's enhanced status. In an effort to remedy this situation—to provide an accessible and attractive format for the publication of Florida-related books—the University Press of Florida has established the Florida History and Culture Series.

The University Press of Florida is committed to the creation of an eclectic but carefully crafted set of books that will provide the field of Florida studies with a new focus that will encourage Florida researchers and writers to consider the broader implications and context of their work. The series includes standard academic monographs, works of synthesis, memoirs, and anthologies. And, while the series features books of historical interest, authors researching Florida's environment, politics, literature, and popular or material culture are encouraged to submit their manuscripts as well. Each book offers a distinct personality and voice, but the ultimate goal of the series is to foster a broad sense of community and collaboration among Florida scholars.

The publication of *The New Deal in South Florida* is timely. Each new generation learns to appreciate the New Deal on its own terms. To aging residents at Century Villages and the Hebrew Home for the Aged, the New Deal evokes memories of youthful idealism and the heroic presidency of Franklin Delano Roosevelt. To high school history students in Miami-Dade County, the New Deal—often confused with the Square Deal and the New Frontier—evokes a long list of alphabet agencies to be memorized. Daily, however, South Floridians are reminded of the New Deal's imprint and legacy: the Orange Bowl, the Coral Gables Library and Community Center, South Beach Elementary and Miami Beach Senior High School, Liberty Square, and hundreds of other projects ranging from public parks to post office murals.

The New Deal in South Florida beckons readers to appreciate one of the most creative and fertile periods in American history. A popular mythology holds that dream states and magical cities are immune to history's dark side. The Great Depression, however, spared neither Florida nor Miami, but out of the social and economic upheaval emerged some remarkably imaginative and enduring responses. John A. Stuart and John F. Stack Jr. vividly demonstrate how the New Deal changed the cultural, political, and physical landscape of South Florida. The authors have edited a compelling and engaging book that should find a wide and grateful audience.

The New Deal in South Florida offers readers some fascinating portraits of 1930s life in South Florida. Several essays address the social ferment that spawned photographic journalism and mural art. The New Deal displayed and magnified populist impulses. While not everyone appreciated or admired post office murals or photographic depictions of jook joints in Belle Glade, almost everyone approved of the ambitious construction or reconstruction of public parks. The Civilian Conservation Corps (CCC) left a rich legacy in today's Royal Palm State Park, Matheson Hammock, and Fairchild Tropical Garden. Historians and African American leaders continue to debate the intentions and consequences of Liberty Square, one of America's first federally sponsored housing projects.

The New Deal almost never happened because of an event in South Florida. In a February 1933 visit to Miami's Bayfront Park, Giuseppe

Zangara, an Italian anarchist, attempted to assassinate the president-elect. Roosevelt survived, and the New Deal was born. One of most original essays draws upon letters written by South Florida clergymen to President Franklin D. Roosevelt, 1935–36. Frustrated by the enormity of problems facing Americans, the president asked clergymen for advice. Their responses represent a poignant but hopeful portrait of Florida.

The New Deal lives!

Gary R. Mormino and Raymond Arsenault
Series co-editors

Acknowledgments

We wish to thank the National Endowment for the Arts for its generous "Heritage and Preservation" grant. Program director Mark Robbins and program specialist Susan Begley offered expert guidance during what turned out to be a very long process. We also wish to thank Raymond Tiechman at the Franklin D. Roosevelt Presidential Library; C. Ford Peatross at the Library of Congress; Eugene Morris, specialist in civil records at the National Archives in College Park, Md.; Dorothy Jenkins Fields, founder of the Black Archives in Miami; Dawn Hugh and Rebecca Smith at the Historical Museum of Southern Florida; Grisel Choter, George Faust, Renee Pierce, and in particular, John Shipley and Sam Boldrick at the Helen Muir Florida Collection in the Main Library of the Miami-Dade Public Library System; Craig Stewart Likness at the University of Miami's Richter Library; Althea "Vicki" Silvera, head of special collections at Florida International University; and staff members of the Claude Pepper Library at Florida State University and of the State Library and Archives of Florida. The Jack D. Gordon Institute for Public Policy and Citizenship Studies at Florida International University and, in particular, Elaine Dillashaw, Kimberly Shaw, Pedro Carvalho, and Hector Cadavid have assisted us from writing the grant proposal to compiling the bibliography.

Colleagues and friends who have helped us in innumerable ways include Adolfo Albaisa, Robin Bachin, Graham Barnfield, Mary Agnes Beach, Nathaniel Quincy Belcher, Gregory Bush, Jeff Donnelly, Adam Drisin, Alice Friedman, Judy Gallion, Alison Isenberg, Pierre Koenig, Jean-Francois LeJeune, Sarah Lowe, Michael and Jane Marion, Aristides James

Millas, Raymond Mohl, Kristopher Musumano, Arva Moore Parks, Barbara Robinson, Allan Shulman, Jewel Stern, and Kim Tanzer. John Stuart offers particular thanks to John Stack for his generous collegiality and abundant intellectual contributions, which have enriched the process of writing and editing the book in too many ways to enumerate. He also extends a heart-felt debt of gratitude to his life partner, Joel M. Hoffman.

We have benefited from many thoughtful exchanges with our contributing authors and from the gracious and enthusiastic support of Professor Gary Mormino of the University of South Florida, the dean of Florida historians. Dr. Thomas Breslin, former director of sponsored research at FIU, Dr. Mark B. Rosenberg, former FIU provost and now chancellor of higher education for Florida, and deans William G. McMinn and Juan Antonio Bueno were particularly supportive along the way. Our editor, Meredith Morris-Babb, endorsed this project from its inception. We have benefited from her wise advice through every stage of the book's long journey.

Finally, the late Jack D. Gordon, founding director of the Gordon Institute and a major figure in Florida politics for more than four decades, urged us to study the public policy dimensions of the New Deal in south Florida. We gratefully acknowledge his interest in the enormous and continuing impact of the New Deal as a pivotal event in the lifeblood of south Florida. Senator Gordon's legacy lives on in the progressive policies he shaped throughout his long and distinguished career in public service.

ONE

The New Deal in South Florida

JOHN F. STACK JR. AND JOHN A. STUART

This book examines some of the most significant social and economic difficulties confronting south Florida during the 1930s and explores the interven-
tions proposed and carried out by members of Franklin Delano Roosevelt's
New Deal administration. In the broadest sense, New Dealers set out to
regain national economic strength by reordering the national landscape and
its resources during the Depression. In order to grapple with the complexities that such a reorganization entailed, this collection of essays looks across
the disciplinary lines of political science and design history to uncover how
the physical characteristics and qualities of life in south Florida were permanently transformed by the impact of New Deal building programs. There
has been much recent scholarly interest in exploring the New Deal in the
South.[1] In south Florida, the tensions were many and involved pressures
upon traditional agricultural interests from the growing urban populations;
the conflicting needs of young working populations with families and growing numbers of retirees; the challenges to ideas of race and community
brought about by sprawling city neighborhoods; the efforts to develop a city
reliant upon tourism that attracts new residents through community services
and amenities; and the difficulties of balancing an image of south Florida as
the fast-paced and edgy winter playground of Jai-Alai, boat races, air shows,
and dog and horse racing with that of serene natural beauty, parks, and
beaches.

The essays presented here explore ways that government, economy, and
visual culture were embraced by the New Deal in its efforts to help south
Florida on its path to become a portrait of a new urban South and, more

generally, a bellwether of postindustrial America.[2] All the New Deal agencies, including the Civil Works Administration (CWA), Federal Emergency Relief Administration (FERA), the Works Progress Administration (WPA), the Public Works Administration (PWA), and the Civilian Conservation Corps (CCC), had lasting impacts upon the physical and political landscape of south Florida. Although historian Jordan Schwarz and others have observed that the New Deal was focused on national transformations, it did so largely through attempts to find more humane and positive approaches to solving problems at the local level by rethinking the relationships between the federal and state governments.[3]

The most important recent contribution to New Deal studies, however, reinforces our own inclinations to join investigations of the built environment with those of the history of politics. This was *Building New Deal Liberalism* by Jason Scott Smith, a historian of political economy. Smith argues that the New Deal public works programs proved to be "an extraordinarily successful method of state-sponsored economic development" that shaped the nation's physical and economic resources in ways it had never before experienced. Smith outlines some of the difficulties that arise when evaluating the impact of the construction of public works during this period. He notes that by "directing so much attention to construction, [New Dealers] supported an economic sector (the construction and building trades) long noted as a bastion of white male employment and discrimination against African Americans and women."[4] In south Florida, an area known to have exceedingly diverse minority populations, these New Deal strategies to engage in construction impact the community in ways that are often difficult to untangle.

While south Florida in the 1930s is largely considered a place of enormous private development through hotels, apartment buildings, and private homes, many of these developments were made possible, located, and ultimately transformed by New Deal policies and decisions. The New Deal legacy in the region remains surprisingly vibrant through evidence of private construction and the existence of large public works projects, some of which, like the Overseas Highway to Key West, were among the largest in the nation. In the 1930s, New Deal initiatives helped to develop a tourist economy in the region, established public housing and laid out patterns of urban growth for decades to come, and offered approaches—albeit some-times questionable by today's standards—to appreciate and control Florida's fragile ecosystem. New Dealers struggled with many issues that remain central to South Florida's contemporary policies: How does south Florida develop a sustainable identity in a culture of transience and disposability? What are the intended and unintended consequences of policies that at-tempt to create permanent communities in the expanding global economies of regional and global tourism?[5] What role does diversity play in building community and citizenship? Historically, attempts to come to grips with these concerns have powerful influences over the policies and have acceler-ated regional patterns of change in economics, commerce, neighborhoods, community building, and other unexpected ways. This story enriches our understanding of the history of the built environment in the region and pro-vides a commentary on the power of public policies to affect a region and to impact its future trajectory for growth and development.

Florida and the New Deal

Although the South was considered by Roosevelt to be the "Nation's No. 1 economic problem" during the New Deal, Florida did fairly well when compared to its northerly neighbors.[6] In fact, the per capita expenditures of the WPA were the highest in Region 3, which consisted of Alabama, Florida, Georgia, Kentucky, Mississippi, North Carolina, South Carolina, Tennessee, and Virginia. It was third in per capita expenditures of the PWA after Virginia and South Carolina.[7] Some of the success Florida enjoyed in acquiring New Deal attention may be attributed to the efforts of Florida senator Claude Pepper, who was arguably one of the most prominent sup-porters of the administration and FDR's close personal friend and ally.[8]

Other reasons for the success of Florida, and more specifically south Florida, however, may be found in its recent history as a region with an economic engine bound to the construction industry. In just a little more than three decades, Miami and the surrounding areas had developed from a one-stop, end-of-the line destination for Flagler's Florida East Coast Railroad, with fewer than 1,000 residents, into an active hub primarily of real estate speculation and construction, tourism, and air and sea transportation. Throughout the land-boom years of the mid-1920s and the inevitable bust of 1926 (and devastating hurricanes of 1926 and 1928) that followed, south Florida provided a playground for the rich and poor as well as a resting place for retirees who wished to enjoy the warm weather unimpeded by the harsh realities of national politics unless they brought greater personal wealth. As the historian Gregory Bush noted, south Florida became something of a national poster child of the speculative real estate "boom" and its seemingly inevitable economic consequences, the "bust."[9] During the early twentieth century, a new urban south Florida distinguished itself from the "old South," which was characterized by the agricultural economy and social norms found in enormous swathes of the state and up into Georgia, Alabama, and Mississippi.[10] Noted historian Gary Mormino points out that the economy of 1920s Florida was tied to the proximity of the land to the beaches and the ocean. This, he observes, became central to popular characterizations of the region and later of the entire state.[11]

Of all the calculated efforts to transform this marshy physical and entrepreneurial landscape of south Florida into a sustainable and thriving community based upon the tourist industry, none were more successful and arguably more problematic than those sponsored by the New Deal. Historians David Colburn and Lance deHaven-Smith stress that "Roosevelt and the New Deal provided the lifeline that kept Florida afloat during the 1930s. In particular, the Agricultural Adjustment Act provided crucial assistance for financially desperate farmers and grove owners. . . . Despite Roosevelt's leadership and aid from the federal government, however, Florida continued to suffer greatly during the Depression, and, while the economy began to stabilize in 1936, no real signs of prosperity were in sight as late as 1939."[12] By the time of the 1931 election, Florida had a reputation for extending its speculative interests to politics. Many members of Miami's business elite were supporting Newton D. Baker for the Democratic presidential candidacy. Some accounts report that "trainloads" of money were needed to coerce Florida's "political panhandlers" into shifting their electoral votes for the governor of New York.[13] This strategy, which won Roosevelt the region and the state, began a strong and often frustrating relationship between the federal government and south Florida based upon the flow of money into the area and the signs of economic recovery and community stability that resulted. It was, however, the policy of the New Deal to spend federal money to expand existing regional economies, and local leaders often guided federal officials to specific projects. In south Florida, this federal patronage propelled the growth in tourism and construction and emboldened local leaders to promote antigovernment views on the economy and unequal racial and social policies that often conflicted with national ideals.

Growth in south Florida differed from that in other parts of the state and from the southern United States. Migratory and highly skilled families of pickers and packers moved seasonally from south Florida up the coast to New Jersey. This meant that south Florida was not greatly helped by federal programs geared to relieve unemployment in agriculture.[14] Most of the region's unemployed laborers were from the building, tourist, and transportation industries. Recent literature on the New Deal in the South, including studies by Douglas Smith, Elna Green, and Roger Biles, do not consider the region in any significant way.[15] The Depression-era problems that arose in south Florida anticipated many of the concerns over community identity, aging populations, transience, and employment later faced by coastal tourist regions of the United States.

The large aging population in the area required concentrated efforts by charitable organizations to coordinate with agencies supplying federal aid. Likewise the early importance of air traffic in the region, which was required to connect the entire length of the state with the rest of the United States and allowed for international travel to Cuba and other nearby foreign countries, highlighted air for the development of the region's airports and seaports.[16] Problems of administering funds throughout the state were compounded by the fact that such diverse communities in Florida had different needs and were often highly suspicious of each other. This book focuses attention on the relationships between location and national expectations in the region's built environment. Enormous issues of housing, transportation infrastructure, connections to South and Central America, the redesign of the city of Key West, and the development of adequate schools and facilities were considerable during this period.

The Florida Clergy Letters

Evidence of the breadth and complexity of conflicting viewpoints on the nature of regional identity may be found in the so-called clergy letters. Following his administration's tradition of reaching out to the American people, and in an attempt to bolster his popularity among religious Americans who were suspicious of the loosening of Prohibition, Roosevelt solicited suggestions about the effectiveness of New Deal programs in a September 1935 letter to clergy throughout the nation, including those from south Florida. The president stated emphatically that "because of the grave responsibilities of my office, I am turning to representative Clergymen for counsel and advice,—feeling confident that no group can give more accurate or unbiased views." He was primarily interested in responses to the recently enacted Social Security legislation, which dealt with three sensitive areas: old age pensions, aid for disabled children, and unemployment insurance. The public works programs were another area of interest; he hoped that they would be "administered to provide employment at useful work." FDR sought information that would make the New Deal programs more effective, requesting that the clergy tell him "where you feel our government can better serve our people." He closed his letter with an appeal to civic engagement: "We can solve our many problems, but no one man or single group can do it,—we shall have to work together for the common end of better spiritual and material conditions for the American people."[17]

It made sense for FDR to look to a distinct subset of community leaders for assistance. The clergy were an obvious if often overlooked constituency, with insight into how local government operated or failed to operate. The president may have believed that the successful implementation of unprecedented social welfare programs depended on a delicate balance among a variety of stakeholders: the emerging federal bureaucracies, state governments, cities, and towns. The New Deal emphasized a vision of cooperative federalism in which states played a major role in the implementation of many federal programs, most notably the CCC, PWA, FERA, and the WPA. The clergy were well positioned to assess the impact of the Depression on families. FDR must have understood that the clergy confronted hurdles that reduced the effectiveness of New Deal programs in small and often isolated communities. His request for information from the clergy also served as a way of creating potential stakeholders at a time when the 1936 presidential campaign was less than a year away. The request for information from selected clergy does not appear to be simply a blatant attempt to garner political support, however. FDR did not solicit information that month from other civic, social, or economic groups. Three months later, when it was suggested that he might contact other civic leaders, including teachers, physicians, conservationists, and labor unions, he replied that he was too busy to undertake another letter writing campaign.[18]

The clergy letters offer a compelling portrait of Florida parishes, neighborhoods, and communities. There is a surprisingly contemporary feel to the letters, perhaps because many reveal insights into the long-standing tensions created as the requirements of tourist-based economic development collided with the need to build viable communities. New Deal programs intensified these conflicts in south Florida as the economic power of FDR's program served as a catalyst for change. There is also an authenticity about the replies to FDR that suggest both an honesty and directness. Addressing complex problems, the letters come to display concerns about economic development, the intrusion of federal programs in local communities, issues of race and racism, and uneasiness about the nature of the welfare state.[19]

Twelve letters from south Florida come from Miami and Miami Beach, one from Ft Lauderdale, and three from Key West. Two letters are from Jacksonville and Belle Glade.

Florida and the Welfare State

Several members of the clergy in south Florida acknowledged the president's concern for their state and region while noting the sea change constituted by the New Deal. "I am particularly interested in the New Social Security Legislation recently enacted for the benefit of our aged people, crippled children, and securing jobs for all who are able to work," wrote the Reverend Oscar Denney of the First Congregational Church in Miami. He added skeptically, "I think the major mission of our government is to help the hungry to feed themselves . . . and encourage them to start a savings account—teach them not to spend all they make."[20]

Writing from rural Belle Glade, the Reverend A. W. Taylor took heart from the president's letter: "To yours of the 24th. I haven't a kick or I haven't a grievance. In fact I think you are doing much better than most of the 'kickers' could do. I say this as one who was in R.I. (Prov.) as a dyed in the wool Republican, who once voted for Mr. Hoover." The message of the New Deal was not lost on Taylor. He applauded FDR's attempt to reach citizens in the grip of the Depression: "But since watching you and what I believe are your honest wishes and efforts for the forgotten man, I hope you get a re-election and intend to vote and speak in your favor."[21]

For one minister living in Key West, which had become a showcase of New Deal activity and embodied the tensions between tourist development and the needs of a local community, New Deal assistance was a lifeline. The Reverend Arthur Dimmick of St. Paul's Church noted how essential federal relief had been to the residents of Florida's southernmost city: "In spite of many blunders due to what were probably unavoidable obstacles and to the shortcomings of individuals, Key West has benefited from the aid of the Relief Administration. The community was virtually destitute. People have been saved from actual starvation which they were not merely facing, but experiencing." Notwithstanding the devastating blow of the September 1935 hurricane that destroyed the Florida East Coast Railroad bridges, the only link between the mainland and the Keys, Dimmick reported that federal assistance had helped to raise morale in Key West: "There is now at least an attitude of hopefulness."[22]

Concerns about the economic health of his community prompted Miami Beach Presbyterian Church pastor William C. Cumming to write to the president on September 30, 1935. Cumming's tone suggested the gulf separating FDR from many of Miami's clergy: "I am writing to say that we [Christian ministers] are not unaware of the heavy burdens that rest upon you and that from time to time we have remembered you in our public prayers before the congregation that you may be given wisdom to know what to do for the real good of the nation." Cumming, formerly of Hendersonville, North Carolina, was direct in his diagnosis of the problems facing the nation. The New Deal's social welfare programs apparently concerned him deeply. He instructed FDR to "balance the budget. Present gains will be engulfed in coming ills if that is not done." He also urged the president to "reduce the tax burden (rather than increase it) for it is becoming too heavy for the people."[23]

For the Reverend John E. Gekeler of Key West, federal restrictions on agricultural production were hard to swallow. He also saw the aims of Social Security as commendable but worried about the weight of bureaucratic inefficiency and red tape. "The Social Security Legislation must be administered for the benefit of the specified groups, and not for the administrators thereof. Often times the opposite seems to be the case at present," he wrote. The evolution of the federal bureaucracy and the modern administrative state weighed heavily on Gekeler: "Industry should be encouraged more and more to assume its portion of the load. The initiative of the individual, which has been such a potent factor in the development of our people, should be fostered. There are many services which government must perform; but there is a large zone of business and industrial life into which it should not enter, and from which it should withdraw. A loosening of all restrictions upon these lines of endeavor would seem to promise helpful results."[24] But there were also serious criticisms of FDR's (and by extension the New Deal's) moral compass. The president's support for the repeal of the Volstead Amendment was a fundamental indictment of his character and his ability to lead the nation for several members of the clergy.

As presiding elder, C. K. Vilet of the Methodist Episcopal Church in South Miami wrote, "The Clergy of our Southland, who tho opposed to the repeal of the 18th Amendment, nevertheless believed in you and your platform and gave you their support. Today our confidence is gone. To have lost faith in confidence in our President and our Democracy is a tragedy. But as we witness the fact that not a single campaign pledge as it related to the repeal of the 18th amendment has been kept what alternative have we?" Vilet blamed Roosevelt personally for failing to live up to campaign promises to protect "Dry States." He railed against the issue of "Federal Licenses for the sale of Whiskey making it next to impossible for us to get a conviction for liquor violation and assisting very materially in thus securing the repeal of our State Constitutional Amendment." Life in Miami had, in fact, deteriorated with the advent of the New Deal. Vilet argued: "Miami has infinitely more saloons and dens of vice today than it had in the most hectic days of Pre-prohibition. Men and women hanging over the bars of saloons twenty four hours in the day and seven days in the week."[25]

The Reverend Cumming called upon FDR to "mitigate the rising curse and peril of intoxicating liquor in this country—and my suggestion is that all liquor advertising be prohibited, for advertising increases consumption and the consequent disastrous effects."[26]

Tourism and Economic Development

By 1925, South Florida was already feeling the effects of a sustained economic downturn. Some of the first signs of recovery ten years later were identified by clergy corresponding with FDR.[27] For Miami pastor H. J. Anger, New Deal legislation proved essential for the recovery of both local and national economies. Anger railed at the recent Supreme Court decisions in *Schechter Poultry Corp v. United States* striking down the National Industrial Recovery Act.[28] Writing to FDR on November 1, 1935, Anger exuded optimism about the expected arrival of tourists in Miami and Miami Beach:

> The tourist season in Florida has as yet not arrived, yet the increase of tourists is conspicuous. The free and liberal spending of the home public, the unprecedented attendance of the working people at the shows and in the six nights of the week wrestling and boxing matches, the increased gasoline sale, the many new automobiles in evidence, the twelve million dollar building program for Miami and Miami Beach, the pastors "and missionaries" again enjoying their old time monthly checks—is evidence to assure you that the New Deal's Face is smiling all over Metropolitan Miami.[29]

Florida's overwhelming dependence on tourism, however, raised a number of significant challenges and, as will be illustrated throughout this book, was not uniformly greeted as a positive development. Resentment toward tourism in Miami formed the gist of the Reverend Daniel Iverson's response to FDR writing from Miami on October 4, 1935. His church, Shenandoah

Presbyterian Church, "The Friendly Bible Church," was located on Southwest Eighth Street, the Tamiami Trail. The trail bisected the Florida Everglades, connecting Miami's Atlantic coast with the Gulf of Mexico in Tampa. Iverson argued that south Florida represented a "unique situation." He wrote, "As you know, we have no large commercial enterprises upon which to build our social and financial structure. The tourist is our chief stock in trade. The tourist season lasts about three months. Consequently, we have nine months when very little is done along the line of producing wealth and much is done to dissipate it." Iverson also questioned whether south Florida's tourist and retirement infrastructure could ever effectively build and maintain viable communities. The problem, as he saw it, revolved around "many citizens that might be called 'natives' who find it difficult to live and to stretch their incomes over a twelve months' period. This is our problem, and it is a practical one. We have too many people past middle age in Miami who live a hand to mouth existence." Seeing in South Florida's growing retirement age populations increasing socioeconomic fault lines, Iverson framed the problem plainly:

> We have quite a few people past middle age who move here for the climate and who have very little to live on. They come with the hope that they will somehow get along. There is no way to keep them out. In a large number of instances, they do not get along, and become a care upon the few *permanent* residents who try to carry on the relief work. The tourists . . . contribute nothing towards their support, and there is no welfare program that covers cases of this kind. So, our local people have not only their own to take care of, but in a great many instances people from other areas.

Iverson urged FDR to provide more federal assistance. Anticipating the massive migrations of retirees to warmer climates and the establishment of Medicare by more than a decade, Iverson recognized the absolute necessity of higher levels of federal assistance. He concluded, "Therefore, it becomes the duty of our national government to consider this as part of their responsibility."[30]

The clergy letters are also useful in highlighting the tensions inherent in attempting to establish viable self-sustaining communities while serving the needs of growing tourist-centered economies. Many of these concerns were expressed in opposition to the lifting of the Volstead Amendment as discussed above, but went well beyond mere opposition to the evils of alcohol consumption. These concerns also express fears of higher levels of federal and state intrusion in local neighborhoods and communities. There was the concern that federal assistance would tilt the playing field in favor of increasingly tourist-oriented economies that were in the years before air conditioning only viable three or four months a year. For the Reverend Arthur Dimmick, Key West epitomized these problems.

Expressing clear misgivings about plans to open up Key West as a tourist destination Dimmick wrote to Roosevelt on October 19, 1935: "There are other projects, however, which seem to me [to] be not practical and not effective." He explained, "The chief of these is to develop the island as a resort for winter visitors. Much money has been sunk in the effort to make this project effective. Thus far, the returns to the community as a whole have not warranted the expenditure of money involved. I feel that this plan is a big mistake."

For Dimmick, Key West was too small to "accommodate a sufficient number of visitors to provide a living for the community as a whole." He also understood that in any plan to increase tourism there would be winners and losers: "As a resort, those in the town profiting most will be holders of real estate already developed (suitable houses, etc.) who least need aid. Unless such real estate holders are forced to pay just taxes on their property, the community as a municipality will be none the better off than at present."

Seeing in tourist development both economic and social disadvantages, he observed that the planned development "is unsound because it does not provide useful profitable employment and occupation for the bulk of the population." Dimmick also articulated concerns about the absence of stable industrial and retail/market capabilities necessary to sustain a tourist enterprise: "The resort business is among the most fickle and is therefore unsuitable as the principal source of revenue of a community where farming and other industries are impossible." There was, too, the realization, even in balmy Key West, that the tourist season was brief. "The shortness of the season for winter visitors leaves the townspeople without profitable occupation for nearly nine months of the year."[31]

In spite of the respectful tone of many of the letters, Florida clergy were not reticent about identifying negative consequences of federal assistance. Writing to the president less than a month after the 1935 hurricane, Key West clergyman John Gekeler saw the New Deal transforming ways of life at the local level, increasing the size and the scope of government—especially the federal government—thus creating a number of problems. By no means unaware of the power of the New Deal to end Key West's physical isolation from Florida through the construction of the Florida Overseas Highway, Gekeler stated:

> Locally the assistance of government toward the rehabilitation of the community is appreciated. Continued aid toward the building of the Overseas Highway, upon which many veterans were engaged at the time of the Labor Day storm, will mean much to Key West and its citizens. The suggestion to erect this Highway with its bridges as a memorial to the men whose lives were lost in that storm is a sound one. In these local projects local men should be given preference where that will not lessen the efficiency of the work.

He also told FDR that an increase in food supplies to Key West was of critical importance citing the scarcity and high cost of food.[32]

Building Communities: Federal versus Local

More than six hundred miles to the north, the Reverend S. D. Walker of the First Methodist Episcopal Church, South, "The Big Downtown Friendly Church" in Jacksonville, complained about the impact of New Deal programs: "The New Deal plans have not worked out as well as our people expected and there is criticism of the regimentation of life." Walker cited a number of specific concerns about the failure of the New Deal bureaucracy. He was most concerned with the negative effects on the local economy.

"Living costs have increased to such an extent that many of our people are doubtful of the final results and the piling up of debt and the raising of taxes are presenting a serious question as to the future." He underscored a sense that the New Deal was moving too fast: "Many people are very much concerned for the Constitution which they regard as the bulwark of their liberties." He added, "Our people also feel disappointed in the results of your action about the saloon business and especially they resent the service of beer in the C.C. Camps [sic]."[33]

The federal intrusion into local communities created special challenges and obstacles for the Reverend John H. Hager writing from Miami. He gave personal testimony citing his involvement in three veterans work camps as the basis for his concern: "The only advice I can honestly give is that the methods of administration must be improved by a change of personnel or closer supervision, and that federal liquor laws sufficient to curb the devastating influence of the present liquor traffic must be passed before you can hope for much lasting results." For Hager, levels of drunkenness were simply out of hand:

> It was a common occurrence with the inhabitants of these camps to become so intoxicated that they became a public nuisance, and on more than one occasion I had to stop my car and wait for veterans to be half carried off the road so I could go on. On one particular occasion one of the veterans was three miles from camp, highly intoxicated, and using very vile language in the presence of several women and girls. When I could not quiet him or persuade him to go on his way I reported the matter to the headquarters office where I was informed that nothing could be done about it unless I could find the local peace officer who at that time was about eight miles away. The beer which was causing this condition was sold in a canteen within the camp, operated by a *member of the Florida State Legislature* who doubtless secured his concession from federal authorities. The canteen was later moved from the actual camp but still maintained just outside the camp.

Hager's view of community building focused on the consumption of alcoholic beverages as an evil to be eliminated entirely. Those concerns also reflected basic fears about how viable communities could be sustained in Miami. Opposition to alcohol was just one concern about rapid social change. Hager concluded: "In my work in Miami I have found the liquor traffic tearing down the spiritual and material welfare of the people to a far greater extent than any Social Security Program could rebuild. Until you reverse your public stand on this question I can hope for little lasting results from social legislation."[34]

William Cumming, the Presbyterian minister from Miami Beach, also asked FDR to help protect the delicate south Florida ecosystem by putting the brakes on the New Deal's penchant for big environmental reengineering: "Discontinue the Florida Sea-level Canal project," he warned, because it "constitutes such a grave peril to the fresh-water supply of South Florida."[35] In the case of Key West, Arthur Dimmick called for the development of a local economy based on the natural environment of Key West and the Florida Keys:

> Although I am not in any sense of the word a student of industrial economy, nevertheless I am convinced that the efforts to set Key West on its feet should be based on what is probably the elementary principle of economics; i.e., the use and development of local natural resources. Surrounded as Key West is by some of the finest fishing waters within the Nation's jurisdiction, the fishing industry is the logical and only characteristic one which can furnish profitable employment to the bulk of the population. Moreover, the business of fishing is about the only occupation that most of them are capable of doing. In referring to the fishing industry I imply also the canning of fish and the preparation of the fish in various different ways.

Dimmick understood that the building of a canning industry in Key West would entail conflicts among fisherman and potential employers in a place noted for its independence of spirit. He called for reliable ties to markets and the construction of facilities capable of sustaining a canning industry, such as icing facilities. He pushed his idea of investing in a viable economic base: "I am convinced that with a certain amount of assistance from outside sources, a fish canning industry could be developed on a paying basis if the fishermen work on some sort of cooperative foundation." He also observed, "Such an industry . . . would provide profitable employment for various classes and groups of people in addition to the fishermen themselves and would go far towards making the town self-supporting and self-respecting." Indeed, the building of community is a theme that recurs throughout the Florida clergy letters.

Dimmick criticized the episodic nature of New Deal assistance seeing "that nothing of a permanently helpful sort has been done." He saw a number of federal initiatives as missing the mark: "The building of an aquarium, the weeding of vacant lots in a tropical climate, the paving of streets, and the building of swimming pools—where the Atlantic Ocean is available as such—all provide temporary employment for several hundreds of persons; but these things are not such as to be to already great degree profit-making and wage-producing." Community-building was something more than a quick fix:

> Playgrounds and playground instructors, as well as other means of developing the physique and morale of the children have been provided and have undoubtedly been a source of improvement. However, this can be of little if any lasting value when the adult population, the bread-winners, are living on a pittance which may cease at any time and when too, they are not becoming able to support their homes and the community in which they live.[36]

Reverend A. W. Taylor in Belle Glade, the town in far west Palm Beach County on the shores of Lake Okeechobee, also urged the president to help settle huge tracks of empty farmland. Taylor was keenly aware of the political and economic power disparities among the small farmers and migrants and large agribusinesses. "It is the brag of our larger farmers here that Government sent in Investigators to see about land settlement, 'but we talked them out of it,'" he stated. In order to assist the economic development of the area, Taylor urged the administration to create more "roads for transportation of crops and escape in time of floods and hurricanes. We only have one at present thru W.P. [West Palm] Beach. Suggest completion of State Road #26 in a direct route to Miami." He also asked for federal assistance in eliminating the Water Hyacinths on Lake Okeechobee, "which completely fill and dam up our Rivers and Canals."[37]

Race in South Florida

South Florida's physical development during the 1930s was intricately linked to the politics and economics of race. The vast, inhospitable, and largely inaccessible waters of the Everglades provided something of a buffer for indigenous Americans who played significant roles in the founding of Miami and other south Florida communities. But Africans from the Bahamas and the descendents of southern slaves, without whose labors the South Florida's physical development would not have been possible, had no such buffers between themselves and white Miamians.[38] The communities of white and black residents were interdependent and yet completely segregated. At the time of Miami's incorporation in 1896, 162 of the 368 men voting for the establishment of the city were black.[39] As agricultural workers, laborers, and servants, black Miamians provided the muscle that contributed to the construction of Miami and Miami Beach. Overtown, a segregated neighborhood adjacent to the Miami's central business district, was the vibrant core of black Miami.[40]

Only two clergy wrote with concerns about race. The Reverend F. D. Sullivan of Gésu Catholic Church in Miami responded to FDR sometime after Oct. 3, 1935, calling the president's attention to the case of a starving mother. Father Sullivan stated: "I am glad you are giving the Negroes of Miami a 'break.' The new plans for a model city in N.W. Miami [Liberty Square] should be a boon to these poor blighted blacks who do not get even the crumbs that fall from the White man's table." Sullivan wrote: "The Catholic Church would like to have opportunity of social and religious service in this new community and I hope Gen Coe will be authorized to cooperate with Bishop Barry of St. Augustine, FL." He also praised the services of "a staunch democrat named John Lovelle," noting that "he could be used for bigger things."[41] The absence of other letters from Catholic priests may underscore the dominance of an overwhelming Protestant state and region. Miami was fundamentally different from the big cities of the Northeast and Midwest and reflects the relatively small size of the Catholic population statewide at that time. It may also suggest that other lines of communication existed with the administration given the prominence of the Church in the major cities of the Northeast and its ethnic Democratic voting bloc. The Catholic Church in Florida had far less influence in secular affairs than its counterparts in Boston, New York, Philadelphia, Baltimore, and Chicago. Virtually the entire state was part of the Diocese of St. Augustine established in March 1870. As with most Catholics in the South, Florida Catholics confronted virulent anti-Catholicism in the early years of the twentieth century, peaking just before America's entrance into World War I. In 1933, the Catholic population of Florida was only 65,767. There were 115 priests serving 61 churches, 41 missions, and 150 stations covering the entire state. There were just 35 schools in the entire diocese.[42]

As a monolithic statewide corporate entity (the archbishop was a "corporate sole"), the Church had far fewer institutional resources to meet the upheavals of the 1920s. The Diocese of Miami was established in 1958 comprised of the sixteen counties in the southern part of the state with a near threefold increase in Catholics estimated at 185,000. Miami also lacked a large vibrant Jewish community in the 1930s. This too affected the nature of local politics. In writing about the relocation of large numbers of Jews to Miami and Miami Beach following World War II, historian Deborah Dash Moore argues that the Miami experience was both strikingly different and alienating for Jews. She noted, "Without the mediating influence of heterogeneous Catholic ethnic groups, Jewish residents confronted directly the Protestant majority for social cues. This majority lacked a visible common denominator of either a shared ethnicity or church hierarchy, presenting Jews with an individualistic and fragmented society." The trajectory of development of local politics owed much to the absence of sizeable numbers of both Jews and Catholics. The individualistic and fragmented character of the Protestant political elite in south Florida laid the groundwork for more decades of conflicts with African Americans and with Cuban refugees. Moore estimates that there were possibly eight thousand Jews living in Miami and Miami Beach during the mid-1930s. Following World War II, Jews arrived in much larger numbers, serving as a crucial catalyst for the civil rights movement in the 1960s, confronting virulent anti-Semitism, and playing a critical role in the development and preservation of Miami Beach in the 1970s and 1980s.[43]

The Reverend Daniel Iverson of the suburban Shenandoah Presbyterian Church due south of the central business district also confronted the issue of race explicitly. His perspective is important because it mirrors both the dominant thinking about the "problem of race" and the future of Miami's poor black communities. Indeed, as John Stuart suggests in chapter 6, the building of the first segregated federally funded housing project in the United States, Miami's Liberty Square, reveals patterns of paternalism, utilitarianism, economic interests, and some measure of social activism that speak volumes about how white Miami perceived and reacted to the black community. Reverend Iverson's thoughts, therefore, provide contemporaneous insight about the Miami community's request for federal assistance to solve the "problems" posed by Miami's "colored population." Systematic patterns of racial exclusion from politics, businesses, and public services—schools, sanitation, the legal system—was a hallmark of white Miami's responses to the presence of blacks since Miami was founded.[44]

Citing the squalor and overcrowding of the "negro quarter [Overtown] in which twenty-five thousand negroes live where there ought to be not more than ten thousand," Iverson laid the blame for these conditions on "an improper attitude towards the race question, politics, and other things of like nature." His concerns about poor treatment of black people were both moral and utilitarian:

> The white people, because of the rapid growth of our city, seem to have overlooked them entirely. Now we have a problem that must be solved. Naturally, the families increase there as they do among the whites, but this quarter is so hemmed in on all four sides so that it is impossible to expand. It is creating a situation the like of which cannot be duplicated in the South. I am a Georgia "Cracker" Democrat, and as a Southerner have studied this situation. In the name of justice and humanitarianism, I believe some place for expansion for the negro is an imperative need.

Iverson attributed an outbreak of an epidemic of Dengue Fever throughout Florida, southern Georgia, and parts of South Carolina and Alabama to living conditions "in our negro quarter." "I am sure you are familiar with the typical Southern negro," Iverson confided to FDR, "It is difficult to teach him sanitation. And no matter how much you teach there is little good to be accomplished as long as he is compelled to live in this tropical climate in such a congested area." Because such highly communicable diseases like tuberculosis are prevalent in the community, "they are subjecting our white families constantly to all kinds of disease." Iverson identified three specific needs: "A place for their delinquent children, hospital space increased at least one hundred per cent, and enough land upon which homes can be built for at least seven hundred and fifty to one thousand families." Iverson asked the president to consider establishing a committee to study how best to address these issues:

> Remember, the average negro has no money to help himself. Our rehabilita-
> tion work program hardly covers his case. Our negroes are largely like our
> Indians. They are our care and responsibility. They are American citizens.
> We cannot deport them. If our homes are compelled to pay prices for their
> services on the terms of the laborer's wage, the homes cannot use them, and
> as a matter of fact, they would not be worth that much as servants, so there is
> our problem. If this were an agricultural community, we could probably solve
> our problem another way, but these negroes are living in the city, and they are
> working as janitors and servants for the whites. Will you please give this your
> personal attention?[45]

Iverson's depiction also suggests the extent to which New Deal programs relied on state and local elites, absent entirely the force of the nationalized civil rights legislation of the 1960s to frame issues that would affect black Miami for generations.

Summary of Chapters

Many of the issues raised in the clergy letters find expression throughout this book, which has been organized into chapters offering diverse perspectives on the region. In the second chapter, "Building Identity," John Stuart focuses on the contributions made by the federal government specifically to south Florida's built environment. He explores these projects as a constructed fabric, whose threads are of various scales and importance, and whose patterns for development remain intact today. These range from FERA's relatively small projects to paint street names onto curb corners in downtown Miami, to more moderately scaled WPA projects to construct community centers, firehouses, police stations, schools, hospitals, and libraries, and finally to the enormous markers of regional identity including Orange Bowl Stadium and the Overseas Highway to Key West. Stuart argues that each of these projects were needed to satisfy New Deal objectives on several different levels. On one level, they addressed the New Deal objective to emphasize local identity through their materiality, construction, location, or activity. They were required, therefore, to enhance the experience of the permanent resident. At the same time, these projects were designed to enhance the tourist experience through an enrichment of the seasonal tourists' needs for schools, or the occasional tourist's interest in the native experience and local activities. Thus, Stuart observes, by promoting a sustainable local economy and encouraging the creation of local identity markers, the federal government was also increasing the number of tourists and potentially reducing the stability of the region. This is one of the paradoxes of the modern American urban condition that seemed to develop early in Miami and has now spread to urban centers across the country.

In chapter 3, Cornell architectural historian and critic of architectural photography, Mary Woods, explores the complex representations of the built communities in south Florida primarily through the work of Farm Security Administration (FSA) photographer Marion Post Wolcott. Woods highlights Wolcott's images of workers and buildings in south Florida in light of the work of commercial photographer Samuel Gottscho. Woods argues for a new visual methodology where changes, survivals, and future prospects of buildings and landscapes can be gleaned from studying and juxtaposing different photographers and photographic genres. The agendas for these three photographers varied greatly. FSA photographers were to capture the plight of the migrant workers and the successes of FSA programs in relieving their problems. Although the FSA project was to capture a "premodern" representation of the South, Woods points out that Wolcott managed to assemble a collection of images that revealed the complexity of a changing south Florida. She highlighted tensions between the modern tourist economies and the agribusinesses that informed the identity of the region. The photographs analyzed in the chapter reveal that these complex tensions also cut across economic and class lines. While Wolcott shot images of black and white migrant workers, Gottscho was exploring the middle and upper classes and the modern architecture in the region that defined Miami Beach. Woods draws critical parallels between the images of the region and the sociocultural environment they depict. She notes that "intangibles like race, class, gender, and values inscribe themselves on spaces and people, inflecting both the photographers' representations of reality and our interpretations of their imagery." These photographs, she points out, reveal the multiple ways in which the New Deal set the stage for Miami's rise as both a Sunbelt city and an international gateway.

Chapter 4 continues the exploration of visual narrative. Marianne Lamonaca focuses on four mural series from south Florida post offices, Miami, Miami Beach, Palm Beach, and West Palm Beach. During the New Deal, the post office was a conspicuous symbol of the federal government and was one of the few federal services used by residents and tourists alike. Lamonaca notes that murals in these spaces provided unique opportunities to "enrich and transmit culture," to reinforce or reinvent community identity. The chapter provides a close look at the processes involved in the selection of the artists and poses a critical commentary on the subject matter for the south Florida projects. Building upon the work of Karal Ann Marling, Virginia Mecklenberg, and Barbara Melosh,[46] Lamonaca examines the murals for insights they offer on a region in transition. In three of the four mural cycles in the chapter, for example, tensions between Native American communities and transplanted communities are present. She points out that the image of Native American communities in the post offices proposed a model for the "acceptance of modernity disguised as an historical narrative." In Miami Beach, for example, the muscular, nearly nude bodies of Native American men fighting Ponce de León and de Soto in *Episodes from the History of Florida* refer simultaneously to the paternalistic New Deal Indian policy outlined in the Wheeler-Howard Act of 1934 and to Miami Beach as a place of cultural contact, bronzed bodies, and athleticism. In fact, the Hollywood fantasy figures in the murals would have been nearly indistinguishable from many of those in the post office itself, thereby blurring the lines further between historical and present identities. Native Americans in other murals were depicted very differently, however. In the Miami post office, Native Americans appear as part of regional trade, bringing goods along the river to the merchants in the city. Finally, in Palm Beach, Native Americans appear in peaceful settlements. Lamonaca points out, these "romantic depictions of industrious and family-oriented Seminoles reassured citizens of Palm Beach that their own traditions were valued and ongoing like those of the Seminoles, despite the fast pace of modern life." Such struggles for local identity during the New Deal were particularly important to an understanding of the origins of many conflicts that still appear today.

The Civilian Conservation Corps (CCC) activities in south Florida form the focus of chapter 5, written by landscape architect Ted Baker. The CCC was one of the first agencies established in Roosevelt's New Deal administration and is a result of the president's long-standing interest in the environment as an expression of regional identity and the need to find immediate employment for tens of thousands of young men who were out of work. Utilizing archival sources, Baker builds upon the work of Faith Rehyer Jackson, *Pioneer of Tropical Landscape Architecture: William Lyman Phillips in Florida* (1997) and A. D. Barnes, *History of the Dade County Park System: The First Forty Years* (1986) to create the first comprehensive view of CCC activities in the region. Baker explores the shift of land use in the region from the predominately private swimming pools and beaches of the pre–New Deal era to the emerging notion of public space and regional identity through several specific CCC projects: the Royal Palm State Park, Greynolds Park, Matheson Hammock, Fairchild Tropical Garden, and the Florida Overseas Highway. The article reflects the ways in which the visionary partnership of two landscape architects, Dade County parks director A. D. Barnes and project superintendent William Lyman Phillips, addressed local and national concerns in the creation of the first subtropical parks system in the United States. Through the local parks, federal and local officials created an image of the region, which in this case was based upon environments of indigenous plant materials, abundant and multiple access to water, and, in the case of Fairchild Tropical Garden, the study of tropical flora. Simultaneously, however, some of the projects, it may be argued, opened the land to further exploitation. Matheson Hammock provided docks for recreational boats, which continue to destroy sensitive areas and animals. Likewise, Greynolds Park with its new use for an industrial mine, while laudatory, may be read as an early example of a glossy public environmental façade that serves to obscure important issues of industrial land use and makes the "cover-up" seem palatable. And finally, the Overseas Highway may be viewed both as enhancing the experience by the visitor to Key West, and as facilitating the breakdown of community identity and the environmental degradation in the Keys by providing parking lots for visitors and landings for increased recreational boaters. As Baker's chapter serves to illustrate, these tensions are embedded in the basic fabric of New Deal activities.

In the last chapter, Stuart highlights the ways in which black and white Miamians from the professional classes worked together—and sometimes at cross-purposes—to construct what many architects and planners in the Federal Housing Division considered to be the most perfect example of density and form for public housing in the United States. Constructed as the first public housing project in Florida, the project immediately ran up against local concerns with the concept of public housing, which, in Miami as elsewhere, was fought by those who wanted strictly defined racial boundaries and feared that profits made from housing people in substandard conditions would be threatened by the subsidized housing. The complexities of building the project in south Florida, however, were made even more apparent by the fact that the white population had multiple motivations for and against the development of the project, while the black population in Miami lacked homogeneous class and ethnic structures. While some of the white players in the housing drama expressed progressive desires for higher standards of living, they were also eager to raise the level of their servants' health so as to lessen their own chances of infection. Likewise, many of the black leaders promoting Liberty Square not only desired better living conditions for the poorer black workers but also were interested in making the historically black downtown area of Overtown into a haven for the middle- and upper-middle-class black population, unimpeded by the crimes associated with the truly poor. The project revealed that the black population in the 1930s, as it still is today, was divided not only along class lines but also lines of ethnicity and national origin. Outcries abounded of Bahamian anti-Americanism within the "black community." One of the biggest concerns for both white and black residents of Miami seemed to be the question of boundaries on future growth in the city. Black leaders were looking for ways for the growing black population to expand, while many white residents demanded large buffers to the east of the project and the addition of a "black" Twelfth Avenue. The chapter ends with an examination of the politics and expectations involved in naming the housing project. Within this discussion alone may be found many of the complex and often paradoxical discussions of race initiated by New Dealers in Washington that continue in south Florida to this day.

As architectural historian Diane Ghirardo notes, in a general sense "New Deal America sought to preserve rather than destroy capitalist economic relations in the building industry." However, from our distance of seven decades, Ghirardo contends, our perspective is necessarily distorted, rendering unclear the "power and urgency of the problems," and the "distress and fear that gripped" Americans who "stood on the brink of terrifying, catastrophic changes."[47] The essays collected here attempt to provide a lens through which these and similar fears—and the responses proposed by New Dealers—may be brought into focus. While the region exhibits rural, suburban, and urban problems of class, race, and identity found in communities across the nation, it is also extraordinary for its diversity of solutions to such problems. As a result of New Deal planning and construction, south Florida arose out of the Great Depression to become one of America's primary postwar playgrounds. For the next seventy years, permanent residents and visitors maintained an unabashed belief—founded in the great boom of the 1920s and capitalized upon by the New Dealers—that the construction of buildings and infrastructure formed the key to community prosperity. Of all the questions underlying this book, perhaps the most pressing involve asking how we measure such prosperity, who benefits from it, and what are its costs. During the 1930s (and the same may be said today), the equation was complex and involved a series of decisions and judgments based upon assumptions about the role of government and private enterprise in the creation of community. The diversity and impact of these judgments will, we hope, be illuminated in the chapters that follow and provide a much-needed perspective on the role of government and the importance of public works to the future of south Florida.

Notes

1. Lisa Kay Adam, "Terrebonne Farms, Louisiana: An Anthropogeographic Study of a New Deal Resettlement" (PhD diss., Louisiana State University Agricultural and Mechanical College, 2000); Ronald Reed Boyce, "Geographies and the Tennessee Valley Authority," *Geographical Review* 94 (Jan. 2004): 23–42; Jeffrey Scott Cole, "The Impact of the Great Depression and New Deal on the Urban South: Lynchburg, Virginia, as a Case Study, 1929–1941" (PhD diss., Bowling Green State University, 1998); Jack Irby Hayes Jr., *South Carolina and the New Deal* (Columbia: University of South Carolina Press, 2001); Virginia Laas, "Reward for Party Service: Emily Newell Blair and Political Patronage in the New Deal," in *The Southern Elite and Social Change: Essays in Honor of Willard B. Gatewood Jr.*, ed. Randy Finley and Thomas A. DeBlack (Fayetteville: University of Arkansas Press, 2002); Louis Mazzari, *Southern Modernist: Arthur Raper from the New Deal to the Cold War* (Baton Rouge: Louisiana State University Press, 2006).

2. For the idea of Florida as a national bellwether, see David R. Colburn and Lance deHaven-Smith, *Florida's Megatrends: Critical Issues in Florida* (Gainesville: University Press of Florida, 2002), 2.

3. Jordan A. Schwarz, *The New Dealers: Power Politics in the Age of Roosevelt* (New York: Alfred A. Knopf, 1993), xi.

4. Jason Scott Smith, *Building New Deal Liberalism: The Political Economy of Public Works, 1933–1956* (New York: Cambridge University Press, 2006), 15, 19–20.

5. The study of tourism during this period is enjoying a recent increase in scholarly interest. See Michael Berkowitz, "A 'New Deal' for Leisure: Making Mass Tourism during the Great Depression," in *Being Elsewhere: Tourism, Consumer Culture, and Identity in Modern Europe and North America*, ed. Shelley Baranowski and Ellen Furlough (Ann Arbor: University of Michigan Press. 2001).

6. Bruce J. Schulman, *From Cotton Belt to Sunbelt: Federal Policy, Economic Development, and the Transformation of the South, 1938–1980* (Durham: Duke University Press, 1994), 3.

7. These figures for the per capita output of the WPA and PWA in Florida were taken from a table in Smith, *Building New Deal Liberalism*, 116.

8. Tracy E. Danese, *Claude Pepper and Ed Ball: Politics, Purpose, and Power* (Gainesville: University Press of Florida, 2000), 110–37.

9. Gregory W. Bush, "Playground of the USA: Miami and the Promotion of Spectacle," *Pacific Historical Review* 68 (May 1999): 29.

10. The period between the 1880s and the 1930s is often called the "Inter-Stage" of southern history, and the "New South" is thought to have developed largely after World War II. See Joseph S. Himes, ed., *The South Moves into Its Future: Studies in the Analysis and Prediction of Social Change* (Tuscaloosa: University of Alabama Press, 1991), vii.

11. Gary R. Mormino, *Land of Sunshine, State of Dreams* (Gainesville: University Press of Florida, 2005), 306.

12. David R. Colburn and Lance deHaven-Smith, *Government in the Sunshine State: Florida since Statehood* (Gainesville: University Press of Florida, 1999), 30.

13. R. H. Gore to Harvey Branch, Dec. 11, 1931, Papers of the Democratic National Committee, Franklin Delano Roosevelt Presidential Library (hereafter FDR Library), Hyde Park, N.Y.

14. See Lorena Hickok to Harry L. Hopkins, Jan. 31, 1934, Group 24, Papers of Harry Hopkins Federal Relief Agency, FERA-WPA Narrative Field Reports, Florida, container 56, FDR Library.

15. Douglas Smith, *The New Deal in the Urban South* (Baton Rouge: Louisiana State University Press, 1988); Elna Green, *The New Deal and Beyond: Social Welfare in the South since 1930* (Athens: University of Georgia Press, 2003); and Roger Biles, *The South and the New Deal* (Lexington: University Press of Kentucky, 1994).

16. See Hickok to Hopkins, Jan. 31, 1934, FDR Library.

17. Letter to the Nation's Clergy from Franklin Delano Roosevelt, Sept. 24, 1935, President's Personal File, 21A (DE–FL), container 6, FDR Library. Responses from clergy are found here as well.

18. Personal correspondence from Alycia J. Vivona, archivist at the FDR Library, July 12, 2005, to John F. Stack Jr.

19. Mormino captures these and other tensions powerfully in *Land of Sunshine*.

20. Oscar H. Denney to FDR, Oct. 7, 1935, FDR Library.

21. A. W. Taylor to FDR, Oct. 14, 1935, FDR Library.

22. Arthur B. Dimmick to FDR, Oct. 19, 1935, 3–4, FDR Library. See also Lester Standiford, *Last Train to Paradise: Henry Flagler and the Spectacular Rise and Fall of the Railroad That Crossed an Ocean* (New York: Crown, 2002).

23. Wm. C. Cumming to FDR, Sept. 30, 1935, FDR Library.

24. John E. Gekeler to FDR, Sept. 28, 1935, FDR Library.

25. C. K. Vilet to FDR, Sept. 26, 1935, FDR Library.

26. Cumming to FDR, Sept. 30, 1935, FDR Library.

27. Michael J. McNally, *Catholicism in South Florida, 1868–1968* (Gainesville: University Presses of Florida, 1982), 51.

28. The U.S. Supreme Court in *A. L. A. Schechter Poultry Corp. v. United States* 295 U.S. 495 (1935) struck down the National Industrial Recovery Act (NIRA) of 1933 on the ground that it constituted an unconstitutional delegation of legislative power to the executive branch. Even Justice Cardozo's concurrence characterized the delegation of legislative power to the executive branch as "not within banks that keep it from overflowing. It is unconfined and vagrant." The evolution of the New Deal's complex political, economic, legal, and institutional framework falls outside the purview of this chapter. But the enactment of the NIRA epitomizes the first 100 days of the administration's effort to bring "industry" stakeholders comprising both management and labor to the table to frame codes of fair competition as a means of stabilizing wages and prices designed to end wage and price declines and reestablish confidence in the nation's industrial economy. Proponents saw the NIRA as a first step in creating a national economy capable of supporting sustained economic growth. Critics saw it as the first stage in the creation of "corporatism" drawing inspiration from Mussolini's Italy. Stephen G. Breyer, Richard B. Stewart, Case R. Sunstein, and Adrian Vermeule, *Administrative Law and Regulatory Policy: Problems, Text, and Cases*, 6th ed. (New York: Aspen, 2006), 40–41.

The political, economic, and institutional struggles of the New Deal are well explored in Paul K. Conkin, *FDR and the Origins of the Welfare State* (New York: Thomas Y. Crowell, 1967); Thomas H. Greer, *What Roosevelt Thought: The Social and Political Ideas of Franklin D. Roosevelt* (East Lansing: Michigan State University Press, 2000); Arthur M. Schlesinger Jr., *The Age of Roosevelt: The Coming of the New Deal* (Cambridge: Houghton Mifflin, 1958); William E. Leuchtenburg, *Franklin D. Roosevelt and the New Deal* (New York: Harper and Row, 1963); Jordan A. Schwartz, *The New Dealers: Power Politics in the Age of Roosevelt* (New York: Knopf, 1993); and Jordan A. Schwartz, *The Interregnum of Despair: Hoover, Congress, and the Depression* (Urbana: University of Illinois Press, 1970).

29. H. J. Anger to FDR, Nov. 1, 1935, FDR Library.

30. Daniel Iverson to FDR, Oct. 4, 1935, FDR Library. See the excellent col-

lection of essays in Randall M. Miller and George E. Pozzetta, eds., *Shades of the Sunbelt: Essays on Ethnicity, Race, and the Urban South* (Westport, Conn.: Greenwood Press, 1988).

31. Dimmick to FDR, Oct. 19, 1935, FDR Library.

32. Gekeler to FDR, Sept. 28, 1935, FDR Library.

33. S. D. Walker to FDR, Oct. 1, 1935, FDR Library.

34. John H. Hager to FDR, Oct. 21, 1935, FDR Library.

35. Cumming to FDR, Sept. 30, 1935, FDR Library.

36. Dimmick to FDR, Oct. 19, 1935, FDR Library.

37. A. W. Taylor to FDR, Oct. 14, 1935, FDR Library.

38. Alejandro Portes and Alex Stepick, *City on the Edge: The Transformation of Miami* (Berkeley: University of California Press, 1993), 41–44.

39. Bruce Porter and Marvin Dunn, *The Miami Riot of 1980: Crossing the Bounds* (Lexington, Mass.: Lexington Books, 1984), 2.

40. Marvin Dunn, *Black Miami in the Twentieth Century* (Gainesville: University Press of Florida, 1997), 144–58.

41. F. D. Sullivan to FDR, after Oct. 3, 1935, FDR Library.

42. McNally, *Catholicism in South Florida*, 42–45, 56. McNally argues that anti-Catholicism did not take hold in South Florida during the 1920s as it did in much of the South because "the rapidly souring post-World War I economic boom riveted South Florida's attention on financial rather than ethnic, religious, or cultural concerns" (50–51).

43. Deborah Dash Moore, *To the Golden Cities: Pursuing the American Jewish Dream in Miami and Los Angeles* (Cambridge: Harvard University Press, 1996), 26, 55.

44. Raymond A. Mohl, "Trouble in Paradise: Race and Housing in Miami during the New Deal Era," *Prologue: The Journal of the National Archives* 19 (Spring 1987): 7–21; Porter and Dunn, *The Miami Riot*, 173–79; Marvin Dunn and Alex Stepick, "Blacks in Miami," in *Miami Now! Immigration, Ethnicity, and Social Change*, ed. Guillermo J. Grenier and Alex Stepick (Gainesville: University Press of Florida, 1992), 41–44; Portes and Stepick, *City on the Edge*, 76–80; and Dunn, *Black Miami*, 144–58.

45. Iverson to FDR, Oct. 4, 1935, FDR Library.

46. Karal Ann Marling, *Wall to Wall America: The Cultural History of Post Office Murals in the Great Depression* (Minneapolis: University of Minnesota Press, 1982);

Virginia Mecklenberg, *The Public as Patron* (College Park: University of Maryland Art Department, 1979); and Barbara Melosh, *Engendering Culture* (Washington, D.C.: Smithsonian Institution Press, 1991).

47. Diane Ghirardo, *Building New Communities: New Deal America and Fascist Italy* (Princeton: Princeton University Press, 1989), 186-87.

TWO

Constructing Identity

Building and Place in New Deal South Florida

JOHN A. STUART

This chapter traces New Deal building projects in south Florida from the late 1920s through the early 1940s, when the United States entered World War II. South Florida grew rapidly during this period, and the portrait that emerges from governmental sources, visitors, and residents is complex and often paradoxical. Located at the tip of the Florida peninsula, the region stood in stark contrast to the rest of the state.

Because of its significance as a tourist destination, some of the best sources for information on south Florida have been northeastern newspapers and magazines including the *New York Times*, the *Wall Street Journal*, and the *New Yorker*. The government provided two important archival sources of visual material that are useful for the study of south Florida. The first was the short-lived and low-budget periodical *Works and Workers of the Florida Works Progress Administration*, designed to instill pride in the WPA workers not only on the projects they had achieved but also to give them a better understanding of the larger contexts and goals of their achievements. The second was the magisterial leather-bound "Survey of the Architecture of Completed Projects of the Public Works Administration," presented to Roosevelt in 1939. Designed to instruct the president on the difference between "bad" architecture and the "good" design sponsored by the PWA, this illustrated report documented government construction activities, which were generally waning by the late 1930s. Such construction projects had an enormous impact on the nation and specifically on the regional identity of south Florida. New schools, community centers, housing, and police and fire stations were central to growing communities. Ports, airports, highways, and roads affected businesses with interests in south Florida. These projects served both the residents and tourists and intensified the differences and the interdependence of one upon the other.

Tourism and the Challenges Leading Up to the New Deal

By the winter of 1925/26, Miami and south Florida had established a reputation as a fun-loving resort environment. The region was known for its beaches, betting establishments, and the relatively free flow of illegal alcoholic beverages. While most visitors came to Florida from neighboring states, there were increasing numbers of tourists who followed the wealthy James and Charles Deering and Carl Fisher from the Midwest and who took Henry Flagler's railroad from the Northeast. Tourism rapidly overtook agriculture as the region's most significant industry. The flow of tourists varied each year depending upon weather-related and economic conditions in other parts of the country. In 1925, the permanent population of Dade County was estimated at 111,352.[1] But during the winter this swelled by nearly 300 percent to over 400,000 residents and tourists, all of whom expected adequate schools, hospitals, roads, post offices, and recreational facilities.[2] These tremendous annual economic swings undermined efforts to stabilize a permanent community.

From the earliest days of the New Deal, federal and state officials attempted to moderate these swings by considering the needs of tourists and local residents. It was hoped that amenities constructed for tourists would also encourage full-time settlement in the region. The Florida State Planning Board articulated this sentiment: "It should never be overlooked that, in providing adequate and interesting recreation for the visitors, Florida, at the same time, is being made a more delightful place in which the permanent resident can enjoy himself. After all, Florida should be equally attractive to its home-folks."[3] In light of this, federal and state spending on public projects was carefully coordinated from the outset with construction in the private sector of hotels, apartment buildings, and individual homes.[4] The coordination of such public and private initiatives was a key component to the region's particularly successful recovery from the Great Depression.

On January 27, 1929, the *New York Times* carried an article entitled "Again Tourists Flow to Florida. In a Land but Lately Ravaged by Boom and Hurricane Runs the Winter Stream That Seeks the Sunlight." The headline underscores Florida's distinction of being one of the few locations to suffer economic difficulty at a time when much of the rest of the country was enjoying unprecedented prosperity. As the journalist points out, the economic devastation in south Florida began with the infamous building bust of the summer of 1926 followed by a devastating hurricane. Some residents considered this confluence of economic and environmental tragedies to be a "heaven sent protest," a cosmic moral outrage against the gambling, illegal drinking, and flamboyant floorshows that visitors came to the region to enjoy. Many Floridians felt that more serious measures were required to eliminate the state's reputation for licentiousness. In response, the Supreme Court of Florida outlawed betting across the state in 1927. The famed horse racetracks in Hialeah and Tropical Park were closed, as were the Coral Gables dog track and the Jai-Alai fronton near the railroad tracks on Northwest 36th Street.[5] Coast Guard clippers increased their patrols of the coastal waters in an effort to cut off the heavy stream of illegal alcoholic beverages coming into the area from Caribbean ports.

Visitors were further discouraged from visiting Florida by another strong hurricane in 1928 that caused millions of dollars in damage. Assessed property values in Miami slid from $389,648,391 in 1926 to $317,675,298 in 1928 at a time when property values across the nation reached record highs.[6] The economic health of the entire state suffered as more than 125 banks failed between 1926 and 1929. State officials turned to agricultural production to compensate for losses felt from the lack of tourism. These efforts were curtailed by an infestation of Mediterranean fruit flies that devastated the citrus crop in 1929.[7] Despite these setbacks, many Americans traveled by automobile to vacation in Miami during the winter of 1928/29.

Although President Herbert Hoover's decision to recover from his successful election of 1928 at the enormous J. C. Penny estate in south Florida placed the region in the spotlight, as many as 80,000 tourists simply passed through Miami that season on their way to Havana, where recreational activities were abundantly available.[8] Travel companies boasted that in Havana "You will thrill to the skill of Cubans playing their favorite indoor sport . . . Jai Alai. You'll strike an eager attitude on the terrace of the Jockey Club . . . and thrillingly anticipate the gait of your favorite—as the thorobreds [sic] flash by."[9]

Between 1926 and 1929, skeletal remains of unfinished buildings littered the south Florida landscape. By 1929, however, some of these projects were being continued or started afresh. The boom period had also left the region with some of the most modern electrical, water, sewage, and fire protection systems of any region in the country, and as one New York Times reporter enthusiastically noted, it had provided the region with "invaluable lessons in city planning."[10] By the mid-1920s, Florida had some of the best highways, numerous new airports, and modernized seaports. These included the new Tamiami Trail between Tampa and Miami and international air service for passengers and mail between Miami and Latin American countries.[11] The new passenger terminal for Pan American World Airways on Dinner Key was considered to be "the first completely equipped station built in America."[12]

The Great Depression dashed hopes that south Florida would be rescued soon from its economic doldrums. In 1931, the Florida East Coast Railroad and the Seaboard Air Line Railroad, businesses critical to bringing building materials and tourists to south Florida, sank into receivership. Florida officials immediately decided to allow racetracks, including those in Hialeah and Tropical Park, to reopen for business, and in June 1931 they made it legal for local governments to use tax dollars to advertise their cities and municipalities.[13] The Florida Supreme Court ultimately determined that public money could be used to advertise what were primarily private hotels and entertainment industries.

Despite an aggressive ad campaign that appeared in the New Yorker and elsewhere during the winter of 1931/32, that winter marked another economic low point for south Florida.[14] The number of tourists to the state as a whole dipped to 500,000, and the value of building permits for residential and commercial construction reached a remarkable ten-year low of less than $400,000.[15] Two important public projects funded by the Hoover administration that year started the flow of federal money back into the area. The first project was the construction of the Jacksonville-Miami portion of the so-called Intracoastal Waterway. This was a protected channel for yachts and pleasure boats that ran along the eastern seaboard of the United States from Boston to Florida. It was announced as part of a $41,577,260 public works program.[16] Over the next several years, the Intracoastal Waterway project would be continued by the War Department, the PWA, and the WPA. Although it was started by Hoover, its completion was a notable achievement of Roosevelt's New Deal.[17] Another public project initiated by the Hoover administration involved a series of improvements to the harbor at Dinner Key, the site of the Pan Am terminal. Although clearly designed to ease travel for those few who could afford it, this Hoover initiative was also continued by Roosevelt.[18]

The beginning of the 1932/33 tourist season brought a promising number of visitors to south Florida, but the season ended as the worst on record for south Florida. The first blow was the federal government's declaration of a mandatory "bank holiday," or bank closing, at the end of January. Without access to their money or certainty of its safety, many tourists returned home.[19] Matters were worsened when on February 15, 1933, Giuseppe Zangara, an unemployed resident of Miami, attempted to assassinate President-elect Roosevelt in Bayfront Park. It was Roosevelt's first visit to Miami in seven years, and he was returning from a successful fishing trip. During his brief address, he noted that he hoped "very much to come down here next Winter," which, after the shooting, he did not do.[20] Although Zangara missed Roosevelt, he injured five others. Mayor Anton Cermak of Chicago died from his wounds, and Zangara was tried for murder and executed in the electric chair.[21] The event suggests that Roosevelt had little contact with the region before his presidency. As president, he occasionally passed through the area on the way to his beloved deep-sea fishing voyages off the Florida coast. Although Eleanor Roosevelt appeared more frequently in the region than her husband, neither seems to have taken a special interest in the area, and it received no extraordinary presidential patronage.

Early New Deal Initiatives

Following Roosevelt's inauguration on March 4, 1933, the famed first 100 days of the new administration brought little immediate relief for the residents of south Florida. The two most significant initiatives designed to aid the nation's unemployed and to create new jobs were the Federal Emergency Relief Administration and the Civil Works Administration. FERA distributed funds to state and local agencies, while the CWA offered direct relief to those without work. By September 1933, nearly one-third of Florida's residents were on relief and the state was nearly bankrupt.[22] Other programs of import to south Florida were the Civilian Conservation Corps and the Public Works Administration, spawned by the National Industrial Recovery Act. Local authorities responded immediately to the opportunity to gain significant federal assistance. By the end of 1933, the federal government had received proposals for several major projects including the expansion of Chapman Aviation Field, the construction of an Overseas Highway to Key West, and the construction of a low-income housing project for black residents. Although the Overseas Highway and the low-income housing would eventually be funded, the projects from Florida were, in general, not "highly thought of" by federal officials.[23]

The winter of 1933/34 brought more tourists to south Florida than any of the previous five seasons. The upturn was heralded in a November 1933 *New York Times* article entitled "Florida Prepares for the Tourist Trade." The first reason for the economic improvement was accorded to the enormous success of the Florida Hall at the "Century of Progress Exposition." The Florida Hall was opened in Chicago on May 27, 1933, and located prominently in the Court of States. Designed by the Miami firm of Paist and Steward, the pavilion reflected a romanticized view of Florida through its Mediterranean-style architecture and ornament. Although somewhat out of sync with the modern "Century of Progress" theme, the Florida Hall proved to be extremely popular with visitors. Over 90,000 requests were made at the pavilion for information pertaining to Florida's winter resort options. Interest in Florida was also boosted by a more general sense of "national recovery and industrial improvement."[24] The second reason was political unrest in Cuba. It began in August 1933 when Cuban president Gerardo Machado fled the country. He was provisionally replaced by New York native Carlos Manuel de Céspedes and ousted almost immediately after a student-led coup swept University of Havana professor of medicine Ramón Grau San Martín into power. Although Grau San Martín would be removed from power in 1934, protests against the "Roosevelt revolution" and "Yankee imperialism" grew under his watch. American warships were moored in the Havana harbor to "protect American lives." That season, Havana was eliminated from lists of travel destinations that still included Nassau, Port au Prince, Cristobal, Rio de Janeiro, and once again Miami.[25]

Economic instability and the depressed value of the dollar against most European currencies added to south Florida's appeal to European travelers. The *Graf Zeppelin*, a German airship replete with swastikas on its fins moored at Miami that year as officials eagerly discussed the possibility of regularly scheduled flights between Germany and south Florida.[26] Domestic connections were immediately improved by the addition of flights between New York and Miami on the Eastern Air Transport Line and by the Orange Blossom Special, which offered the first and only completely air-conditioned trains—cooled "like a Roxy cathedral"—to south Florida.[27]

For visitors arriving in Miami between January 25 and March 17, the Hialeah racetrack would be open for business, and the bars, nightclubs, and restaurants offered various diversions.[28] More visitors, however, did not mean huge increases in revenue for south Florida businesses. A writer for *Business Week* noted that the 1933/34 tourist season "had been good as to numbers but the customers squeezed their nickels hard."[29] The numbers, however, proved encouraging enough, as an extraordinary $9 million was invested in private building over the course of 1934 in preparation for the next season.

Lorena Hickok

During the winter of 1933/34, with the New Deal less than a year old, FERA head Harry Hopkins decided to evaluate the effectiveness of federal relief efforts by listening to local voices. He hired Lorena Hickok, a journalist formerly with the Associated Press and a close friend of Eleanor Roosevelt, to report back to him from cities and towns in thirty-four states across the nation. Hickok had a forceful and intelligent nature, and she reported to Hopkins what she learned from people of various walks of life in a series of remarkable letters.

Hickok's portrait of Miami is particularly valuable for its lack of sensationalism and boosterism. Upon her arrival in January 1934, Hickok focused on "the resort business," which she noted was "better this year than it had been in years—but still there are thousands out of work." Despite this, Hickok was not particularly generous with her assessments of Miami. "I am not fond of Miami. Principally because I do not like tourists. But Miami likes them. And, by all accounts, Miami should!"[30] She sketched quickly, effectively, and with some degree of humor, a portrait of the activities taking place around her. "The streets of Miami are a mess, what with hundreds of out-of-state automobiles, whose drivers are either smart alecks trying to pass everything on the road or timid old gentlemen who never signal you what they're going to do because they don't know themselves, and what with tourists from New York in white flannel pants—and why must tourists, especially tourists from New York City, be so damned arrogant!—walking all over you." The season she reported on, however, was more complicated than it first appeared, and she admitted that it was too early to make an evaluation. Contrary to the raving announcements in the newspapers that 1933/34 was best season Miami had ever seen, individual merchants, hotel managers, and those involved in real estate provided more reserved opinions. She noted that south Florida was already a popular destination for vacationers of limited means. She informed Hopkins that lower- and medium-priced hotels were full every night. Higher priced accommodations at $5 to $6 per night, however, were still easy to find without reservations. Suites at $14 per night were not filling up at all, and the $150 deluxe suites at the Biltmore were not "selling any too well." But hotels were only one of the options for accommodations available to tourists. The others were private homes with rooms open to tourists and campgrounds designed to accommodate automobiles and tents. Hickok reported, "The tourist homes—private houses where they take 'em in—the automobile camps, and apartments renting at $50 or $60 a month ARE full. Real estate men differ in their opinions as to the value of this business. The general feeling seems to be that it's better for Miami that these places should be filled up than for the big winter hotels to be doing a capacity business, because this means that the money will stay in Miami, even though there isn't so much of it, whereas, if the big hotels got it, it would go North—just now to mortgage holders."

Hickok discovered that area hotels had hired anywhere from 1,000 to 1,500 individuals, in spite of the fact that "many of the larger hotels bring most of their help down from the North." In addition, the stores had hired about 500 workers and were continuing, along with the hotels, to hire an additional 150 employees per week. Unethical practices were reported. In one case, a businessman reported that managers in a large department store had made most of their employees "'junior executives,' so that they could work them just as many hours as they liked."

The region had unique economic issues, or as Hickok put it, "Miami has a funny unemployment problem." She observed that unlike much of the rest of the South, for whom agricultural unemployment was critical, 40 percent of Miami's unemployed were bricklayers, carpenters, and other types of builders who had been financially successful during the boom years. They had purchased homes in the area, then had run out of work with the bust and the Depression. She complained to Hopkins, "Now there's no building going on down there, and they're stranded." Hickok made it clear to Washington that construction was central to the regional economy in south Florida.

By the end of her stay, Hickok reported that the 1933/34 tourist season "was nothing to write home about."[31] She observed, however, a sense of optimism among businessmen in south Florida. One of the merchants she spoke with told her, "One thing that CWA started and that a good tourist year is continuing . . . is a great improvement in the morale of Miami businessmen and people generally."[32] This optimism encouraged significant new construction in the region before the close of 1934.[33] The demand for inexpensive housing was soon met with vigorous private construction in Miami Beach, primarily south of Lincoln Road.[34]

The FERA and the PWA

During the spring and summer of 1934, the PWA began construction projects in the region. They engaged over 5,000 workers, which proved to be a new ten-year high in employment.[35] In June 1934, the Housing Division of the PWA approved a project for African American residents, Liberty Square, to be constructed and financed by the federal government. Although the project would not break ground for nearly two years, it added to the momentum of recovery in the region and spread the benefits of the PWA to Miami's black population.

Expectations for the 1934/35 tourist season in south Florida ran high after the relative economic successes of 1933/34. Advertisements for the region focused heavily on increasing the numbers of middle-class visitors. In January 1935, the City of Miami Beach advertised itself in the *New Yorker* as a place where "Smart America Spends the Winter."[36] The ad highlighted the fact that more than $8 million in building construction had been completed over the past year for accommodations "in every class." It promised vacationers "actual saving through fuel and heavy-clothing economies." Miami Beach marketed itself as a glamorous resort available at moderate prices with affordable accommodations for all. It was also promoted as a healthy modern city with plenty of sunlight. The construction boom of 1934 in Miami Beach marked the beginning of one of the largest in the country during the Depression. Over the next six years, seasonal apartment buildings built in the art modern style would form the core of the historic Art Deco district in Miami Beach.

Seasonal fluctuations in the tourism-based economy were also beginning to ease a bit by 1934. The author of a March 9, 1935, article in *Business Week* entitled "Florida Comeback (not 'Boom')" suggested that two new components of the south Florida economy were aiding this new stability: summer tourism and the sale of modest homes on suburban lots. The article reported that homes were no longer "palaces" but residences for "middle-aged people who have retired on sufficient means." On Miami Beach alone, over 280 new homes had been built in 1934 at the (relatively high) average construction cost of $15,000.

Appearances of renewed prosperity were deceiving, however, and a 1935 article in the *Nation* pronounced that "all [was] not well underneath." Extreme poverty still existed in the midst of the widely reported new wealth and growth despite the FERA programs available to local residents. Many jobs required long hours at extremely low pay. Employees in some restaurants, for example, were required to work twelve hours every day of the week. With transient camps full, more than eighteen workers per day without homes or jobs were regularly sent back across the Dade County line. Conditions were so uneven that a reader wrote *The Nation* owner, Oswald Garrison Villard, whose grandfather was the anti-slavery campaigner, William Lloyd Garrison, that "there is more slavery in Florida today . . . than when Lincoln at the instigation of your ancestor freed the slaves."[37]

By 1935, Roosevelt's New Deal came under attack for not helping those most in need. Indeed, the housing programs, for example, of the PWA, FERA, and the newly minted WPA were primarily intended to help skilled workers who were already employed. Robert C. Weaver, an advisor on race relations to the Department of the Interior during the New Deal, later noted that the system failed those who were without "enough income to buy food and clothing of the barest minimum standards."[38] South Florida was no exception.

By 1935, FERA activities in south Florida included a decade of much-needed construction and repairs to the region's infrastructure. FERA funds were used to repaint and repair bridges crossing the Miami River, including that at 36th Street. They were used to create a federal highway between Miami and Homestead, to restore the roadway into Matheson Hammock, to construct a new access road to the Municipal Airport facilitating visitors to the popular International Air Races, and to paint street signage on curbs in the city of Miami. Likewise, Miami's Central Park was cleared, filled, redesigned, and replanted with FERA funds. A much-needed playground was installed for Miami's black residents in Liberty City, and public areas around the Coast Guard station on Dinner Key were replanted. Civic buildings, including the top portion of the Dade County Courthouse, the Coconut Grove Elementary School, the Miami firehouse and training tower, and parts of Jackson Memorial Hospital were repaired and repainted. An additional floor and new wing were added to the existing structure of the Kendall Home Hospital and a laboratory wing for medical research was completed at Jackson Memorial Hospital.

FERA funds were also used to construct independent structures. These tended to utilize local building materials in the service of functional and

FIGURE 1. Training tower for the Miami Fire Department, Northwest Seventh Avenue, FERA, 1935. Courtesy of the FPC.

FIGURE 2. Laboratories at Jackson Memorial Hospital, FERA, 1935. Courtesy of the FPC.

FIGURE 3. Custodian's home at the Plant Introduction Center on the site of the Chapman Field military base, FERA, 1935. Courtesy of the FPC.

straightforward designs. One such project was the 1935 custodian's home at the Plant Introduction Center, an institution established by David Fairchild on the site of the Chapman Field military base. The single-story building with an overhanging white tile roof sported exterior walls of rough-cut native oolitic limestone and a large screened area. The Biscayne Park community house, now the community police station, was constructed from local pine logs, and surrounded by screened porches. It was furnished by chairs and benches made from rough-hewn pine logs and branches. The large open interior meeting space could be heated on cool winter evenings with a coral rock fireplace. Rusticated hanging lamps, wall sconces, and floor lamps provided additional illumination. The construction materials, simple rectilinear plan, and wide eaves linked the national New Deal activities with building traditions found in the region and informed the identity of Biscayne Park, which would pride itself on its natural environment and accompanying success as a bird sanctuary.

FERA was also critical to the process of enhancing south Florida's reputation as a center for public sporting events through the construction of grand-

FIGURE 4. Biscayne Park community house, FERA, 1935. Courtesy of the FPC.

FIGURE 5. Interior of Biscayne Park community house, FERA, 1935. Courtesy of the FPC.

FIGURE 6. New York Giants Stadium in Flamingo Park, Miami Beach, FERA, 1935. Courtesy of the FPC.

stands and bleachers. These included grandstands erected at Flamingo Park in Miami Beach, the winter home of the New York Giants baseball team, and bleachers for spectators at the International Air Race. Completed in 1935, such projects may be considered precursors to the more ambitious $320,000 PWA construction project on what was known as the Miami Municipal Stadium, the Roddy Burdine Stadium, or the Orange Bowl. That project came to Miami through Colonel Horatio Hackett, a celebrated army football star. Hackett was the director of the Housing Division during the negotiations for Liberty Square, when he came into contact with Miami officials.[39] The sleek new 23,000–seat structure, replete with lighting for nighttime play, was heralded as "the most complete, in accommodations for teams, for patrons, and the press, in the country," and it brought national recognition to the region through the famed Orange Bowl games and other winter sports activities.[40] One federal official noted that such projects were a "credit on the city" and "attracted nationwide interest."[41]

FIGURE 7. Aerial view of the Orange Bowl, also known as Miami Municipal Stadium and Roddy Burdine Stadium, PWA, 1937. Courtesy of NARA.

FIGURE 8. New seating at the Orange Bowl, PWA, 1937. Photograph by Frances E. Lee. Courtesy of NARA.

The WPA

In April 1935, Congress approved the Emergency Relief Appropriation Act of 1935 that inaugurated the Works Progress Administration (renamed Works Projects Administration in 1939), which finished many projects begun by FERA. Between May and December 1936, Florida WPA administrators in Jacksonville published a low-budget, picture-intensive monthly journal entitled the *Works and Workers of the Florida WPA*. Its unnamed editor claimed that the journal favored pictures of "men at work," in an effort to "furnish information concerning WPA operations to those who chiefly are responsible for the success attained—the workers themselves."[42] Pictures or names of skilled laborers are rarely included. Specific architects, landscape architects, and engineers are never mentioned. The journal attempted to create a pride in work and a sense of ownership of projects produced by the WPA workers themselves. Countering critiques that WPA jobs were trivial and meaningless, the editor claimed that the WWFWPA would convince workers themselves and their communities of their projects' value. This, in turn, would make "that project . . . a success not only in actual physical completion, but in the mind of the man who did the work." The documentation of valuable work would serve to "bridge the gap between the present and the day when they [the WPA workers] can return to their regular places in private industry."[43]

The journal featured projects ranging from sewing classes and roadwork to park maintenance and building construction. In this sense, the WPA in Florida followed the trend of the rest of the nation, which, according to historian Jason Scott Smith, spent 75 percent of its funding on "highways, streets, public buildings, airports, public utilities and recreational facilities." Florida enjoyed the highest per capita WPA expenditures of all the states in Region 3, which included Alabama, Georgia, Kentucky, Mississippi, North Carolina, South Carolina, Tennessee, and Virginia.[44] The Florida WPA offers a particular glimpse of what south Floridians envisioned for the future of the region since municipal representatives selected specific projects to be undertaken.[45]

Schools received "preferred classification" for funding in south Florida. By October 1936, the Florida WPA augmented the work started by the PWA and FERA to complete 204 school buildings. Eight were constructed in WPA Florida Region 3, which included Miami, Miami Beach, Coral Gables, and surrounding communities, representing 10 percent of all active district projects. Of the schools funded by the WPA in Miami, the one most widely publicized and representative of New Deal objectives was Shenandoah Elementary School. Construction began in December 1935 on a site where children "had to travel long distances for their education." The WWFWPA commented that "so rapidly was this community [of Shenandoah] built up and settled during the spring and summer of 1936, the capacity of the school when built was already too small." The simple two-story reinforced concrete structure accommodated fourteen classrooms arranged along open-air corridors. These took advantage of the warm climate and protected children from sun and rain between classes. The narrow building afforded much-needed cross ventilation in a time before the installation of air conditioning. Despite the overcrowding, the project was hailed as a success, and writers for the WWFWPA commended it for its high levels of safety and efficiency, as well as the rare level of cooperation between "the workers and their foreman, Fred Frensdorf."[46]

Other school projects in the region included kindergarten and high school buildings in Key West and St. Lucie. One school in Miami, presumably in Liberty City near Liberty Square, was constructed for black students. Writers for the WWFWPA proudly reported that all the employees on that construction project were black except the project superintendent and the timekeeper.[47] Although black supervisors worked for the WPA in other parts of the nation, Miami residents resisted this change in the existing racial structure of labor.

Schools were placed to help orchestrate the spreading of populations into new regions and to enhance conditions for learning in areas that were already densely populated. Such overcrowding in schools was typical for

FIGURE 9. Shenandoah Elementary School, Miami, WPA, 1936. *WWFWPA*.

Miami Beach. There, it was noted, "the capacities of the elementary and high schools, prior to the completion of this project [by the PWA], were not sufficient to care for the children of the normal population. The influx of winter tourists residing in Miami Beach created a deplorable shortage of room for the children attending the schools, necessitating the use of three tent classrooms to relieve the congestion."[48] South Beach Elementary School and Miami Beach Senior High School, both PWA projects designed by August Geiger, boasted open-air hallways similar to those found at Shenandoah. This arrangement of classrooms along open-air corridors became a hallmark of New Deal school architecture in the region. Their stripped-down monumentality and arched walkways had strong associations with "Mediterranean style" architecture of the 1920s and the development of what some have called a regional style.[49] Many of these schools were adorned with one of six plaster plaques of children at play designed by Joan Van Breeman for the Federal Arts Project. These were cast by the Plaster

FIGURE 10. Walkway connecting buildings at Miami Beach Senior High School, designed by August Geiger, PWA, 1939. Photograph by Francis E. Lee. Courtesy of NARA.

Casting Department of the Sculpture Group of the Federal Art Project and were placed in nearly 150 schools and public buildings in Dade County and the surrounding region.[50]

Community Buildings

According to the writers of the WWFWPA New Deal community buildings were designed to result in "healthier, happier, and more successful living" and enable "people to enjoy a social life broader than in their individual homes." The Recreation House in North Miami was one such example.

Designed along the lines of the FERA–funded Biscayne Park Community House, the Recreation House in North Miami was constructed of Dade County long leaf pine anchored and tied with concrete and steel. In a gushing report on the project, the foreman noted that each of his workers took "great joy in knowing that he was a part in bringing into existence this building" and that in at least three cases, the project provided a means for workers to "establish themselves in private industry."[51] Dade County pine was also used in the Wynwood Park Community Center, noted for the economy of its construction. The structure consists of stone columns that support pine logs sealed with concrete. The center had a large recreation room and two classrooms to be utilized "to aid the development of backward youths."[52]

The most elaborate of all the community center projects was the Coral Gables Library and Community House, currently the Coral Gables Woman's Club. "Vigorously and enthusiastically sponsored by" the City of Coral Gables, the center used native oolitic limestone for the floors and walls, with exposed pine roof trusses overhead. Nearly finished by November 1936, the

FIGURE 11. North Miami Recreation House, WPA, 1936. *WWFWPA.*

FIGURE 12. Wynwood Park Community Center, Miami, WPA, 1936. *WWFWPA.*

FIGURE 13. Masons with the Federal Arts Project carving one of a series of thirteen limestone plaques depicting the wildlife of Florida for the Coral Gables Library and Community House, WPA, 1936. *WWFWPA.*

FIGURE 14. *Migration*, designed by Dewing Woodward for the Coral Gables Library and Community House, WPA, 1936. *WWFWPA*.

Library and Community House was acclaimed as "an outstanding architectural contribution to that city." As the same WPA writer, Maurice Feather, noted, the limestone cladding of the buildings added "much to the beauty of this resort city on the East Coast." The limestone connected the natural local environment not only to the local community who used it but also to a wide range of tourists who came to south Florida to enjoy the many qualities of the area that the limestone represented. One observer commented, however, that this "superlative material" was used all too rarely in the "paradise of the stucco artist." Such connections to the landscape were enhanced by a series of thirteen carved limestone plaques depicting birds, fish, and other wildlife "familiar to residents of the Miami area."[53]

The Coral Gables Library and Community House was the site of *Migration*, a series of murals designed by Dewing Woodward, superintendent of the Easel Group of artists under the auspices of the Federal Arts Project. He was aided by Coral Parker, Will Wynn Jones, Harold Lawson, Wilfred Don Stiles, Dumain Weaver, and Maud Holme. *Migration* featured a family of Seminole Indians floating across marshes on their way to "fresh haunts and habitations." Flying birds and native plants suggested the history of south Florida as the "progression from the old to the new."[54]

George Merrick and the Dade County Planning Board

The WPA was structured around what its chief administrator, Harry Hopkins, described as "a decentralization of activity and responsibility."[55] Requests for WPA funding that came from local organizations were sorted and prioritized at the local and regional levels according to the type of project and the availability of workers. Then they were forwarded to the state and federal levels. Federal officials preferred funding proposals from states and localities that had adopted the system of regional and statewide agencies. As described in a bulletin from the National Resources Committee, "Definite preference should be given to projects which are endorsed by local planning agencies where they can be carried out with the classes of labor that are available."

One influential local governing body was the Dade County Planning Board. Governor David Sholtz appointed members of the planning board and requested their first meeting on November 29, 1935.[56] George E. Merrick, developer of Coral Gables, was elected chairman. One of the board's first duties involved the reevaluation of approximately 150 WPA projects in Dade County. The board approved the continuation of all the school projects and approximately 20 others that they thought served "vital civic needs." They maintained strong connections to O. A. Sandquist, their regional WPA director. The board's primary objective was to create a six-year plan for Dade County. Projects were separated into categories of importance. Priority status was granted to Shenandoah Elementary, Earlington Heights School, Homestead "Negro" School, and a project that added hurricane shutters to all schools. Other priority projects included the Riverside Community Center, a so-called Dormitory for Delinquent Colored Children, and the creation of "parkways" for Southwest Third Avenue and Coral Way.[57] The projects reflected the county's ongoing need to accommodate its enormous and fluctuating population growth.

Other projects promoted by the planning board under Merrick included the planting of a large botanical "coloured" park in the southern part of Dade County, the establishment of the Fairchild Tropical Garden in Chapman Field, and the digging of regular canals for European-style canoe club camps for "tourists and homefolks."[58] While nothing seems to have come of the idea for the canals, the botanical park may exist in the Miami Fruit and Spice Park, and Fairchild Tropical Gardens has become an institution of international importance.

By the time the six-year plan was formulated, its estimated cost ranged from $50 million to $100 million. The plan was lauded in the *Miami Tribune* as "comprehensive" and as including "improvement of every segment of the county." Since most beaches in Dade County were privately owned, the writer at the *Tribune* was particularly impressed that the plan called for three public bathing facilities, one designated for members of the black community, who, it was noted, had no public access to any of the area beaches.[59]

Recovery and Growth after 1936

While the Planning Board was looking at the future of the county, public and private building in south Florida had escalated by the end of 1936. The year marked the completion, or near completion, of Greynolds Park, Ida Fisher Elementary on Miami Beach, North Beach Elementary, numerous roads and bridges, a WPA Federal Art Gallery in the Old Miami Post Office, and Liberty Square.[60] Likewise, private construction continued at a feverish pace. Thirty-seven new hotels were added to the approximately 150 already existing in the area. For visitors who could not afford hotels or preferred other accommodations, there were five hundred furnished apartment buildings and a dozen trailer parks. Since most of the beaches were private, tourists gathered at the Bath Club, Surf Club, and in cabañas at the Beach Cabaña Club and the Everglades Cabaña Surf Club. Fishermen were accommodated especially well at the Key Largo Club. For evening entertainment, tourists had the choice of four dog race tracks, the Royal Palm Club on Biscayne Bay, the Palm Island Club, Villa Venice, and the Town Casino. Three flights per day brought visitors from New York to Miami. With a stop in Charleston, South Carolina, the trip took seven hours one way and cost $129.20, twice the expense for a twenty-six-hour ride on the deluxe air-conditioned trains, the Florida Special and the Orange Blossom Special.[61]

The expansion of entertainment in south Florida to include "strip-tease dancers, private 'clubs' where anything goes, and heavy-tariff gambling emporiums" met with local resistance. Some of this came from the Ku Klux Klan, which had been reactivated in Miami in 1921. The Klan terrified many local club owners when 175 of its members raided the La Paloma nightclub in November 1937 and searched for Al Youst, the club owner. As reported in the *New York Times*, "Every civic club of the Miami area is sure to approve the Klan's militant stand against too rough divertissement which has characterized the city's night life from 1934." The *Times* reporter then struck at the core of the conflict between seasonal tourist economies and permanent residents. He commented that natives want "Miami to be a substantial community, depending less on tourist dollars than on year-round activity. They deplore that you can shoot a cannon down Flagler Street at high noon in mid-Summer and injure no one, but you can't inch your way through the same main thoroughfare in January."[62]

According to the *Times* report, the Klan raids provided only a temporary and partial return to the more modest days of Miami. Nightspots like the French Casino, the Palm Island Club, and the Club Ha-Ha closed for the winter 1936/37 season. Visitors, however, could still count on placing their bets at the racetracks in Hialeah and Tropical Park, at the dog tracks, and the Jai-Alai frontons.

In 1936, federal officials noticed that south Florida was enjoying what the *New York Times* characterized as "perhaps a little more" than "her full measure" of national prosperity. Many feared that south Florida would experience another "boom" as building starts reached new highs of over $28 million in 1936, a total that would soar to $100 million in private construction before 1940.[63] Even though the 1936/37 season was tempered by serious flooding in the Ohio River valley and an unusually warm winter in the Northeast, the high levels of unemployment had ended among skilled construction workers in the region. In December 1937, the *Wall Street Journal* reported that Miami Beach was a city with "no factories; no cemeteries; no billiard parlors; no basements; no wall paper on any walls; no trailer camps, and no unemployment."[64] For all its peculiarities as an atypical post-industrial American city, Miami Beach and much of south Florida could be considered a model of New Deal economic success.

This strong economic recovery stimulated rumors that relief funds for WPA projects in the region were no longer needed. Sandquist and others argued, however, that despite outward signs of prosperity in the construction and tourist industries, other populations were still in need of relief. These included women heads of household, older mechanics who, it was argued "are now being displaced by younger mechanics coming from the North," and white-collar workers ages fifty to seventy.[65] Until mid-1937, WPA projects continued to provide relief work for a broad range of south Floridians, including those in the healthy construction industries. After 1937, national cutbacks in the WPA and the virtual elimination of the PWA meant that few new federal projects would be started.

The Overseas Highway to Key West

Key West provided a stark contrast to the economic story of the south Florida mainland. Heralded in March 1935 as a model of New Deal recovery, the island suffered a series of setbacks. The first was the deadly Labor Day hurricane of 1935. The storm killed hundreds of veterans and civilians working on the federal construction of the Overseas Highway between Lower Matecumbe and Tavernier Keys. It washed out railroad tracks, bridges, and federal veterans camps on Matecumbe and Islamorada Keys.[66] The Florida East Coast Railroad declared bankruptcy in July 1936, which left Key West accessible only by infrequent boat service and flights (three times per week from Miami) until March 1938. The storm also broke water mains from Miami, severely limiting viable tourist activity on the island.

Reconstruction of the island city took place at a feverish pace. In March 1937, Key West again become the focus of national attention. A new $500,000 naval base provided a much-needed boost to the local economy. Money and tourists trickled in as contracts were written for continued work on the Overseas Highway. Sponsored by a $3.6 million loan, the highway project was one of the last to be initiated by the PWA. It was also one of the largest engineering projects—along with the Hoover Dam and the Tennessee Valley Authority—to be undertaken anywhere in the country by New Deal authorities. Train service was eliminated entirely, as a new two-lane highway covered the 12.9 miles of existing railroad bridges, which had been widened to accommodate automobiles. Pieces of train track were reused as guardrails along the bridges and served as reminders of Henry Flagler's ambitious plans. An additional 19.7 miles of coral reef was paved to meet the existing bridges. The ride by car was estimated to take only four or five hours, and this opened the Florida Keys to the middle-class American automotive tourist. Debates ensued over how the Overseas Highway would alter the Keys and their culture. The focus was on the historically rich, yet relatively inaccessible Key West. One commentator suggested that the island was a "Sleeping Beauty" waiting for the "magic touch of the overseas causeway." Others questioned whether Key West would retain "her slumbering charm" when awakened by the annual flood of more than 100,000 automobiles expected to arrive on the new causeway. The older part of the island had been built to maximum density, forcing new development to "have to spread over the keys to the north." As noted in the *Times*, the battle for the city's identity "holds the seeds of a whooping family war. The blue-blooded ladies of Key West are proud of the old town as it is. They love its esthetic beauty, its charming old salt-crusted dwellings of mixed Nantucket, West Indian and Virginia Colonial architecture. . . . They do not want the awakened Sleeping Beauty stripped of her colorful rags and done over in modern dress. Before they reach some compromise on the subject with their merchant banker and land-owning husbands, some tender shins should be barked."[67]

In March 1938, the 106–mile highway opened. Photographic images of the roadways and bridges along the highway abounded. In newspapers and on postcards, its crisp, clean bridges, many of which had once supported railroads, were depicted marching over calm seas and across tranquil island enclaves. Photographs of the highway are both poetic and descriptive, implying connections between the flow of automobiles and the flow of the tides beneath them. As one journalist commented, this was "the only highway in the world by which the motorist actually goes to

FIGURE 15. The reuse of train tracks as guardrails along the Overseas Highway to Key West, PWA, 1939. Courtesy of NARA.

FIGURE 16. The Overseas Highway built upon the existing railway bridges, PWA, 1939. Courtesy of NARA.

sea in his car . . . [providing] one of the most unusual and scenic drives in America."[68]

The Overseas Highway was part of a much larger social and cultural agenda that had developed around Roosevelt's 1936 Good Neighbor Policy toward Latin America. This was made explicit in a radio address broadcast nationally from the opening ceremonies.

> The fact is, this highway to Key West is only the beginning of an even more ambitious and far-seeing highway program . . . with the ultimate aim of connecting the eastern section of the United States and Canada with Cuba, Mexico, Central and South America . . . this branch of the Pan-American highway will carry traffic southward through Florida to Miami and then by this new Overseas highway to Key West and thence over the Cuban National highway 120 miles to the western tip of Cuba and thence by ferry 110 miles to the Yucatan peninsula and from Yucatan southwestward some 500 miles to Guatemala City . . . . At Guatemala City it will connect with the main road of the Pan-American highway en route to South America which enters Mexico at Laredo, Texas.[69]

Or as the chief of the Division of Highways summarized it for the *New York Times,* "With the opening of the Overseas Highway . . . the first critical step has been taken toward a motor tour through lands touching on the Gulf, which was the theatre of much of America's early history."[70]

This New Dealer "grand tour" through American history around the Gulf of Mexico embodied the administration's political and economic visions for the region. Although well intentioned, the plans overlooked the ways in which sensitive social and cultural environments might be altered by invasion of American motorists. New Dealers, however, were confident in the ambassadorial abilities of the American motorist. Tourists were to race from modern Miami to cosmopolitan Havana, across Mayan and Aztec ruins, through sprawling Mexico City and the quaint French Quarters of New Orleans, and grasp the complex interrelations of the cultural heritages they were passing. This New Deal vision helped establish south Florida's physical and ideological position in the region for decades to come.

FIGURE 17. Miami Beach Post Office, October 1938, designed by Howard Cheney for the Treasury Department. Courtesy of NARA.

FIGURE 18. Coral Gables Police and Fire Station, designed by Paist and Steward, WPA, 1938. Photograph by author.

Despite the gradual move away from New Deal construction initiatives by the late 1930s, several important public buildings were completed. The Miami Beach Post Office was designed by Howard Lovewell Cheney and competed in 1939. Its construction was sponsored by the Miami Beach Chamber of Commerce and the Procurement Division of the Treasury Department, headed by Henry Morgenthau Jr.[71] Educated at the Armour Institute of Technology in Illinois (renamed in 1940 the Illinois Institute of Technology with an architecture school headed by Mies van der Rohe) and at the University of Illinois, Cheney responded to President Roosevelt's stated desire that federal edifices be "returned to simpler forms, returned to practical architecture, which, at the same time, has beauty."[72] Cheney was particularly mindful of public gathering space, which he had been exploring since his 1928 project in Chicago for the Sixteenth Church of Christ Scientist. That church's classically proportioned and detailed exterior hid an expansive white, barrel-vaulted interior.[73] The simplicity of that interior space foreshadowed the entry rotunda in Miami Beach, which, with its curved walls lined with post boxes, central fountain, wall murals, and lantern, became one of Miami Beach's most elegant public entryways in what the *Miami Herald* would claim as "a contemporary reinterpretation of Mediterranean architecture."[74] While designing the Miami Beach Post Office, Cheney developed two better-known works: the monumental and cleanly classical Court of Peace and Federal Building at the 1939 World's Fair and the simple and modern Washington National Airport (1940).[75]

Two fire stations, one in Coral Gables and the other in Miami Beach, were late works that exemplified the range of New Deal architectural solutions to similar projects. The 1938 Coral Gables Police and Fire Station was designed by Harold D. Steward. The building was clad in local oolitic limestone quarried near the site.[76] The limestone forms a uniform skin that highlights the building's simple volumetric forms and its Mediterranean-style bell tower. The clean building surface flows into sculpted busts by Jon Keller of firemen placed on piers surrounding the large doors for the fire engines.[77]

Local architects Robert Law Reed and Edwin T. Reeder designed the 1940 PWA-funded Miami Beach Fire Station No. 3 located on Pine Tree Drive.[78] The project featured a central truck room and a six-story drill tower flanked by two-story wings on either side, which reflect the scale of the surrounding modern residential neighborhood.[79] The fire station was one of the most ambitious public buildings undertaken on Miami Beach. Described in the *Architectural Record* as a "multi-use" project, the plan reveals space for two fire trucks with dormitories above, the city's central fire alarm, a training station, and a two-bedroom residence on the north side for the fire chief.[80] The station's white brick surfaces, two-story massing, light colored shutters, and rounded entry portico gave it a potentially ambiguous identity as either a home or a public facility. A comparison between this sleek modern fire tower, with its white stucco walls and glass block, and the more traditional tower constructed by FERA in Miami (see fig. 1) reveals something of the government's role in the regional design shift toward industrial forms and details that took place during the second half of the 1930s. This distinguished Miami Beach, in particular, from other parts of south Florida and grew into an aesthetically unified urban fabric that became the prevailing identity of the city.

Conclusion

Federal funding made Miami a more livable city for residents and visitors. This had the salubrious effect of strengthening the fabric of community in the city, providing more schools, better roads, and hospital facilities and even making south Florida a "safer" place through the construction of shelters and improved storm notification technologies during hurricane season.[81] Yet it also made Miami more vulnerable to the waves of tourists arriving in the area for relief from the winter cold. The New Deal may be seen as institutionalizing change in south Florida. It ensured that the region would flourish with an influx not only of wealthy tourists but also of the middle-class and working-class tourists who would contribute to the character of the place by making use of the new public facilities. Public construction was closely intertwined with private construction. During World War II, the

FIGURE 18. Coral Gables Police and Fire Station, designed by Paist and Steward, WPA, 1938. Photograph by author.

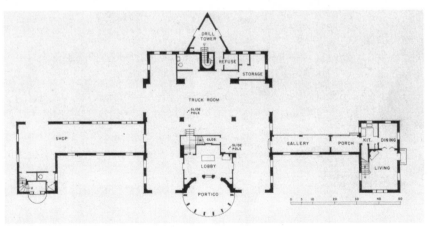

FIGURE 19. Miami Beach Fire Station, designed by Robert Law Weed and Edwin T. Reeder, PWA, 1940. *Architectural Record* (April 1940).

convenience of the airports, harbors, and roadways, along with the plentiful guest accommodations in the area, guaranteed south Florida's success as one of America's premier military training grounds.

Notes

1. Florida State Department of Agriculture, *Fifth State Census for 1925*, Florida Department, Main Library, Miami-Dade Public Library System.

2. *Polk's Miami and Miami Beach Directory 1926* 14 (Jacksonville: R. L. Polk, 1926), 21.

3. Florida State Planning Board, *Summary Report (Mar. 7, 1934–Dec. 31, 1936)* (Tallahassee, 1937), 23.

4. See Jean-Francois LeJeune and Allan T. Shulman, *The Making of Miami Beach, 1933–1942: The Architecture of Lawrence Murray Dixon* (New York: Rizzoli, 2000).

5. The old Coral Gables dog track was reopened for horse racing in 1931. See *Wall Street Journal (WSJ)*, Sept. 22, 1931, 14; and Hans von Briesen, *Why Not Know Florida? An Informal Guide for the Motorist* (Jacksonville: Drew Press, 1936), 97.

6. Writers' Program of Florida, *Planning Your Vacation in Florida: Miami and Dade County, Including Miami Beach and Coral Gables* (Northport, N.Y.: Bacon, Percy and Daggett, 1941), 63.

7. Durward Long, "Key West and the New Deal, 1934–1936," *Florida Historical Quarterly* 46 (Jan. 1968): 209.

8. "Again Tourists Flow to Florida," *New York Times Magazine*, Jan. 27, 1929, SM3.

9. Advertisement for the Cunard Havana Service, *New Yorker*, Feb. 18, 1930, 58.

10. "Again Tourists Flow to Florida."

11. Writers' Program of Florida, *Planning Your Vacation in Florida*, 63.

12. "Passenger Terminal, Pan-American Airways, Inc., Miami, Florida," *American Architect* 136 (July 1929): 76.

13. Writers' Program of Florida, *Planning Your Vacation in Florida*, 63; "Florida Prepares for Tourist Trade," *NYT*, Sept. 19, 1933, E6.

14. For early advertisements for Miami, see *New Yorker*, Dec. 12, 1931, 42, and Jan. 2, 1932, 55.

15. Michael Gannon, ed., *The New History of Florida* (Gainesville: University Press of Florida, 1996), 319.

16. "$41,577,260 Funds for Public Works," NYT, Sept. 14, 1932, 6.

17. For the completion of the Intracoastal by the WPA, see Gannon, ed., *New History*, 318. For work on the project by the PWA, see Office of Government Reports Statistical Section, "Florida," vol. 2, State Data, 1940, Claude Pepper Library, Florida State University, S201/box 153A/F1, 30. See also National Emergency Council, "Report by Lt. Col. Brehon Somervell," *Statewide Coordination Meeting of Federal Agencies Operating in Florida. Held at Mayflower Hotel, Jacksonville Florida Apr. 6, 1936, Corps of Engineers, War Department*, 20B.

18. National Emergency Council, *Statewide Coordination Meeting of Federal Agencies Operating in Florida*, 20C.

19. Lorena Hickok to Harry L. Hopkins, Jan. 31, 1934, Group 24, Papers of Harry L. Hopkins, Federal Relief Agency Papers, FERA-WPA Narrative Field Reports, Florida, container 56, Franklin Delano Roosevelt Presidential Library and Research Center, Hyde Park, N.Y. (hereafter FDR Library).

20. "Roosevelt's Miami Speech Just before the Shooting," NYT, Feb. 16, 1933, 3.

21. "Zangara Receives 80–Year Sentence," NYT, Feb. 21, 1933, 1.

22. Alan Johnstone, *Report to the State*, Sept. 1, 1933, FDR Library.

23. Chapman Field was rejected for PWA funding. In January 1934, there was "little enthusiasm" for funding the bridge to Key West. This, however, would soon change. See Hickok to Hopkins, Jan. 31, 1934, FDR Library.

24. "Florida Prepares for Tourist Trade. Advertising Campaign, Recovery and International Situation Expected to Help. Dollar Drop Also an Aid. State Planning Wide and Varied Attractions for Anticipated Influx of Visitors," NYT, Nov. 19, 1933, E6; Joel Hoffman, "From Augustine to Tangerine: Florida at the U.S. World's Fairs," *Journal of Decorative and Propaganda Arts* 23 (1998): 64.

25. "Plea of Cubans Exiled Here Stems Anti-American Tide," NYT, Sept. 17, 1933, E1, E8; *New Yorker*, Jan. 20, 1934, 55.

26. "Florida Prepares for Tourist Trade," NYT, Nov. 19, 1933, E6.

27. For Eastern Air Lines and the Orange Blossom Special, see "Air Lines and Clipper Ships," *New Yorker*, Jan. 20, 1934, 55; an Orange Blossom Special advertisement, NYT, Dec. 8, 1933, 28; Gannon, *New History*, 434.

28. John A. Stuart, "Exoticism Meets Pragmatism: An Interview with Paul Silverthorne on His Mural Painting and Interior Design in South Florida in the 1940s," *Journal of Decorative and Propaganda Arts* 23 (1998): 361–81.

29. "Florida Comeback (Not 'Boom')," *Business Week*, Mar. 9, 1935, 16, 18.

30. Hickok to Hopkins, Jan. 31, 1934, FDR Library.

31. Hickok to Hopkins, Feb. 5, 1934, FDR Library.

32. Hickok to Hopkins, Jan. 31, 1934, FDR Library.

33. Oswald Garrison Villard, "Florida Flamboyant," *Nation*, Mar. 13, 1935, 295.

34. For example, see L. Murray Dixon's The Royal Arms (1934) on Miami Beach. LeJeune and Shulman, *The Making of Miami Beach*, 56, 74–75.

35. Office of Government Reports Statistical Section, *Florida* 2 (1940): 31, Claude Pepper Library, Florida State University, S201/box 153A/F1.

36. *New Yorker*, Jan. 16, 1935, 111.

37. Villard, "Florida Flamboyant," 295.

38. Robert C. Weaver, "Negroes Need Housing," *Crisis* 47 (May 1940): 138.

39. "Opening of Roddy Burdine Stadium Is Set for Tonight," *Miami Herald*, Sept. 24, 1937, 1A.

40. "Survey of the Architecture of Completed Projects of the Public Works Administration," Album VII (1939), National Archives and Records Administration, College Park, Md. (hereafter NARA), RG 135, box 4.

41. Ibid., Album VII, p. 628, NARA, RG 135, box 7.

42. *Works and Workers of the Florida WPA* (hereafter WWFWPA) 1, no. 1 (May 1936): 2; WWFWPA 1, no. 2 (June 1936): 6.

43. WWFWPA 1, no. 1 (May 1936): 2.

44. Jason Scott Smith, *Building New Deal Liberalism: The Political Economy of Public Works, 1933–1956* (New York: Cambridge University Press, 2006), 87, 116.

45. For this virtually unique organization of the WPA in Florida, see WWFWPA 1, no. 1 (May 1936): 8.

46. WWFWPA 1, no. 4 (Aug. 1936): 5; .1, no. 6 (Oct. 1936): 10, 11; 1, no. 8 (Dec. 1936): 3.

47. WWFWPA 1, no. 8 (Dec. 1936): 18.

48. "Survey of the Architecture of Completed Projects of the Public Works Administration," Album VII, p. 601, NARA RG 135, box 7.

49. Beth Dunlop, "Inventing Antiquity: The Art and Craft of Mediterranean Revival Architecture," *Journal of Decorative and Propaganda Arts* 23 (1998): 190–207.

50. WWFWPA 1, no. 7 (Nov. 1936): 3.

51. WWFWPA 1, no. 4 (Aug. 1936): 7.

52. *WWFWPA* 1, no. 2 (June 1936): 7. The structure is still in use in Wynwood Park, although it has been reclad in stucco.

53. Maurice Feather, "Some Observations on Building in Florida," *Pencil Points* 18 (Oct. 1937): 615; *WWFWPA* 1, no. 1 (May 1936): 6.

54. *WWFWPA* 1, no. 7 (Nov. 1936): 9.

55. Harry Hopkins, "National Radio Address," July 17, 1935, unbound manuscript in Works Program, May 1935–May 1936, Columbia University Business Library.

56. *First Report of Dade County Planning Board*, Apr. 29, 1936, Merrick Archive, box 1, HMSF.

57. Works Program for Ensuing Year as Approved by Dade County Planning Board, Aug. 13, 1936, Merrick Archive, box 1, HMSF.

58. "Approval Given to 30 Projects by Dade Board," *Miami Daily News*, Oct. 31, 1936, 13.

59. "Dade Board Approves Huge Expansion Plan," *Miami Tribune*, Oct. 1, 1936, 3.

60. "Paist Tribute is Paid by District WPA Head," *Miami Tribune*, May 4, 1937.

61. *New Yorker*, Jan. 16, 1937, 53–54.

62. "Miami Night Life Loses 'Hot Spots,'" NYT, Nov. 22, 1937, 2.

63. "Miami, Miami Beach, and Jacksonville Report Gains in Nearly All Categories," *WSJ*, Jan. 19, 1937, 7; Writers' Program of Florida, *Planning Your Vacation in Florida*, 63; "Prosperity, but No Boom, Please, Says Florida. All That Glistens in Her Sun Is Not Yet Gold. But Her Hope of Substance Is Burgeoning," *NYT Magazine*, Feb. 28, 1937, 12.

64. "Miami Beach Boasts It Has No Unemployment," *WSJ*, Dec. 13, 1937, 10.

65. O. A. Sandquist to Merrick, Dec. 18, 1936. Merrick Archive, box 1, HMSF.

66. Joseph Hyde Pratt, *Weekly Report Feb. 14–20, 1935*, Group 24, Papers of Harry L. Hopkins, Federal Relief Agency Papers, FERA-WPA Narrative Field Reports, Florida, container 56, FDR Library.

67. Meyer Berger, "Old Key West Awakes," *NYT Magazine*, Mar. 21, 1937, 10–11.

68. "Motorist Goes to Sea in Own Car Traveling Overseas Highway from Miami to Key West," *WSJ*, Dec. 12, 1938, 9.

69. "Highway Links Canada to Cuba," *Miami Herald*, July 3, 1938, 3C.

70. "Encircling Gulf by Car," NYT, Feb. 5, 1939, XX7.

71. *Miami Herald*, May 2, 1937.

72. Franklin Delano Roosevelt, "Remarks at the Dedication of the New Post Office at Poughkeepsie, N.Y. October 13, 1937," *Public Papers and Addresses of Franklin D. Roosevelt* (New York: Macmillan, 1941), 438.

73. "Sixteenth Church of Christ Scientist, Chicago, Ill.," *American Architect* 134, no. 2548 (July 5, 1928): 21–22.

74. Allan Shulman, "Miami Beach between World's Fairs: The Visual Culture of a Modern City," *Making of Miami Beach,* 54–55.

75. For the Court of Peace, see *Pencil Points* 20 (Sept. 1939): 605–14; for the Washington National Airport, see Howard Cheney, "Washington National Airport: Howard Lovewell Cheney, Consulting Architect," *Architectural Record* 90 (Oct. 1941): 48–57.

76. Limestone for this structure was taken from the same quarry as that used to construct the Keys Memorial Monument on Matecumbe Key. See "Coral Gables Begins New Police Station," *Miami Herald,* Mar. 4, 1938, 7C.

77. Metropolitan Dade County Office of Community and Economic Development, Historic Preservation Division, *From Wilderness to Metropolis: The History and Architecture of Dade County, Florida, 1825–1940 (Miami: Metropolitan Dade County,* 1982), 146.

78. For the PWA, see "Nearing Completion Is This $75,000 Fire Station," *Miami Herald,* May 14, 1939, 3C.

79. LeJeune and Shulman, *The Making of Miami Beach,* 54.

80. "New Multi-Use Fire Station at Miami Beach," *Architectural Record* 87 (Apr. 1940): 46–48.

81. "Florida Feels Safer: Science Has Improved the Detection of Hurricanes and Building of Shelters," *NYT,* Oct. 1, 1939, 147.

THREE

Migrants, Millionaires, and Tourists

Marion Post Wolcott's Photographs of a
Changing Miami and South Florida

MARY N. WOODS

After eight years in the artistic hothouse of Paris, photographer Berenice Abbott returned to New York City in 1929. Struck by the city's startling juxtapositions of the old and new, Abbott began to document what she called "a changing New York" with support from the Works Progress Administration. Almost three decades later, she took her project on the road, now photographing a changing America she found along U.S. 1. Spanning the East Coast from Maine to Florida, this interstate highway brought many to Miami and Miami Beach. And Abbott did some photographs of south Florida while traveling on it. But the region clearly failed to stir anything like the "fantastic passion" she felt for New York City.[1]

And yet the cities and countryside of south Florida experienced changes in the 1930s and 1940s as striking as any Abbott found in New York. Working in tandem with private interests (local, national, and even international), the New Deal transformed urban and rural life in south Florida. And photographs taken by New Deal agencies reveal just how profoundly federal programs affected the region. They recast traditional tourism in Miami Beach, and they abetted corporate agriculture in the fruit and vegetable fields outside Miami and Palm Beach. The New Deal depended on publicity to win support for this unprecedented intervention into private lives and businesses. And photography was crucial in winning support for New Deal programs in an era when mass circulation picture magazines like *Life* and *Look* shaped public opinion. Moreover, because Florida rebounded from the Depression before other areas of the country, its recovery in the mid-1930s was a story that the New Deal especially wanted to tell through texts and images.[2] The Historical Section of the Farm Security Administration (FSA), headed by Roy Stryker, sent photographers John Collier, Dorothea Lange, Carl Mydans, Gordon Parks, Arthur Rothstein, Howard Hollem, and Marion Post Wolcott to north, central, and south Florida during the 1930s and 1940s. Their photographs illustrated official government reports and publications, but the FSA also encouraged newspapers, magazines, books, and exhibitions to use them. As John Stuart has observed to me, "New Deal photography became, in a sense, a way for the government to understand itself and the scope of its endeavors."

Marion Post Wolcott's FSA photographs are featured here for several reasons. First, compared with FSA colleagues like Walker Evans and Dorothea Lange, her work is still relatively unstudied and unappreciated. Second, her photographs of south Florida are especially intriguing because they were both typical and atypical of FSA imagery. Post Wolcott, as was expected of FSA photographers, documented the desperate times of Americans during the Depression. In south Florida she photographed the plight of migrant workers who sought work in the fields and packing houses there. She also photographed what she called "FSA cheesecake": improvements in housing, nutrition, sanitation, and medical care that FSA programs brought to migrant workers and their families.[3] But she also depicted the idle rich in Miami, Palm Beach, and Miami Beach, anomalous subjects among the craftsmen, shopkeepers, tenant farmers, sharecroppers, and migrant workers who dominated the FSA files (see figs. 21, 22). Furthermore, her works subverted as well as served the purposes of New Deal propaganda. While many of her photographs celebrated the New Deal, others made visible the fault lines of race, gender, and class just below the surfaces of south Florida tourism and agribusiness (see fig. 23). And these divisions were issues that federal officials preferred to obscure rather than confront.

Her photographs revealed Miami and south Florida as places apart and yet tied to modern America. They interwove times past and present. Yet these images also traced the outlines, however faintly, of a future Florida that New Deal programs helped to create: the Sun Belt powerhouse of the postwar era. To sharpen this focus on future times, the architectural photographs of Samuel Gottscho are juxtaposed with Post Wolcott's government work.

FIGURE 21. "Migrant agricultural workers waiting in line behind truck in the field, for pay for day's work, near Belle Glade," 1939. Marion Post Wolcott. Courtesy of the FSA/OWI.

Gottscho, a commercial photographer, was also active in Miami and south Florida during the late 1930s and early 1940s. Working for architects, property owners, and real estate developers, he documented the importance of the private sector's partnership with the New Deal. Since private developers and New Deal bureaucrats together laid the foundations for south Florida in the postwar era, analyzing Post Wolcott's imagery alongside Gottscho's seems an especially apt strategy. Finally, considering what was absent from their photographs is as telling as what was present. These photographs registered the present moments, preserved the past, and occasionally predicted the future. Previous studies of FSA pictures have focused on the artistic, political, and cultural implications of documentary photography. Although informed by this scholarship, what follows is another exploration of FSA photography:

FIGURE 22. "Entrance to one of Miami Beach's better hotels." Roney Plaza, Miami Beach, April 1939. Marion Post Wolcott. Courtesy of the FSA/OWI.

FIGURE 23. "Miami employment office, Miami, Florida." January 1939. Marion Post Wolcott. Courtesy of the FSA/OWI.

how it can reveal but also conceal change, survival, and destruction of urban and rural environments in Miami and south Florida.[4]

Post Wolcott and the FSA Project

Roy Stryker hired Post Wolcott in 1938. She was a modern woman. Her mother was a political activist and birth control advocate, and Post Wolcott was a working woman and fervent New Deal supporter. Experienced as a freelance and staff photographer for New York and Philadelphia publications, she was no novice when she came to work at the FSA. Photographer Paul Strand had praised her to Stryker as a someone "of considerable experience who has made a number of very good photographs on social themes in the South and elsewhere."[5]

Urban life was an uncommon subject for the FSA files. Its principal interest was, of course, rural or small town America. FSA photography focused on documenting the economic and environmental crises in agriculture and celebrating New Deal remedies, if not solutions, for problems afflicting rural families.[6] But Stryker was also determined to create an archive of American life, not just publicity shots for government programs. In the early 1960s, Post Wolcott recalled his vision of an FSA archive:

> Along with our political awareness and our interest in trying to make a comment simply, and forcefully, and directly on our national scene, Roy widened our horizons by constantly plugging and urging us to record, to document America from the historians,' sociologists,' and architects' point of view. Constantly we were asked and asking of ourselves, "In what direction are we going; are we doing the whole job? How can we fill in the gaps, round out the file, also photographing some of the beauty, grandeur, lush quality of the USA?"[7]

The project was fundamentally about portraits of Americans, how "to confront people with each other, the urban with the rural, the inhabitant of one section with those of other sections of the country in order to promote a wider and more sympathetic understanding of one another."[8] Moreover, Stryker insisted that his photographers document everyday life. He later wrote: "There are pictures [in the FSA archive] that say labor and pictures that say capital and pictures that say the depression. But there are no pictures of sit-down strikes, not apple salesmen on street corners, not a single shot of Wall Street and absolutely no celebrities."[9]

Other FSA photographers also worked in Florida, but Post Wolcott provided the most extensive coverage of the state, and south Florida was her particular focus. She photographed there from 1938 until 1941, working in such agricultural centers as Belle Glade, Moore Haven, Canal Point, and Homestead. But she also turned her camera, at Stryker's suggestion, on the resort cities of Miami, Miami Beach, and Palm Beach.[10] As a woman, outsider, and government employee, she brought particular insights as well as blind spots to her photography of south Florida.

Her style and working methods were common to both documentary and commercial photographers of the time: sharply focused, richly detailed, and strongly contrasted images. She shot primarily with black-and-white film but also experimented with Kodachrome (an early color film) in her Florida work. (See plate 3.) The dramatic angles, foreshortened views, and abstracted forms of European avant-garde photography from the 1920s did not seem to interest photographers during the Depression. Such concerns seemed irrelevant and self-indulgent to many amid the grim realities of the period.[11] In a 1938 exhibition entitled "American Photographs" at the Museum of Modern Art, Walker Evans was praised for "no trick shots" and his "straight, puritanical stare." Nevertheless, Evans himself called this work a "documentary style." It was not just a simple, unaffected way of seeing but also an "art" and "style" with all the implications of deliberation and consciousness those terms implied.[12]

Photographer Henri Cartier-Bresson spoke of the art of photography as "the decisive moment." It was, he wrote, "the simultaneous recognition in the fraction of a second, of the significance of an event as well as of a precise organization of forms which gave that event its proper expression."[13] Some of Post Wolcott's south Florida photographs seemed to live in Cartier-Bresson's "decisive moment." But others alluded to a rich and complex layering of time, place, and people within the frame of a single image. This was what Berenice Abbott recognized as photography's remarkable power to depict " the intersection of human beings and solid architectural construction all impinging upon each other in the same time." Furthermore, some of Post Wolcott's photographs captured the temporal slippages where, Abbott said, you can see " what the past left you and . . . what you are going to leave the future."[14] Post Wolcott's images often elided "decisive moments" of the present with past and future times.

The temporal dimensions of south Florida's built environment were especially rich and complex given its fabricated past, or more aptly legend, which architects and planners created for their wealthy clients in Miami, Palm Beach, and Miami Beach during the late nineteenth and early twentieth centuries. Shunning the regional vernacular, these designers crafted a mythical architectural past through an eclectic blend of Islamic, Italian, and Spanish precedents. They called it the Mediterranean Revival (see fig. 22).

FIGURE 24. Façade of Pinecrest Apartments, Miami Beach, photograph by
Samuel Gottscho, 1936. Courtesy of Avery Architectural and Fine Arts Library,
Columbia University.

By the 1930s, however, Miami Beach designers reinvented the city again, building a huge district of modern buildings in a distinctive tropical variant of streamlined Art Deco (see fig. 24). The machine age rather than the nostalgic pleasures of past styles became the language of New Deal hopes for the city's future.[15]

Beyond southern Miami and western Palm Beach were the vast farmlands where white and black migrants labored in the fields and packing houses. Here, too, was a strange mix of the old and new. The Old South traditions of racism, poverty, and stoop labor still characterized life and work in south Florida. New Deal policies, however, favored the consolidation of farms into huge corporate holdings. And these agribusinesses employed modern media, processing, and technologies alongside the oppressive yet traditional southern ways. Fruits and vegetables picked and processed by migrant laborers were prepared, refrigerated, transported, and promoted for national and global markets. The Old South was enfolded within the New South.[16]

Photography was the ideal medium to capture what architect Allan Shulman has observed is "a tradition of transience and an easy susceptibility to change" in Miami and Miami Beach.[17] And Post Wolcott's subjects were also transients: either migrant laborers who sought seasonal work in the fields and packing houses of Homestead, Belle Glade, Moore Haven, and Canal Point or tourists who vacationed in the hotels and resorts of Miami, Miami Beach, and Palm Beach. Even the millionaires who built estates in south Florida were transient, "snowbirds" escaping the frigid winters of the Midwest and Northeast. Transience and mobility were tropes of modernity, the experiences of modern life. Since the nineteenth century, historian Marshall Berman has argued, "To be modern is to be part of a universe, in which, as Marx said, 'all that is solid melts into air.'" It was also, Berman noted, "to live a life of paradox and contradiction. . . . It is to be both—revolutionary and conservative . . . longing to create and to hold onto something real even as everything melts. We might even say to be modern is to be antimodern."[18] By Berman's definitions, this commingling of the Old and New Souths that Post Wolcott found in Florida was a fundamentally modern phenomenon.

Migrant Workers

Post Wolcott shared Roy Stryker's commitment to recording everyday life. And she was sensitive to the seasonal changes and rhythms of south Florida. Writing from Belle Glade in 1939, she explained how this town of bean fields and packing houses took on

> a completely different aspect when the crops are coming in and the transient labor is here and trucks and carloads of pickers are in the streets. . . . There are many things to photograph around the *packing houses* which give a good picture of their lousy existence and general life and health, etc., as around their homes and shacks. I don't remember that we have very much of this. I don't mean just showing various operations of the packing and grading processes. I mean the life of the packing houses—the hanging around, the "messing around," the gambling, the fighting, the "sanitary conditions," the effects of the *very* long work stretch, with rest periods, their "lunch"—etc. Then I must get some good pix of the picking in the muck—It's also different from *anywhere* else and different at the height (or near it) of the season."[19]

The punishing and impoverished lives of migrant camps and farm towns Post Wolcott captured lay only miles beyond the fabled estates and resorts of Miami and Palm Beach. As an early twentieth-century postcard emphasized, south Florida was about hotels, resorts, and tourism, but it was also about agriculture (see fig. 25).

Peas, beans, celery, tomatoes, strawberries, and sugar cane were all important cash crops. A state brochure from 1940 underlined the importance of agriculture to the economy:

> Florida is a vast agricultural empire with Citrus as King and Vegetables, Queen, and with a retinue of general agricultural crops and tropical fruits that is truly amazing. From an agricultural output of $14.5 million in 1914, Florida today has 2 million acres in farms and groves . . . to produce a farm income of $285 million a year—and this on only 6 percent of the land of the state.[20]

The rail and shipping lines that brought tourists to south Florida carried back fruit and vegetable crops to national and international markets. Long

FIGURE 25. Postcard from the early twentieth century. Courtesy of the Historical Museum of Southern Florida.

before air conditioning became common in buildings, refrigerated cars prevented Florida produce from perishing before reaching consumers. Yet south Florida was extolled to tourists as a naturally "air-conditioned state" where "summer spends the winter."[21] And air conditioning for hotels and apartments was uncommon until after the postwar era. Just as the transport of Florida agricultural products depended on modern technologies and engineering, so did their cultivation. South Florida fruits and vegetables were grown, in large part, on land created by draining the Everglades during the early 1900s.

While Post Wolcott did photograph some of the citrus groves and factories of central Florida, she concentrated on the fields and packing plants in the southern part of the state. The FSA was the only federal agency focusing on migrant workers. Transient agricultural laborers were now black and white rural families rather than the single men imported from Mexico, Japan, India, and the Caribbean as contract laborers before the Depression. Ironically, New Deal programs of crop allotment and scientific farming also benefited corporate and large individual landowners. Dispossessed from the land by mechanization, ecological disasters, and government programs, former tenant farmers and sharecroppers became "an army of migratory farm laborers," in the words of an FSA report from 1940. They had "little chance for more than a few months' work" in any one place.[22] These workers were part of what Dorothea Lange and Paul Taylor called a modern-day exodus. In *American Exodus*, their 1939 study of migrant laborers in text and image, they wrote: "Now our people are leaving the soil again. They are being expelled by powerful forces of man and of Nature."[23] Working for only a few weeks at a time, migrant laborers and their families barely subsisted as they followed the harvests from east to west and from south to north across the country.

There were simply too many migrants for American agriculture to absorb during the Depression. An April 1939 *Fortune* article on migrant labor, "I Wonder Where We Can Go Now?" estimated that a million farm workers and their families were on the road each year, looking for seasonal work in fruit and vegetable fields. Living conditions in the labor camps and tent cities erected by workers quickly became squalid, and malaria, typhoid, and malnutrition were common. Built on the peripheries, these camps were invisible until writers, photographers, and social scientists like Lange, Taylor, John Steinbeck, Erskine Caldwell, and Margaret Bourke-White explored them in books and photographs. Bourke-White and Caldwell's *You Have Seen Their Faces* appeared in 1937, and Steinbeck's *The Grapes of Wrath* came out two years later. By 1939, congressional committees and the Roosevelt administration were also investigating the problems of migrant workers.

FSA photographs of seasonal laborers were reproduced in government reports, newspapers, magazines, and books and displayed at fairs, churches, schools, museums, and libraries. All this exposure made migrant workers the one American agricultural problem that gripped the public imagination.[24] Visitors' comments from an April 1938 exhibition of FSA works (part of an international exposition of photography held in New York City) testified to the power of these images: "Excellent and vivid portrayal. "Far better than reams of the written word." "Have never witnessed more clear depiction of things as they are." "Photos so graphic the legends were unnecessary." And "Wake up smug America! Give them more of these pictures." These reactions recalled those caused by Jacob Riis's photographs in the late nineteenth century. Riis had used photography to reveal conditions in the tenements of New York's Lower East Side in his *How the Other Half Lives* (1890). Nearly half a century later, the FSA project gave rural poverty in America a compelling face. It was a fitting tribute when one visitor to the New York exhibition wrote, "Something real—lets one half know how the other half live."[25]

Before the Depression, Bahamians and African Americans had worked the fields of south Florida. Wages were relatively good, as Florida agriculture prospered first from World War I military contracts and then during the expansive economy of the 1920s. The warm winters attracted sharecroppers and tenant farmers from surrounding states when there was no work in their own fields. Migrant work was initially a supplement to their incomes. Farmers brought their families for the balmier weather as well as the additional money, and white men worked as supervisors in the fields and packing houses. In the fruit and vegetable fields, black Bahamian migrants earned wages unobtainable in their island's stagnant economy.[26]

The citrus season in central Florida lasted six to seven months, allowing workers to reside there for half a year or even permanently. By contrast, work in the pea, celery, lettuce, bean, and tomato fields and packing houses of Dade and Palm Beach counties was for only a few weeks.[27] The conditions in south Florida that Post Wolcott documented in the 1930s and 1940s were as difficult as those recorded by Steinbeck, Taylor, and Lange in California. During harvesting season Belle Glade, Pahokee, Canal Point, and Homestead became frontier boom towns filled with trucks, automobiles, and railroad cars. Migrant workers crowded into bars, stores, juke joints, and movie theaters. Housing was particularly scarce, and living conditions were deplorable.

But Zora Neale Hurston, a novelist and folklorist who worked on the Federal Writers' Project in Florida, captured something else about migrant life in her novel *Their Eyes Were Watching God* (1937). Her black migrant workers found freedom, license, and excitement in the farming communities of south Florida. Like her protagonist Janie Crawford, many migrant workers came from staid farms and small towns of Arkansas, Georgia, Alabama, and northern and central Florida. Janie fled south to the Everglades, escaping a suffocating life in central Florida, with her younger lover, Tea Cake. In a town like Belle Glade, she and Tea Cake thrived, finding hard work in the Everglades muck (known as black gold) but also passion, friendship, and community in the migrants' quarters. Wolcott's images capture the life that people like Janie and Tea Cake lived in the fields, shotgun houses, and juke joints clustered around Lake Okeechobee.[28] Compared to the demurely posed and dressed white "worker" shown harvesting celery in an early-twentieth-century Florida postcard, the FSA photographs of African American migrant laborers were another world, startling in their reality and immediacy. In Post Wolcott's photographs, south Florida was no longer an idyllic Old South where crops were magically harvested by either invisible or lily-white hands. (See fig. 26 and plate 4.)

Overlaid onto the traditions of racism, stoop labor, and grinding poverty were also signs of modernity's incursions into this Old South. Post Wolcott's images recorded how jazz, dance, cinema, fashion, automobiles, and advertising were transforming southern life and folkways. These were signs

FIGURE 26. "Migrant workers cutting celery, Belle Glade, Florida." January 1941. Marion Post Wolcott. Courtesy of the FSA/OWI.

that regional traditions, individuality, and particularity were at risk. As Stuart Kidd argues, the 1930s and 1940s were a "watershed between the South's plantation system and the modernized and diversified economy of the Sun Belt." Post Wolcott's photographs of the streets, bars, juke joints, and movie theaters made visible what Kidd sees as "the homogenizing cultural agencies of radio and cinema and centripetal economic forces of transportation, chain stores, and national sales organizations [that] were turning Southern towns into satellites of metropolitan American."[29] South Florida was at the forefront of this burgeoning and modernizing South, with an economy based on mass tourism and agribusiness. As the authors of the Federal Writers' Project guide to Florida (which was subtitled *A Guide to the Southernmost State*) wryly observed: "Politically and socially Florida has its own North and South, but its northern area is strictly southern and its southern area definitely northern. In the summer, the State is predominantly southern

FIGURE 27. "Juke joint and bar in the Belle Glade area." February 1941. Marion Post Wolcott. Courtesy of the FSA/OWI.

FIGURE 28. "Juke joint and bar in the Belle Glade area." February 1941. Marion Post Wolcott. Courtesy of the FSA/OWI.

FIGURE 29. "Movie theater, Moore Haven, Florida." January 1939. Marion Post Wolcott. Courtesy of the FSA/OWI.

by birth and adoptions, and in winter is northern by invasion."[30] Wolcott's images and Hurston's writings indicated that the agricultural fields of south Florida, like the tourist destinations of Miami, Palm Beach, and Miami Beach, were also invaded by popular culture, industrialization, and the relaxed mores and morality of the modern world (see figs. 27–30).

But such images of a "new" Old South found little favor with Stryker for publication. Only one photograph from Post Wolcott's southern Florida migrant series, in fact, appeared in the "Agriculture" section of the FWP's state guide of 1939. Viewed from behind, a white mother and daughter from Indiana marched off to pick beans in Homestead (see fig. 31). Here Post Wolcott surrounded the two women with lush fields and a magnificent sky

FIGURE 30. "Osceola migratory workers picking up mail in Belle Glade." June 1940. Marion Post Wolcott. Courtesy of the FSA/OWI.

filled with white clouds. Framed to form a strong diagonal through the landscape, they did not stoop but walked erect with their baskets. Although Post Wolcott rarely depicted smiling migrants at work in the fields or packing houses as other photographers did for such government publications as the Florida Guide, her image of the mother and daughter was still a benign and picturesque view of fieldwork. It was a rare image for her, recalling sanitized views of Florida agriculture from picture postcards and state promotional brochures. It projected a comforting view of agricultural labor in a New Deal publication designed to stimulate investment and tourism.

Post Wolcott interviewed and photographed these new migrants (white and black farmers, tradesmen, and even small businessmen) forced onto the road by economic and ecological disasters. In Belle Glade she met the white Indiana barber whose wife and daughter she photographed picking

FIGURE 31. "Mother and daughter from Indiana, picking beans, Homestead."
January 1939. Marion Post Wolcott. Courtesy of the FSA/OWI.

FIGURE 32. "Migratory laborers' camp near packing houses, Canal Point, Florida." April 1939. Marion Post Wolcott. Courtesy of the FSA/OWI.

beans. He chastised his daughter, Post Wolcott wrote in her field notes, to pick faster as she worked in a nearby row. Apparently straight-faced, the father told Post Wolcott that a doctor had advised him to take his child south to improve her health in the Florida sunshine.[31]

As migrants like these continued to arrive, the governor warned his colleagues in surrounding states that there were no more farm jobs in Florida. Stationed at state lines, police turned back those without any visible means of support. Once the crops were picked, "hobo expresses," railroad cars full of migrant workers, were sent out of state. As one boy told a *Fortune* reporter in 1939, "When they need us, they call us migrants. When we've picked their crop, we're bums and have to get out."[32] Camps and tent cities of migrant workers along roads leading to Miami, Miami Beach, and Palm Beach were injurious to tourism (see fig. 32). The harsh realities of south Florida's rural economy now impinged on the fantasies necessary for its tourist industry.

But winter was the season for both migrants and tourists in south Florida. Post Wolcott arrived, like the migrant workers, ahead of the harvest in the winter of 1938/39. Timing was of the essence for both migrant workers and FSA photographers. Thus she and the workers had to wait until the crops ripened for picking. Since work in the fields and packing houses was on hold, Post Wolcott photographed life in the streets, boarding houses, bars, and juke joints. She also took her first pictures of Miami.

Towns like Belle Glade and Homestead became packed during the harvests. Black migrants, an FSA report noted, "usually move in with families who are permanent residents of the Negro quarter. This section of town is "always full of shiny new automobiles against a background of dance halls, bars, and unpainted shacks." In the captions she wrote for her photographs, Post Wolcott noted the bars, stores, juke joints, and even movie theaters doubled as boarding houses (see figs. 33, 34).[33] But there was also a community here for black migrants, which Hurston depicted in *Their Eyes Were Watching God*. It was a familiar landscape of wooden buildings: stores, churches, shotgun houses, and juke joints (see fig. 35).

White migrants had no such community to absorb them. While some picked the crops, others worked in the packing houses on assembly lines (jobs usually denied black workers), packing and canning the produce for shipment. Yet conditions there were as grim as those in the fields. Temperatures were sweltering, and packing house workers often stood in water. Children and adults worked day and night shifts in the rush to ship perishable vegetables. White migrants lived in shacks, boarding houses, tourist camps, trailer parks, and tent cities. A few had electricity and even poignant vestiges of domesticity like plants, tattered awnings, and screen doors, as evident in Post Wolcott's photograph (see fig. 36). Perhaps these were the quarters of packing house supervisors, who received higher wages, near Belle Glade. But most migrants, white and black, lived in overcrowded and unsanitary conditions. Post Wolcott noted in her captions that African Americans continued to live in housing condemned by the Belle Glade board of health. Many white migrant families built ad hoc structures from

FIGURE 33. "Every available building is used for rooming houses in overcrowded Negro section, Homestead, Florida." January 1939. Marion Post Wolcott. Courtesy of the FSA/OWI.

scraps of wood, metal, and canvas they scavenged. Weekly wages ranged from $2 to $15 with living expenses for a small family averaging $9. It was a life of "bare subsistence."[34]

While many were defeated (victims of a surfeit of unskilled field and factory labor), some of the migrants Post Wolcott photographed were not beaten down. These people were proud and even defiant as they confronted her camera. As Nicholas Natanson has observed of photography, "There is a critical difference between images of the hard-pressed and images of the pathetic; the latter may evoke a view of only condescension, establishing a typical relationship between powerful and powerless."[35] However, as Post Wolcott confessed to Stryker, the beaten down were easier to photograph:

FIGURE 34. "Street in Negro section, Belle Glade, Florida." January 1939.
Marion Post Wolcott. Courtesy of the FSA/OWI.

FIGURE 35. "Negro church, Homestead, Florida." January 1939. Marion Post Wolcott. Courtesy of the FSA/OWI.

FIGURE 36. "Housing for white migratory workers near Belle Glade." January 1941. Marion Post Wolcott. Courtesy of the FSA/OWI.

> I've decided in general that it's a helluva lot easier to stick to photographing migrants, sharecroppers, tenants, "niggers,"—clients—and the rest of those poverty-stricken people, who are depressed, despondent, beaten, given-up. Most of them don't object too strenuously or too long to a photograph or picture. They believe it may help them, or they may get something out of it—a little money, or better houses, or a government loan.[36]

Such "easy" subjects justified what Natanson has characterized as New Deal conservatism, which was about "paternalism that came from the government" rather than worker activism across racial lines, like the Southern Tenant Farmers' Union, that threatened established powers.

Some of Post Wolcott's most striking subjects encountered her as equals, like the young white man, out riding with his friends in an automobile, who smiled for her and her camera (see fig. 30) or the black man in a Belle Glade juke joint (see fig. 28) whose gaze challenged her right to be there photographing him. This man was an individual; he had agency. This image did not present African Americans as pathetic victims, the portrayal favored in New Deal photography. Nor was it a comforting image like the group portraits of black college students, boy scouts, and church congregations compiled in 1943 for the *Florida Negro*, another Federal Writers' Project.[37] Post Wolcott's man in the juke joint was too challenging for white America.

Other pictures derived their impact from the invisibility of Post Wolcott. A woman (see fig. 27) was irrepressible as she danced in front of a juke joint, oblivious to the camera. These images depicted spaces that people constructed for themselves in streets or automobiles or juke joints. Here they shaped what Natanson has called "functioning minds, capable of creating the social and cultural patterns that helped to mitigate, circumvent, and occasionally avoid the daily rebuffs and disasters, providing meaning, form, substance, and pleasure."[38]

In these photographs Post Wolcott's subjects were individuals. Unlike the iconic portraits of Lange's migrant Madonna or Evans's white Alabama sharecroppers, Post Wolcott's images might be understood as landscape views vibrantly inhabited by people. Single figures or groups were shown in the contexts of their streets, stores, dwellings, or places of entertainment (see figs. 27, 28, and 34). These pictures were often exterior rather than interior views. Her status as a single woman photographing alone in the South may, in part, have necessitated composing a view from outside and at a distance.

Lange and Bourke-White did not usually work alone in the field. They collaborated with husbands or partners when they photographed. A woman alone in the South was a cause for concern and comment. Stryker fretted and worried about Post Wolcott, advising her to dress conservatively and conduct herself with decorum and caution. He wrote she should not wear pants and exotic headscarves or be out alone at night. As a single white woman she had to be especially careful about interviewing and photographing African Americans lest she endanger them. This was still the Jim Crow South where cross burnings, night rides, and lynchings were common occurrences. Even white men had to be circumspect. Arthur Raper, who studied social and economic issues in southern agriculture, was arrested in Georgia when he was overheard addressing a black man as "sir."[39] New Deal staff members who were openly sympathetic to Africa Americans in the fields and towns endangered themselves and their subjects in the Jim Crow South. The Ku Klux Klan openly paraded in Miami streets and counted city policemen among its members. And Miami, Miami Beach, and Palm Beach were among the most racially segregated cities in the United States.[40]

So Post Wolcott usually kept her distance, perhaps choosing to photograph with a small and less obtrusive Leica camera as well as her larger Speed Graphic or Rolleiflex camera.[41] Close-up views were taken when she could control the circumstances, shooting New Deal "cheesecake" at the Osceola and Okeechobee Camps that the FSA built for white and black migrant families, respectively, near Belle Glade. Here her subjects had to be amenable because they were recipients of public aid on government property. Yet these staged publicity shots were what Post Wolcott resented most about her FSA assignments. Finding her more malleable than photographers like Evans or Lange, Stryker depended on Post Wolcott for FSA publicity materials like camp residents attending school, being inoculated against typhoid, canning vegetables for themselves, and assembling for town meetings.[42] Such "feel good" imagery appeased administrators and politicians, buying Stryker the time, staff, and funding he needed to build his FSA archive of everyday life.

Yet keeping her distance may have created opportunities for Post Wolcott that her fellow FSA photographers were not forced to explore. Lange and Evans isolated individuals or groups from their surroundings. More spontaneous interactions between individuals were also lost. Catching informal yet complex choreographies of daily life became possible only when the photographer worked with a small and unobtrusive camera and stood at a distance. Framing literally and figuratively the "big picture," Post Wolcott often created still images that were what cinematographers refer to as "master shots." Sally Stein has observed of Post Wolcott that "she was especially attentive to informal group interactions for the way they expressed some of the bonds and boundaries within a community. This interest precluded the common pictorial strategy of moving in close; and, as a result, much of her imagery studying group dynamics is less sensationally dramatic."[43] Distancing herself, Post Wolcott gave her images a spontaneity, immediacy, and verisimilitude that the heroic portraits of Lange and Evans lacked.

It also led to informal and overall compositions (see figs. 26, 27, and 28) characteristic of a radical modernism that eschewed control, hierarchy, and monumentality.[44] Here Post Wolcott was most free of staged "FSA cheese-cake." She brought a modern eye and aesthetic to images that, ironically, better suited Stryker's desire for the real and everyday life of his beloved traditional America. Yet he was apparently oblivious to her achievement; he used very few Post Wolcott photographs in such celebratory publications as *In This Proud Land*, the 1973 volume dedicated to the FSA archive. Yet Stryker needed her FSA "cheesecake" for government reports, publications, and exhibitions. The first critics and historians of FSA photography under-estimated Post Wolcott, too, dismissing her, until Stein's pathbreaking article of 1983, as merely a "romantic 'city girl' in a predominantly male group of seasoned social observers."[45]

Yet it was probably not just Post Wolcott's modern aesthetic but her explorations of the fault lines fracturing America that gave Stryker pause. She made visible inequities and disparities of race, class, and gender in her best images. The south Florida work, in particular, traced differences in rural, urban, and small town landscapes with both drama and subtlety. Unlike many FSA photographers, she showed inequities as ubiquitous and inescapable, manifesting themselves not only in migrant camps and small towns like Belle Glade and Homestead but also in Miami (called the Magic City for its seemingly overnight development) and exclusive resorts of Palm Beach and Miami Beach. Her photography threatened, as both Stein and Kidd have astutely noted, the traditional myths and values of a premodern and resilient American society that Stryker was determined to enshrine in the FSA archive. This was what confused young men and women needed during World War II to inspire and motivate them, Stryker wrote in 1940, pictures of "the tool maker, expert farmer, the fine teacher, even the good politician" rather than celebrities and entertainers. Stein writes that Stryker's America was rooted in myths about "the concept of the integrity of the individual; the concept of responsible leadership; the belief in self-government; the concept of individual liberty and opportunity."[46] And Post Wolcott's biting imagery often questioned rather than affirmed his ideals.

Moreover, her South was often about the inroads of modernity into the region. The South for Stryker and FSA photographers like Evans and Lange was compelling precisely because modernity had seemingly bypassed it. As Kidd has written: "The region's premodernity invited an alternative construction that was more comforting in the contexts of the Great Depression and escalating global tensions: namely, that the South was a repository of American traditions and values." The small towns, churches, farms, historic architecture, and community traditions of the South were "terra incognita" for FSA photographers who were from East and West Coast cities. The FSA project was

> an opportunity to travel the country as a government employee [that] was
> both revelatory and educational. The American heartland became as much
> an imaginary space as it had been for the 19th-century landscape painters, for
> whom geographical discovery opened up a range of creative possibilities. For
> the photographers the natural and human environments of the South pro-
> vided a touchstone for the modern world of mass and motor in which they
> lived and worked. . . . For them, the South was a stimulating antidote to the
> predictable, anonymous, and modernized cities with which they were associ-
> ated professionally. Man's traces on the southern landscape, in contrast, were
> personalized, rooted in history, and culturally authentic.[47]

For Stryker, who had lived and worked on small ranches and in mining towns in Kansas and Colorado, the South represented the survival of American community, democracy, and individuality, all (he believed) imperiled by modernity. The FSA file was an archive for a vanishing America.[48] Marked by change, diversity, urbanism, popular culture, and commercialism, Post Wolcott's south Florida was at odds with Stryker's vision of both the FSA file and America. Her photographs of Miami and south Florida were complex, showing a region that was and was not the traditional South. As Post Wolcott wrote Stryker, her slacks, which he fretted would upset and

provoke conservative southerners, were perfectly acceptable for white wom-
en to wear in the fields and resorts of south Florida (see fig. 31).[49]

Millionaires and Tourists

If Belle Glade and Homestead showed the incursions of modernity into
the countryside, Miami and Miami Beach were truly modern metropolises.
They swelled with tourists from the Midwest, Northeast, Cuba, Europe, and
Latin America during the winter season. As a *Fortune* reporter observed in
1936:

> In winter Miami forgets it is a southern city, so long as the profits of forgetful-
> ness are rich. . . . they [the tourists] bring their pleasures and their morals with
> them from the North. They are mostly of the metropolitan world that finds its
> entertainment on Broadway. . . . In Miami's business district are the same lofty
> skyscrapers that Manhattan has, sunk often twenty-five feet underground into
> the soft coral rock, without Manhattan's narrow confines to excuse them. . . .
> The biggest Manhattan stores like Saks, Best and Company, and Jay Thorpe
> have Miami Beach branches during the winter season.[50]

Ironically, it was Stryker who suggested Post Wolcott shoot "a little of
some of the tourist towns, which will show up how the 'lazy rich' waste their
time; keep your camera on the middle class, also," as she waited for the harvest in south Florida.[51] Although she photographed Miami and Palm Beach,
Post Wolcott concentrated on Miami Beach. Here she found both the traditional playground of the wealthy and a new destination for middle- and
even working-class tourists. Miami Beach, as Allan Shulman has written,
was a "miniature metropolis, a city devoted entirely to leisure," all within
easy reach of her camera.[52]

Its Mediterranean Revival hotels and mansions were Post Wolcott's most
frequent subjects, as she followed Stryker's instruction to depict the pastimes
and places of the "lazy rich" and middle class. She documented the exte-
riors and interiors of private homes owned by millionaires like the former
president of Gillette Safety Razor (see figs. 37 and 38). The Roney Plaza
on Collins Avenue was another subject for Post Wolcott. She documented

FIGURE 37. "Wealthy residential section, Miami Beach." April 1939. Marion Post Wolcott. Courtesy of the FSA/OWI.

FIGURE 38. "Cocktail bar in home of former president of Gillette Safety Razor Company, Miami Beach." April 1939. Marion Post Wolcott. Courtesy of the FSA/OWI.

the crisp elegance and sophistication of its guests framed by the Spanish Renaissance entryway (see fig. 22).

But Post Wolcott alluded to realities just beyond the carefully crafted stage sets of the Roney Plaza. Her photograph of the Roney Plaza forms a striking pendant to the image of a young woman leaving a Miami employment office (see fig. 23). The Mediterranean Revival fantasies created for wealthy white tourists, such as the man in the white suit at the Roney Plaza, functioned smoothly because of black maids, porters, cooks and gardeners. Residing in Overtown (so called because it was just over the railroad tracks from downtown Miami), African Americans worked in the Miami Beach and Palm Beach hotels and estates. But they were prohibited from living there (except in servants' quarters) or even swimming there. Curfews and pass laws mandated how and when they could and could not appear in the exclusive enclaves of white Americans.[53]

In a sly image, she also captured the luxurious coddling and lassitude in the cabanas along the private beaches of hotels like the Roney Plaza (see fig. 39). Here a man being served brunch provided her with an opportunity to explore class differences. The guest was sprawled in an unbuttoned shirt on a hot and sunny day, while the waiter wore a suit, rather elegantly, and stood at attention as he served. The tan lines at the waiter's wrists, indicating many days spent working in the sun, contrasted with the guest's white, vulnerable skin.[54] There was no eye contact between the two men. While service entailed decorum and attention, privilege allowed self-absorption and informality.

Post Wolcott photographed other haunts of the wealthy, like Miami's Hialeah Racetrack, built in 1925 and remodeled in 1930. She captured a postcard-perfect view of the racetrack, designed around a lushly land-scaped lake stocked with imported flamingoes, and a grandstand view of elegantly dressed millionaires worthy of the Ascot Derby scene from My Fair Lady. But she also depicted a crush of gamblers around the Hialeah betting windows that was more Damon Runyon than Cecil Beaton. Profits from Hialeah's pari-mutuel windows were especially important to Florida because legislators refused to enact income and inheritance taxes, deeming them detrimental to the economy.[55] Post Wolcott tried to photograph inside

FIGURE 39. "Winter visitor being served brunch in a private club, Miami Beach."
April 1939. Marion Post Wolcott. Courtesy of the FSA/OWI.

Miami and Miami Beach gambling casinos, which enriched both gangsters and the municipalities, but she was thrown out when her camera was spotted. *Fortune* reported in 1936 that gambling profits were essential for any Miami entertainment establishment, dependent on a tourist season of only a few months.[56]

Post Wolcott's photographs of the Roney Plaza and Miami Beach estates alluded to the city's fabricated past. It was a past, however, from only a few years earlier. Before hotels of the 1920s like the Roney Plaza, the city had been a winter home for millionaires like Edsel Ford and Harvey Firestone. Fortunes from the automotive industry allowed such men to build Mediterranean Revival mansions north of Lincoln Road, the Fifth Avenue of Miami Beach. Carl Fisher, an Indiana millionaire whose wealth came from automobile headlights, created Miami Beach from an unprepossessing swampy and mosquito-infested sandbar in 1915. But even the wealthy could be displaced, albeit at a handsome profit. The Firestone estate was sold in 1926 to developers who constructed the Roney Plaza, the first resort hotel on the ocean rather than bay side of Miami Beach. Imported from New York City, the Roney Plaza architects were Schultze and Weaver, who specialized in luxurious hotel properties like the Waldorf-Astoria Towers in New York and the Biltmore in Coral Gables, Florida.[57]

By 1939 when Post Wolcott photographed it, Mediterranean Revival buildings like the Roney Plaza were fast becoming old Miami Beach. A new city of streamlined Art Deco hotels, stores, cinemas, gasoline stations, and apartment buildings designed for working- and middle-class tourists and retirees was rising (see figs. 24, 40). This feverish development drove Miami and Miami Beach's recovery from the Depression in the mid-1930s. Architects and developers now pinned their hopes on a machine-age future rather than a Mediterranean Revival past. Miami Beach had excluded Jewish Americans in the 1910s and 1920s. Now it welcomed developers like the Grossinger family, resort owners from the Borscht Belt of the Catskills outside New York City, who created hotels, resorts, and restaurants for Jewish Americans. Miami Beach, like Manhattan, was engaged in what historian Max Page has called the creative destruction of cities. Structures become economically obsolescent, they are demolished, and then a new urban identity is constructed, only to be consumed and reinvented yet again.[58] Even by Manhattan standards, south Florida's creative destruction was especially feverish. As Allan Shulman has noted, Miami Beach's "makeovers" were remarkable for their frequency and sudden design shifts.[59]

The Miami that Post Wolcott photographed with only a few exceptions was about the past, the south Florida that Henry Flagler and Carl Fisher had created for snowbird millionaires from the Northeast and Midwest. Perhaps her fixation on Miami's gilded Mediterranean Revival past was appropriate given that it too was fading by the mid-1930s. Since the FSA archive was about preserving a vanishing America on film, Miami Beach millionaires took their place alongside tenant farmers and sharecroppers from the Everglades and Mississippi Delta. However, two of Post Wolcott's photographs alluded to the present and future Miami Beach. She photographed

FIGURE 40. "Even the gas stations are on an elaborate scale, often modern in design, resembling hotels." Miami Beach, April 1939. Marion Post Wolcott. Courtesy of the FSA/OWI.

the sweeping porte-cochere of a Gulf gas station, a rare image in her work of the streamlined Art Deco designs then transforming Miami Beach (see fig. 40). In her caption she marveled that even the gas stations in Miami Beach were modern and elaborate structures, resembling the Art Deco hotels, which she chose not to photograph. Ironically, the Gulf station she documented was, in fact, a hotel. Designed by the modern architect Igor Polevitzky, it literally married the streamlined Art Deco style with what had inspired it, the aerodynamic forms of the automobile.[60]

This photograph also alluded to the automobile's importance to Miami Beach's transformation during the New Deal era. The city now staked its future on mass tourism, not class tourism. This change was also evident in her photograph looking up Washington Avenue in south Miami Beach (see fig. 41). Cars and Greyhound buses (the latter's neon sign visible on the right) brought middle- and working-class tourists, especially Jewish Americans from New York and Chicago, to Miami Beach. Here they patronized familiar sounding establishments like the Times Square Cafeteria and Blackstone Hotel (the former's neon sign is on the right and the latter's tower is in the background). The Blackstone was a fitting symbol of the new Miami Beach as the first hotel to accept Jewish Americans as guests.[61]

Since this streamlined Miami was largely the creation of the private sector, its portrait was appropriately the work of New Yorker Samuel Gottscho (1875–1971), a commercial architectural photographer. A traveling salesman for twenty-three years, Gottscho made photography his profession when he turned fifty in 1920. Since he had always been interested in houses and

FIGURE 41. "One of Miami's streets showing small shops, signs, and tourist bureaus." Miami Beach, April 1939. Marion Post Wolcott. Courtesy of the FSA/OWI.

gardens, Gottscho built his professional career around architectural photography.[62] He later wrote: "I dedicated myself to learn to make good pictures which would please them [architects and landscape architects], for with their blessing, I would be able to interest their clients as well."[63]

He first photographed Long Island estates and then worked for architects like Raymond Hood photographing Art Deco skyscrapers in New York City. Romantic nocturnal views of the "architecture of the night" (a term coined by Hood, who dramatically lit his own skyscrapers) became a Gottscho specialty.[64] It was a sure sign of south Florida's economic recovery when, as Jean-François LeJeune and Allan Shulman note, Gottscho began working there in the mid-1930s.[65] Following his Long Island clients southward, he photographed their Mediterranean Revival estates in Miami Beach and Palm Beach. But Gottscho also depicted the new Art Deco Miami Beach for architects like L. Murray Dixon, Igor Polevitzky, and Thomas T. Russell.

Buoyed by New Deal programs and American and European investors, Miami Beach recovered in 1935 from the economic collapse that had crippled south Florida since 1926. It became the fastest growing community in the United States, with a per capita building rate twenty times higher than the next city, Washington, D.C. Construction in the Miami area, valued at $2.5 million in 1932, rose to $14 million in 1935.[66] Five years later, *Architectural Forum* reported (in an article aptly titled "Boom over Miami Beach") that construction crews were working day and night to complete 41 new hotels and 166 apartment buildings for winter tourists. "Money has poured in from France, Belgium, Cuba, seeking safety in Florida's southernmost tip."[67]

Foreign and American investors found their money went much further in the 1930s. Edward Doherty, head of the Cities Services petroleum empire, purchased Mediterranean Revival resorts—the Biltmore Hotel in Coral Gables and the Roney Plaza in Miami Beach—at bargain prices.[68] New resort designs based on Manhattan skyscrapers began to rise north of Lincoln Road along Collins Avenue.[69] Spaced at fairly regular intervals along the beach, these hotel towers fell, an *Architectural Forum* reporter noted, "into a pattern of which Le Corbusier would approve. Eleven to fifteen stories each, braced against the hurricane, using steel and reinforced concrete,

FIGURE 42. Albion Hotel, photograph by Samuel Gottscho, 1940. Courtesy of the Gottscho-Schleisner Collection, PPD, Library of Congress.

each holds aloft its distinctive bid for attention—name, tower, pinnacle, or what have you."[70]

Gottscho captured all these qualities to their best advantage in his photographs. Long before *Miami Vice*, the Michael Mann design-driven television series from the 1980s, Gottscho portrayed Miami Beach as a city of speed, glamour, and sexiness. His nocturnal views of hotels like the Albion were especially provocative (see fig. 42). Here Igor Polevitzky and Thomas Triplett Russell's sleek, white ocean liner of a building gleamed and shimmered, dominating the night as streaks of light, like Futurist force lines, raced across the street in Gottscho's long exposure. In the courtyard of the Albion (see fig. 43), Polevitzky and Russell designed a raised swimming pool (its depths visible through portholes strategically placed at eye level),

FIGURE 43. Albion Hotel pool and beach with cabanas, photograph by Samuel Gottscho, 1940. Courtesy of the Gottscho-Schleisner Collection, PPD, Library of Congress.

surrounded by an artificial beach with cabanas. Gottscho's angled and elevated view made clear how the architects moved the real beach, which was several blocks east of the hotel, to the Albion's courtyard.

Equally glamorous was Gottscho's detail of the Atlantis Hotel terrace. Here black glass panels (modern and luxurious materials so characteristic of Art Deco) reflected Miami Beach's fabled expanses of sand and palm trees on the façade of L. Murray Dixon's Atlantis Hotel (see fig. 44). The building literally became a movie screen, projecting constantly changing images of Florida fantasies.

Gottscho's imagery made clear these were buildings designed for an urbane, wealthy, and sophisticated clientele. The hotel guests were the real-life Tracy Lords of *The Philadelphia Story*, gone south for the winter season.

FIGURE 44. Detail of Atlantis Hotel terrace facing the ocean, photograph by Samuel Gottscho, 1936. *Architectural Record* (July 1936). Courtesy of the Avery Architectural and Fine Arts Library, Columbia University.

Architects like Dixon, Polevitzky, and Russell created stage sets as modern and glamorous as any designed for Fred Astaire and Ginger Rogers in the Hollywood musicals of the 1930s. *Fortune* observed in 1936 that Miami Beach streets were "definitely smart, as smart as Palm Beach's streets," but this smartness was different, a modern, machine-age one, based on "sleek motors . . . [and] clumps of willowy women in frail evening gowns, that are the unmistakable insignia of Manhattan, Boston, and Philadelphia." This Florida, the writer John Dos Passos wrote, appeared "fabulous and movie-like, a place where cities were built in three months."[71]

But Art Deco sets and costumes of Hollywood movies stimulated the dreams of more modest Americans. And Miami Beach built a modern resort for them, too. Smaller real estate players developed new properties in a machine age modernism that drew on not only avant-garde European designs but also New York commercial and residential typologies.[72] These architects appropriated the garden apartment typology (developed in European and American housing developments) for south Miami Beach below Lincoln Road. Low-rise, walk-up units oriented around courtyards were familiar to working- and middle-class New Yorkers who inhabited such complexes in the Bronx, Queens, and Brooklyn. Although the colors, materials, ornaments, and landscaping were tropically inspired, small hotels and garden apartments like Dixon's Pinecrest Apartments were a home away from home for these New Yorkers (see fig. 24). Financed by loans from New Deal agencies like the Federal Housing Administration and Reconstruction Finance Corporation, these small units were intended for tourists and retirees with modest incomes.[73] Many were union members from the New York garment trades who came to Miami Beach on vacations only recently won through collective bargaining sessions. And their unions also invested pension funds in these properties.[74] Yet Post Wolcott did not photograph these buildings. Corporate welfare for hoteliers and real estate developers was perhaps not the sort of New Deal program that the Roosevelt administration wished to publicize. Yet it was a success story: a modern utopia built for and, in some cases, by industrious American workers.

Miami

Neither Gottscho nor Post Wolcott documented the infrastructure of highways, schools, water treatment plants, and harbor facilities that the Public
Works Administration (PWA) sponsored in south Florida. As noted elsewhere in this collection, these PWA projects were essential in rebuilding
both the tourist and agricultural economies. The PWA hired freelance photographers like Francis Lee or unidentified staff members to record these
projects for internal reports, government publications, newspapers, and
magazines. And these photographers sometimes depicted PWA works with
great verve, as Lee did in his series on the Overseas Highway linking Miami
to the Florida Keys. But they also dutifully recorded more prosaic PWA
projects like small community centers. Yet Miami was still the magic city;
its new PWA-financed harbor facilities included berths for the yachts of millionaires. While neither the aesthetic tour de forces of Gottscho nor Post
Wolcott's compelling human stories, these photographs documented the
scale, ambition, and cost of PWA initiatives in Miami and Miami Beach.
The budgets for public projects in those two cities totaled $5,630,438, an
amount far exceeding PWA funds allocated to any other Florida county or
even surrounding state. The New Deal was clearly betting on Miami and
Miami Beach as engines for recovery not only in Florida but also in the
Southeast.[75]

Apart from these PWA images, Miami was something of a photographic
stepchild in the 1930s and 1940s. Neither Gottscho nor Post Wolcott gave
it the attention they devoted to Miami Beach or the Everglades. While the
builders and architects who employed Gottscho were at work in Miami
Beach, the FSA concentrated primarily on agricultural workers outside
Miami and Palm Beach. Miami possessed neither the urban glamour nor
the rural grittiness that drew Gottscho and Post Wolcott. Composed of
shopkeepers, tradesmen, businessmen, professionals, and service people,
the working city of Miami went largely undocumented. Photographers and
their employers seemed to agree with a 1936 *Fortune* assessment of the city
as a wasteland, "a flat morass covered with grass and scrubby trees, snakes
and shallow pools of stagnant water, on whose coastal brim flourish resorts

for tourists. Miami's only salable product is its climate, that and the unlimit-ed license it offers pleasure-bent guests." But Miami was also where tourists and retirees unable to afford even the small Art Deco hotels and apartments of Miami Beach went. According to *Fortune*, northwest Miami was "the section for the masses." Here were "the retired shopkeepers and manufac-turers, men old and tired, who have settled in Miami on their savings to wait for death in the sun." Here retirees cautiously spent their time and sav-ings in the Florida sunshine. A Post Wolcott photograph of the downtown post office hinted at this other Miami (see fig. 45). Against the imposing neoclassical façade, an older and decidedly frumpy woman warily eyed a young woman in an exuberant floral print dress. Here a midwesterner from a Grant Wood painting or Sinclair Lewis novel confronted the license and glamour of the city across the bay, Gottscho's booming Miami Beach. Like the older woman in Post Wolcott's picture, Miami, the writer for *Fortune* continued, was "decorous compared with Miami Beach. Its inhabitants are older, they have less money to spend, and it is to them sufficient holiday to be in Florida at all during the winter months that are so cold in Indiana and Michigan."[76]

Another rare image of Miami by Post Wolcott was the photograph of an African American woman leaving an employment agency (see fig. 23). It al-luded to Overtown, known as the Harlem of the South, where most African Americans had to live. Here they were allowed to live, work, shop, dine, and be entertained.[77] It stood apart from a Miami and Miami Beach that, nonetheless, depended on Overtown residents to make those white cities possible.

Although Stryker later said he wanted FSA photographers to depict ur-ban life, southern cities like Atlanta, Birmingham, Charleston, Mobile, and Miami were not well represented in the FSA archive. This remained true even as FSA photographers began to shoot urban scenes for the new Office of War Information in the 1940s. Moreover, African Americans were prob-lematic subjects for Stryker. He believed photography of them was less us-able, fearing its dissemination would anger southern legislators and lose the FSA congressional support. While Miami's Overtown had its slums, it also possessed schools, churches, businesses, hotels, restaurants, and nightclubs.

FIGURE 45. "Miami Post Office." January 1939. Marion Post Wolcott. Courtesy of the FSA/OWI.

But photographs about Overtown and its signs of racial pride and uplift, like Post Wolcott's pointed commentaries on race and class, were too threatening for Stryker's white audiences in the 1930s and 1940s. Neither found a place in the articles, books, and exhibitions that the FSA prepared for general dissemination.[78]

Conclusion

Studying Marion Post Wolcott's and Samuel Gottscho's photographs from the 1930s and 1940s, we see how the New Deal profoundly affected lives and the built environment in Miami and south Florida. These two photographers documented traces of the past that have persisted into the present day. They also captured what Evans called the present "passing out of history" into the past.[79] They highlighted curious mixtures of the North and South, tradition and modernity that converged in Miami and south Florida. Post Wolcott and Gottscho provided glimpses of a future Miami, a Sun Belt city, beginning to draw populations and investment away from old industrial centers in the Midwest and Northeast. Understanding what photographers like Post Wolcott and Gottscho did and did not see in a changing Miami and south Florida, we can discern what the New Deal chose to promote and what it preferred to ignore, its capacities for change as well as conservatism.

Notes

1. Bonnie Yochelson, *Berenice Abbott's Changing New York* (New York: New Press and the Museum of the City of New York, 1997), 1, 9; Julia Van Haaften, *Berenice Abbott, Photographer: A Modern Vision* (New York: New York Public Library, 1989), 69.

2. Maren Stange, *Symbols of an Ideal Life: Social Documentary Photography in America, 1890–1940* (New York: Cambridge University Press, 1989), xvi, 109–11. On Florida's recovery, see "Paradise Regained," *Fortune*, Jan. 1936, 34–45, 92–94, 99–100, 102.

3. Marion Post Wolcott to Roy Stryker, Jan. 21, 1940, Marion Post Wolcott Papers, Center for Creative Photography, University of Arizona; Sally Stein, *Marion Post Wolcott: Some Thoughts on Some Lesser Known FSA Photographs* (San Francisco: Friends of Photography, c. 1983), 9.

4. See Stange, *Symbols of an Ideal Life*; William Stott, *Documentary Expression and Thirties America* (Chicago: University of Chicago Press, 1986); James Curtis, *Mind's Eye, Mind's Truth: FSA Photography Reconsidered* (Philadelphia: Temple University Press, 1989); Carl Fleischauer and Beverly Brannon, eds., *Documenting America, 1935–1954* (Berkeley: University of California Press, 1988); and Michael Carlebach and Eugene F. Provenzo Jr., *Farm Security Administration Photographs of Florida* (Gainesville: University Press of Florida, 1993).

5. Stein, *Marion Post Wolcott*, 44–48; Carlebach and Provenzo, *Farm Security Administration Photographs of Florida*, x–xi.

6. *How the Farm Security Administration Is Helping Needy Farm Families* (Washington, D.C., 1940), 1, Avery Architecture and Fine Arts Library, Columbia University; Roy Stryker interviews with Richard Doud, Oct. 17, 1963, and June 13 and 14, 1964, typescript, Archives of American Art, 1–3, 7–14.

7. Post Wolcott's response to a query from Stryker on her recollections of the FSA project, Stryker Papers, Library of Congress microfilm. Stryker wrote to several of the FSA photographers in the 1960s, perhaps gathering materials for *In This Proud Land*, his 1973 collection of project photographs.

8. Memorandum, Still Photography Unit—Section I, n.d. (1935–37?), Stryker, microfilm.

9. Stryker, "The FSA Collection of Photographs," in *In This Proud Land*, ed. Roy Stryker and Nancy Wood (Greenwich, Conn.: New York Graphic Society, 1973), 8.

10. Robert Snyder, "Marion Post Wolcott and the FSA in Florida," *Florida Historical Quarterly* 65 (Apr. 1987): 458–59, Carlebach and Provenzo, *Farm Security Administration Photographs of Florida*, ix–xi.

11. Curtis, *Mind's Eye, Mind's Truth*, 5–6; Stott, *Documentary Expression and Thirties America*, 200–220.

12. See Curtis, *Mind's Eye, Mind's Truth*, 5, 11, and 23 for Evans's influence and reviews of his 1938 exhibit. See Leslie Katz, "Interview with Walker Evans," *Art in America* 59 (Mar./Apr. 1971): 87, for Evans's comments on documentary style.

13. Henri Cartier-Bresson, *The Decisive Moment* (New York: Simon and Schuster, 1952), n. p.

14. Abbott quoted in Melissa McEuen, *Seeing America: Women Photographers between the Wars* (Lexington: University Press of Kentucky, 2000), 266, 269.

15. Beth Dunlop, "Inventing Antiquity: The Art and Craft of Mediterranean Revival Architecture," and Allan Shulman, "Igor Polevitzky's Architectural Vision for a Modern Miami," *Journal of Decorative and Propaganda Arts* 23 (1998): 190–206, 334–59.

16. Carlebach and Provenzo, *Farm Security Administration Photographs of Florida*, 1–20; Pete Daniel, "New Deal, Southern Agriculture, and Economic Change," in *The New Deal and the South*, ed. James C. Cobb and Michael V. Namorato (Jackson: University Press of Mississippi, 1984), 37–61; and Raymond Arsenault, "The End of the Long Hot Summer," in *Searching for the Sunbelt*, ed. Raymond Mohl.(Knoxville: University of Tennessee Press, 1990), 176–211.

17. Allan Shulman, "Building and Rebuilding: The Making of Miami Beach," in Jean-Francois LeJeune and Allan Shulman, *The Making of Miami Beach, 1933–1942: The Architecture of Lawrence Murray Dixon* (New York: Rizzoli, 2000), 38.

18. Marshall Berman, *All That Is Solid Melts into Air: The Experience of Modernity* (New York: Penguin, 1988), 13–14.

19. Post Wolcott to Stryker, Jan. 1939, Marion Post Wolcott Papers, Center for Creative Photography, University of Arizona. Post Wolcott's emphasis in original.

20. "Learn More about Florida" (Tallahassee: Florida Department of Agriculture, 1940), brochure, Historical Museum of South Florida, 7.

21. Arsenault, "The End of the Long Hot Summer"; "Miami: Metropolis of the Tropics," (Miami: City of Miami, 1938); "Miami Beach Is Calling You" (Miami: Miami Chamber of Commerce, 1930), travel brochures, and *Miami: The Magic City* (n.d.), souvenir viewbook, all from The Wolfsonian Museum Library, Miami Beach.

22. "I Wonder Where We Can Go Now?" *Fortune*, Apr. 1939, 91, 112, 119; *How the FSA Is Helping Needy Farm Families*, 2, 12. See also Daniel, "New Deal," and Carlebach and Provenzo, *Farm Security Administration Photographs of Florida*, 1–5.

23. Dorothea Lange and Paul Taylor, *An American Exodus: A Record of Human Erosion* (New York: Reynal and Hitchcock, 1939), 5.

24. *How the FSA Is Helping*, 12.

25. "FSA Picture Comments," typescript, c. 1938, Stryker microfilm, Library of Congress.

26. "I Wonder Where We Can Go Now?" 94; Raymond Mohl, "Black Immigrants: Bahamians in Early 20th Century Miami," *Florida Historical Quarterly* 65 (Jan. 1987): 271–97.

27. "Florida Migrant Workers," undated FSA typescript, Stryker microfilm.

28. Hurston, *Their Eyes Were Watching God* (1937; rpt., New York: Harper Perennial, 1998). A juke joint was a roadside bar and dance hall. Juke comes from the Gullah (referring perhaps to Angola and thus a West African dialect spoken by some southern African Americans) for bad, wicked, and disorderly. Juke joints were sometimes brothels, too. But to juke also means to dance. See "Juke," *American Heritage Dictionary*, 3rd ed. (Boston: Houghton Mifflin, 1996), 976.

29. Stuart Kidd, "Begrudging Aesthetics for a New South: The FSA Photography Project and Southern Modernization, 1935–1943," in *Technologies of Landscape*, ed. David Nye (Amherst: University of Massachusetts Press, 1999), 127.

30. Federal Writers' Project, *Florida: A Guide to the Southernmost State* (New York: Oxford University Press, 1939), 3.

31. Post Wolcott, caption, FSA photograph #LC-USF34–050977–E, Jan. 1939, FSA/OWI Collection, Library of Congress.

32. Charlton Tebeau, *A History of Florida* (Coral Gables: University of Miami Press, 1971), 403: "I Wonder Where We Can Go Now?" 91.

33. "Florida Migrant Workers," undated FSA typescript, and Post Wolcott, caption, FSA photograph, #LC-USF34–050507–D, Jan. 1939, FSA/OWI Collection, Library of Congress.

34. Post Wolcott, caption, FSA photograph #LC-USF34–050489, Jan. 1939, FSA/OWI Collection, Library of Congress; "Florida Migrant Workers," FSA typescript.

35. Nicholas Natanson, *The Black Image in the New Deal: The Politics of FSA Photography* (Knoxville: University of Tennessee Press, 1992), 24.

36. Post Wolcott to Stryker July 28/29, 1940 (?), Post Wolcott Papers, Center for Creative Photography, University of Arizona.

37. See Natanson, *Black Image*, 83, for quotation on New Deal paternalism. See illustrations in *The Florida Negro: A Federal Writers' Project Legacy*, ed. Gary W. McDonogh (Jackson: University Press of Mississippi, 1993).

38. Natanson, *Black Image*, 27–28.

39. Stein, *Marion Post Wolcott*, 7–8; Stryker to Post Wolcott, July 14, 1938 or 1939 (?), Jan. 13, 1939, and May 11, 1939, Post Wolcott Papers; and Natanson, *Black Image*, for Raper, 193–94, 239.

40. Mohl, "Black Immigrants," 287–89, 296, and his "Pattern of Race Relations in Miami since the 1920s," in *The African American Heritage of Florida*, ed. David R. Colburn and Jane L. Landers (Gainesville: University Press of Florida, 1995), 346–48.

41. Paul Hendrickson, *Looking for the Light: The Hidden Life and Art of Marion Post Wolcott* (New York: Knopf, 1992), 7; Snyder, "Marion Post Wolcott and the FSA in Florida," 465–67.

42. Stein, *Marion Post Wolcott*, 9; Natanson, *Black Image*, 75.

43. Stein, *Marion Post Wolcott*, 6.

44. Joan Ockman, "Architecture in a Mode of Distraction: Eight Takes on Tati's *Playtime*," *Any* 12 (Nov./Dec. 1995): 20–27.

45. Stein, *Marion Post Wolcott*, 3.

46. Ibid., 4; Kidd, "Begrudging Aesthetics," 123–24; and see letter to Arthur Rothstein, July 8, 1940, for Stryker's comments, quoted in Curtis, 20.

47. Kidd, "Begrudging Aesthetics," 119–20, 122.

48. Ibid., 120–21.

49. Defending her wearing of pants, Post Wolcott wrote Stryker that in south Florida, "the idle rich, winter and year round residents, migrants, and Negroes, especially when you are pickin' . . . all these women wear trousers. My slacks are dark blue, old, dirty, and not too tight—okay?" Post Wolcott to Stryker, Jan. 1939, Post Wolcott Papers.

50. "Paradise Regained," 35, 38, 94.

51. Stryker to Post Wolcott, Jan. 13, 1939, Post Wolcott Papers.

52. Shulman, "Building and Rebuilding," 38.

53. Mohl, "Pattern of Race Relations," 327–39, and Dorothy Jenkins Fields, "Tracing Overtown's Vernacular Architecture," *Journal of Decorative and Propaganda Arts* 23 (1998): 323–33.

54. Stein, *Marion Post Wolcott*, 4.

55. Tebeau, *A History of Florida*, 397.

56. "Paradise Regained," 36, 99; Snyder, "Marion Post Wolcott and the FSA in Florida," 468.

57. Shulman, "Building and Rebuilding," 21–22.

58. Deborah Dash Moore, *To the Golden Cities: Pursuing the American Dream in Miami and Los Angeles* (New York: Free Press, 1994), 1–20, 21–52, 63–67, for Jewish Americans and Miami Beach; Max Page, *The Creative Destruction of Manhattan* (Chicago: University of Chicago Press, 1999), 251–60.

59. Shulman, "Building and Rebuilding," 21–22.

60. Shulman, "Polevitzky," 341.

61. The Blackstone admitted Miami Beach's first Jewish Americans guests in 1929. See Bill Wisser, *South Beach* (New York: Arcade Books, 1995), 57.

62. Samuel H. Gottscho, "My Life in Photography," unpublished typescript, 1957 (?),1–3, Avery Architecture and Fine Arts Library, Columbia University, and Jean-François LeJeune and Allan Shulman, "Samuel H. Gottscho and the Photography of Miami Beach," in *The Making of Miami Beach*, 226.

63. Samuel H. Gottscho, "Seventy-one Years, or My Life with Photography," unpublished book typescript and photographic album, c. 1968, folders v and vi, n.p., Prints and Photographs Division, Library of Congress.

64. Dietrich Neumann, *The Architecture of the Night* (Munich: Prestel, 2002), 6–7.

65. Shulman, "Gottscho," 226.

66. Shulman, "Building and Rebuilding," 38; and "Paradise Regained," 40.

67. "Boom over Miami Beach," *Architectural Forum* 73 (Dec. 1940): 10.

68. "Paradise Regained," 102.

69. Shulman, "Building and Rebuilding," 12, 22–27.

70. "Boom over Miami Beach," 10.

71. "Paradise Regained," 102; and John Dos Passos, *The USA: The Big Money* (Boston: Houghton Mifflin, 1937), 231, quoted in Shulman, "Building and Rebuilding," 14.

72. Shulman, "Building and Rebuilding," 12, 22–27.

73. Jean-François LeJeune, "Lawrence Murray Dixon and His Colleagues," in *The Making of Miami Beach*, 170.

74. Moore, *To the Golden Cities*, 1–52, 63–67.

75. *Photographic Report to the President of the United States: Survey of the Architectural Completion of Projects of the Public Works Administration*, 1939, NARA, RG 135–SA, PWA Records, album 40, box IV, o–629–30, o–632

76. "Paradise Regained," 35, 37.

77. Fields, "Tracing Overtown," 330–32.

78. Natanson, *Black Image*, 14–15, 61, 71–72, 76.

79. Evans quoted in Katz, "Interview," 87.

FOUR

Whose History Is It Anyway? New Deal Post Office Murals in South Florida

MARIANNE LAMONACA

Hundreds of people pass through the Miami Beach Post Office on a typical day. Does anyone notice the large oil painting on the wall above the rows of brass mail boxes? And if they do, what do they make of this writhing composition of brawny male figures and rearing horses? Do they know why the mural was placed there? It is inscribed "C. Hardman '40," the artist's signature and the date it was completed. It stands alone, without an explanatory label or commemorative plaque.

Post office murals produced in south Florida during the Great Depression under the auspices of the U.S. government, such as the mural in the Miami Beach branch, are a living legacy of an unprecedented period of federal support for the arts. This essay focuses on four murals: Denman Fink's *Law Guides Florida Progress* (1941) in Miami, Charles Russell Hardman's *Episodes from the History of Florida* (1940) in Miami Beach, Stevan Dohanos's *Legend of James Edward Hamilton, Mail Carrier* in West Palm Beach (1940), and Charles Rosen's *Seminole Indians and Two Landscapes* in Palm Beach (1938). The south Florida murals present historical events and persons (*Episodes from the History of Florida* and *The Legend of James Edward Hamilton, Mail Carrier*), living history (*Seminole Indians*), and contemporary life within an historical continuum (*Law Guides Florida Progress*). Three of the murals are still on view in their original settings, and the Dohanos murals remain on view in West Palm Beach, but not in their original location.[1]

This essay examines the murals by considering the process by which the artists and subjects were chosen, the themes presented, and the public re-

FIGURE 46. Hernando de Soto's attempted conquest, from Charles Hardman's *Episodes from the History of Florida*, 1940. Courtesy of NARA.

sponse to the murals at the time of their inaugurations. While I began by examining the visual clues found in the murals themselves, I have based my analysis within the broad political, social, and economic context of the period. The textual records preserved at the National Archives in Washington, D.C., include correspondence between the Treasury Department's Section of Painting and Sculpture and the artists, newspaper clippings, photographs of preliminary studies, and other documents.[2] These have brought to light some of the specific matters related to the commissioning of the murals. Previous scholarship on Section murals has helped me to shape my own argument affirming the Section's acceptance of modernity cloaked in historical narrative.

The New Deal art programs shared the idea that public art could enrich and transmit culture, that art could and should be democratic and speak to the ordinary citizen, and that the federal government had a responsibility to provide cultural as well as material assistance during a period of almost overwhelming national hardship. Local post offices were concrete links between the people and the federal government. The murals played an important role in presenting images that reflected community histories, values, and aspirations while assuring citizens that the government was interested in their welfare.

The New Deal and the Arts

To keep the nation's artists working during the Depression, Franklin Delano Roosevelt established several art programs, each with different criteria.[3] The Roosevelt administration recognized that dramatic steps must be taken to solve the country's economic crisis (at the nadir, 25 percent of the nation's working population was unemployed). It enacted reforms and new regulatory practices in industry, agriculture, finance, labor, and housing. In order to build consensus for these policies, artists were employed to portray the direct correlation between government programs and the public good.

The Treasury Department's Section of Painting and Sculpture, under the leadership of Edward Bruce (1879–1943), commissioned all four south Florida murals. The Section, as it is generally known, was officially established in October 1934 and funded through allocations from the Procurement Branch of the Treasury Department, which at that time was responsible for constructing and embellishing public buildings.[4] Bruce established a formula for funding that theoretically set aside 1 percent of the construction funds for new federal buildings for decoration, although in practice the allocations were much less. Bruce's ultimate goal was to establish a permanent federal art patronage program. He and Holger Cahill, director of the Federal Art Project of the Works Projects Administration, laid the groundwork for later percent-for-art legislation and the National Endowment for the Arts.[5]

Unlike other New Deal art programs such as the Public Works of Art Project (1933–34), the Works Progress (later Projects) Administration, and the Federal Art Project, Section awards did not consider artists' economic situation. Instead, artists were chosen based on their professional merits alone. Susan Valdes-Dapéna convincingly argues that the Section "regularly awarded commissions for small post offices to artists who had done well in a competition for a larger commission but had not won. This created a loophole in the process through which the Section could reward artists who not only produced quality work but with whom it was easy to work—artists who had avoided controversy and worked well with local postmasters and publics, and artists who had complied with the Section's suggestions."[6] The program provided artworks for new federal buildings, such as courthouses, post offices, and administrative offices, and awards were made through anonymous competition or by direct commission. When the program was established, Bruce and his close advisor Forbes Watson (1880–1960) set down its philosophical guidelines:

To secure suitable art of the best quality for the embellishment of public buildings;

To carry out this work in such a way as will assist in stimulating, as far as practicable, development of art in the country and reward what is regarded as the outstanding talent which develops;

So far as consistent with a high standard of art, to employ local talent;

To endeavor to secure the cooperation of people throughout the country interested in the arts and whose judgment in connection with art has the respect of the Section in selecting artists for the work to be done and criticism and advice as to their production;

In carrying out this work, to make every effort to afford an opportunity to all artists on the sole test of their qualifications as artists, and accordingly, to encourage competitions wherever practicable, recognizing the fact, however, that certain artists in the country, because of their recognized talent, are entitled to receive work without competition.[7]

The Section defined a series of steps that would help ensure that the completed mural conformed to their quality standards. In competition announcements and award letters, the Section requested "a simple and vital design." Because the Section paid the artists in increments, the step-by-step process allowed the Section to maintain control over the final project. Once commissioned, the artist usually made contact with the postmaster of the community where the mural was intended for installation. Often, this initial contact led to other community groups such as the local chamber of commerce or a committee selected to oversee the mural project. From discussions with community stakeholders, the artist would develop an idea for the mural. Sometimes controversies arose with government officials or local committees. Because the artist would be paid only when the mural was successfully installed, the artist took seriously anything that prevented installation. It was left to Section officials to reconcile with the artist or the community any differences that arose. Scholars such as Barbara Melosh have convincingly argued that the Section chose a middle ground that did not upset prevailing notions of gender, race, and class.[8] The Section mural program attempted to convey the progressive aims of the New Deal. Administrators hoped that the murals would convince citizens that the increased intervention of the federal government into areas such as welfare, agriculture, and labor reform benefited their local communities.

First, the artist submitted a preliminary sketch for the proposed mural to Section officials. The Section often counseled artists about the overall composition and scale of the mural because the artist may not have had prior mural-painting experience. Once approved, the artist continued to develop the design until a scale drawing was produced in color. The color sketch often included the architectural elements of the site, such as counters, doorways, and windows. Once approved, the artist developed the full-scale cartoon and then the final mural. Most artists painted the mural on canvas with oil paint or oil/egg tempera, a medium popular during the 1930s, and then installed the mural in the building.[9] A few artists used true fresco, whereby pigments were applied directly to wet plaster.

The Section worked with artists to accurately portray a community's local flora and fauna or major trade. Sometimes Section officials suggested petty changes that might involve a figure's placement in the overall composition or the depiction of someone's facial features. Section murals were produced under a centralized bureaucracy in Washington, D.C. Because administrators tended to promote consensus, the murals often presented a conservative view of American life, one that would be accepted by the majority of the community.

In order to disseminate information about the program, the Section periodically published its *Bulletin*, which announced upcoming competitions, the recent awarding of projects, and the completion of others. The *Bulletin* provided guidelines for artists interested in submitting sketches for competition. For example, in *Bulletin* 2, the Section provided a list of subjects from the history of the U.S. Postal Service that were then being addressed in national and local projects. These included American historical episodes; delivery scenes; colonists; the newest delivery methods via trains, airplanes, bicycles, and motorcycles; outside activities, such as hauling mail or the arrival of glad news; and abstract qualities, such as speed, responsibility, courage, and courtesy.[10]

In 1939, the Section of Fine Arts announced the Forty-eight States Competition. The goal was to bring art to the most remote rural communities in the United States. Conceived of as a huge publicity campaign to garner support for the program, the winners were revealed in a 1939 *Life* magazine article. Although the competition was successful, many towns protested the portrayals of their local customs and trades. Artists were encouraged to do research about a community before embarking on a mural design. Artists who conducted secondhand research in libraries might not always find the kind of information that would give specificity to a town's portrayal. Some, especially those not from a particular locale, would paint stereotypical images of farmers, Indians, and cowboys, often employing imagined or Hollywood-inspired conceptions of local conditions. Subsequently, the Section fostered collaborations between each winning artist and the townspeople in order to produce a mural that characterized the interests and aspirations of their community.[11]

Post Office Murals in South Florida

The south Florida murals demonstrate how the Section functioned. Only one of the four south Florida murals, Denman Fink's *Law Guides Florida Progress*, was awarded through competition; the other three were direct commissions based on sketches the artist had submitted in competition or on the artist's record of achievement. Although the Section indicated that it would "employ local talent," Fink was also the only local artist commissioned in south Florida. However, the local community was involved in other ways: the jury for the Miami post office competition was composed of

Florida residents and the building's architects; the Miami Beach Chamber of Commerce advised Charles Hardman on a suitable subject; and a Palm Beach historian informed Charles Rosen about Seminole life and customs.

Edward Rowan (1898–1946), assistant chief of the Section, was responsible for much of the day-to-day responsibilities of the program, serving as Bruce's liaison to the artists and the community. His letters provide a vivid account of the government's involvement in artistic production. The Section's desire to control the final product so as not to cause any local indignation may best be conveyed by a comment written by Rowan to Hardman regarding his sketch for the Miami Beach Post Office mural: "The only suggestion offered is that the lower extremities of the two rearing horses be turned in order to avoid the necessity of portraying their sexual organs in so prominent a way."[12] Today this comment seems at once odd and innocent, yet it crystallizes the difficulties that a centralized Washington bureaucracy faced in promoting democratic interaction between the government, the artist, and the local community.

The federal government developed a mechanism for communities to work with Section administrators and the artist to shape their shared identity. The murals were one way to give specificity and local relevance to the new federal bureaucracy that many citizens saw as encroaching on individual lives and local politics.[13] The buildings that the murals embellished were themselves public works projects. In Palm Beach and Miami Beach, the post offices were under construction as the mural commissions were being made. In Miami and West Palm Beach the murals were installed within large, mixed-used federal buildings that attested to the growing civic responsibilities of this rapidly developing region.

Mural art was not new in south Florida in the 1930s. Many citizens would have been familiar with the decorative murals that adorned chic hotel lobbies, luxurious ballrooms, and ornate movie theaters. These murals defined spaces where identities could be reinvented within an exotic landscape or a historical narrative. The Section murals were also opportunities for reinvention. They provided a platform for the federal government and the community to visualize their shared history and aspirations. Historian Karal Ann Marling used the term *American Stuff* to describe murals such as Stevan

Dohanos's *Legend of James Edward Hamilton, Mail Carrier* that were "defiantly provincial and deliberately obscure." Hardman found himself especially challenged when asked to present a subject for his Miami Beach mural, replying that this area of Florida has "very little historical background." The majority of the murals in Florida's northern counties depict traditional rural labor scenes such as logging and farming. Included are murals such as Denman Fink's *Harvest Time—Lake Wales* and George Snow Hill's *Long Staple Cotton* and *Cypress Logging*. These portrayals of local industries served to affirm community values by highlighting their productivity and recalling more prosperous times. Almost all of the remaining Florida murals, including the ones under discussion, fit into the history category. Michael Zimny posited that the south Florida murals depicted historical themes because they would appeal to a growing tourist industry in that part of the state.[14] Florida's Spanish history was thoroughly exploited in the state's promotional campaigns. At the U.S. World's Fairs from the 1890s to the 1930s, Florida's presence was proclaimed in displays and with architecture that evoked the Spanish settlement of the territory. At the 1939 New York World's Fair, "The Florida Pavilion . . . took the form of a Mission-style church. Like the exhibits erected at Chicago in 1893 and 1933, the 1939 pavilion is again evocative of Florida's colonial past and the upscale developments of Palm Beach, Miami Beach, and Coral Gables."[15] According to architectural critic Beth Dunlop, "Spanish sold." During the 1920s architectural boom in south Florida, the Spanish idiom was most widely quoted. The Spanish heritage of the region was heralded by the tower of the Miami News Building, which resembles the Giralda tower in Sevilla, Spain, and in the luxurious Mediterranean Revival residences built in Palm Beach by Addison Mizner, Maurice Fatio, and their contemporaries.[16]

Law Guides Florida Progress

The Miami Post Office and Courthouse mural was the first Section mural to be commissioned in south Florida and the last to be installed. The reasons for this are varied, but they help to explain how the local community and the government interacted when planning and executing a public mural. Built during the Hoover administration in the early years of the Depression, the Miami Post Office, Courthouse, and Federal Building was dedicated on July 1, 1933. Coral Gables architects Phineas Paist and Harold D. Steward received the commission, benefiting from new government guidelines that gave priority to local architects and labor. As was customary at the time, the architects recommended an artist to carry out a decorative scheme for the building. Paist and Steward chose Denman Fink (1881–1956) to paint a twenty-five-foot mural in the main courtroom. Fink and Paist were longtime collaborators for the City of Coral Gables, so it was only natural that the architects turned to Fink for this important mural. Fink was the artistic director of the planned community of Coral Gables as well as an art professor at the University of Miami. He submitted a sketch and a $6,000 bid in 1935, but a contract was never executed.[17] Rowan explained the circumstances to Judge Halsted Ritter, whose court chamber the mural was to adorn:

> The design for the proposed mural by Mr. Denman Fink of Miami, for the courtroom in the Miami Federal building, was shown to the Section of Painting and Sculpture. The quality was not equal to that of most of the winning designs which are submitted to the Section under our competitive method. This is not saying that Mr. Fink could not create the equal of the work which we are placing in Federal buildings, but he did not achieve that quality in the particular sketch submitted. Mr. Fink will have an opportunity of submitting another design in the regional competition.
>
> It happens that the Federal building at Miami is on the old program and there are no funds available at the present time for this decoration. If such funds become available in the future, the Section will hold a regional competition to secure an artist to do the work.[18]

More than five months later, an internal memo from assistant superintendent of the Section Inslee A. Hopper to Rowan indicated "there is a reservation of $6,000 for mural painting set up on the Miami Post Office and Court House. . . . Mr. Fink, painter recommended by Judge James A. Wetmore, is considered by Mr. Dows below the standard maintained by the Section. A competition can be started practically immediately."[19]

With monies available in November 1935, it is unclear why it took between December 1936 and February 1937 for the competition to be announced.[20] Of the $6,000 Hopper claimed to set aside for the mural, only $3,800 was actually provided to "cover the complete cost of execution and installation." Artists residing in the southeast region including Florida, Louisiana, Arkansas, Mississippi, Alabama, Georgia, South Carolina, North Carolina, Virginia, West Virginia, Kentucky, Tennessee, Maryland, and the District of Columbia were invited to compete for the commission. Eve Alsman Fuller, director of the Federal Art Project in Florida, headed the committee. Fuller was responsible for organizing the jury for the competition, which included the building's architects Paist and Steward, Beatrice Beyer William, an artist at the State College for Women in Tallahassee, and S. Peter Wagner, an artist in St. Petersburg. Fuller had misgivings about the architects serving on the jury. Rowan assured her that "it will be quite proper for Mr. Paist to be a member of your committee as the local committee serves merely in an advisory capacity to the Section and the final decision is not made until all the sketches have been carefully studied by the members of the Section together with the recommendations of the advisory committee."[21]

The Section recommended that "whatever subject is selected, the artist emphasize Florida, drawing from her unmeasured wealth of history and experience. Subject matter should deal with some phase of contemporary justice, local history, past or present, local industry or pursuits, or customs and commerce service. Federal buildings are a concrete link between every community of individuals and the Government, and in addition to mail service through such departments as postal savings, money orders, etc., functions importantly in the human structure of the community. As distinguished and vital a conception as possible along such lines is desired."[22]

After the jury met to review the works on March 15, 1937, Eve Fuller reported that the jury had quickly eliminated forty-eight of the sixty sketches. The twelve remaining were ranked, and the top three were sent on to Section officials in Washington, D.C. Among the three selected works was Fink's submission. Soon after the sketches were sent to the Section for review, Paist and Steward wrote to Hopper expressing their personal opinions that "the work of No. 3 was evidently the work of a matured artist, pictured the purpose of a painted panel back of a Judge of a Federal Court, was in scale and color, well adapted to the room, and could be understood by the public at large." Within the context of the debacle surrounding the previous nonawarding of the mural commission, the architects must have surely felt that their persistence would be understood and indulged. More revealing, however, is a comment the architects made about some of the other works in "a very modern manner. . . . Anyone of these three men could probably paint a good decoration in any manner if it is essential to be modern."[23] Whether or not they were merely being defensive, the remark reveals their anxiety about having a "modern" mural in their courtroom. Fink was nearly sixty years old at the time of the competition. His complex composition, realistic figuration, and decorative color scheme were more in keeping with the ornamental style of the 1920s than that of the more abstracted forms of the late 1930s.

Later, Eve Fuller received a brief letter from Edward Bruce, chief of the Section, announcing that "none of the sketches submitted seemed entirely suitable," and the competition was closed without the awarding of a contract.[24] The news that Fink was not awarded the commission was soon followed by another affront to the artist. As was the usual practice when a jury did not find a suitable project through competition, the Section offered the mural to someone else. The Section asked New York artist Charles Chapman, who had distinguished himself in the competition for a mural for the auditorium of the new Interior Department Building, to submit a design for the courtroom. The Section's decision unleashed a torrent of protests. The letters that survive in the National Archives confirm how politically charged the awarding of a mural commission could be. The Section received letters from leaders of the Democratic Party in Florida and Washington, D.C., including Congressman J. Mark Wilcox, Senator Charles O. Andrews, and Senator Claude Pepper, a Roosevelt supporter and sponsor of a congressional bill to create a permanent government-sponsored art program.[25] Other letters arrived from art associations and art critics in Florida. The Section held firm in its decision, citing its conviction that no suitable work was found through the competition. Steward wrote to Rowan that "it happened that the period in which the original sketches

FIGURE 47. Jury for the 1937 Miami Post Office mural competition. Denman Fink's entries are marked with the number 3. Architect Phineas Paist stands at the far left. Courtesy of NARA.

were prepared was during the season that Mr. Fink's time was taken up with local clients, and he was unable to give the work the thought and time that the project required. I personally know that he is capable of doing a far better job than the sketch submitted would indicate."[26] In an internal memorandum dated October 1, 1937, Ed Rowan reported that he had telephoned Chapman "to find out his attitude on the Miami job and whether or not he had done any work on the designs."

> Mr. Chapman states that Fink is one of his best friends and according to Chapman is an artist who has achieved some very fine murals. He assures us that Mr. Fink is a capable artist; "an exquisite draftsman and excellent colorist." Mr. Chapman also said that he would be mentally relieved to have Mr. Fink given another chance at the decoration in question and that he would be willing to wait for some other appointment under the Section.[27]

Chapman's candor may have paved the way for the Section to reopen the Miami competition. While Chapman offered his friendship with Fink as the justification for declining the Section's award, surely the political in-fighting and discontent surrounding the awarding of the commission con-tributed to his decision.[28]

The outcome of all the political posturing was a new, slightly modified competition announcement: the award was $3,650 and the pool of applicants was limited to Florida, Alabama, Georgia, and South Carolina. Organizers brought back the same jurors, with Alexander Orr Jr. replacing the recently deceased Phineas Paist. Orr was a Miami city commissioner (later Miami mayor) and the owner of a company that specialized in heating and refrig-eration systems and that was engaged in the finishing work for the Miami post office building. As in other competition announcements, the Section indicated that artists of meritorious designs not chosen for the Miami com-petition would be invited to submit preliminary mural studies for several other southern post offices.

The jury for the second competition met on May 9, 1938. This time Ed Rowan went down to Miami for the judging. Again the jury selected Denman Fink. The Section agreed and moved swiftly to get the commission under way. "Fink presented the most comprehensive subject matter in relation to Miami," according to Rowan. "Further his color was the most appropriate for the room."[29] Rowan sent Fink an official offer letter on June 6, 1938. In it, he made several suggestions about the composition of the mural:

> In studying your design this office felt that while the color was possibly the most appropriate and harmonious for the room there was a tendency to over crowding. Elimination of certain of these elements would certainly improve the design. The area which was considered the most attractive in your sketch was on the right, in which you depict the Seminole Indians. Some of the fruit, certain of the negro figures, etc., could be eliminated without loss of theme. It was also felt that the rather trite symbols of Justice in the central part of the composition could be eliminated and the figure of the Judge approached by the mother and child and the workmen could be raised in the composition to take the place of these elements.
>
> Before authorizing you to proceed with the full size cartoon of this work, I suggest that you work up a black and white in the same scale as the color

FIGURE 48. Denman Fink's sketch for *Law Guides Florida Progress*, which he submitted in the second Miami Beach Post Office and Courthouse competition in 1938. Courtesy of NARA.

sketch indicating the slight revisions requested in this letter. I might add that these revisions were suggested by the Committee meeting in Miami.[30]

The Section's suggestions were attributed to the "Committee meeting in Miami"—people Fink knew who had lobbied for the commission. It is likely that Rowan did not want to further alienate or offend the artist. When Fink responded to Rowan's letter, he provided a just reason for not complying with one suggestion and graciously yielded to the Section on another: "As to the matter of the fruit—the placing and quantity of it in relation to the washing and sorting machine is as true to packing house usage as my space for that feature of my composition allowed. To indicate much less would fail, I fear, to get across the amplitude of a full crop activity. The impression of a packing house at that time is indeed one of abundance." Perhaps Fink had thought it necessary to include the symbols of justice—wings, a disembodied hand holding a sword, and two stone tablets—to comply with the themes presented for the competition, as he added, "It will be a great satisfaction to me to eliminate the symbolism you mention. It was to me a disturbing element in my scheme, and I am glad to have you feel as you do about it."[31] Fink submitted his color sketch for the mural almost nine months later, incorporating the revisions suggested by Rowan.

Fink took longer than expected with his work, and the final cartoon was approved on October 26, 1939. Fink's reason was that the "large number of figures involved in this composition has consumed vastly more time than I anticipated." He also noted that "with its 11' × 26' dimensions you will see that the figures in the entire central area are considerably over life size."[32] Fink's health seems to have been a factor in the delays, too. When Edward Bruce "stopped off at Coral Gables" to see Fink, he wrote a memorandum asking to approve another extension: "He has had a very bad year with arthritis and in view of the bad weather he has suffered so much he hasn't been able to start to paint."[33]

When Fink submitted a written description of the mural to Washington, he revealed his own professional concerns about the mural. It appears that he subordinated the subject matter to his own creative and aesthetic issues. He wrote, "I discarded the idea of using an historical subject for the mural because I felt that while the depicting of an episode in the State or City history would be of great interest, I was of the belief that such a selection of subject matter would impose upon me considerably greater restriction on my treatment of the panel from a decorative point of view." He continued, "The subject which I have carried out (Florida's natural and cultural development under the guidance of Law and Justice) gave me a much greater latitude for the decorative element of the mural aside from the subject matter. It also did not limit me to the presentation of a single episode which would have been handicapped by the necessity of accuracy of place and dress which at times can be a thorn in the flesh of a muralist." Fink's comments attest to his self-assurance as a professional muralist. While it seems wholly appropriate that he described the mural as a decorative embellishment to the architecture, he may also be vindicating himself. The building's architects, Paist and Steward, had chosen Fink to do the mural for the courtroom before the Section was ever involved. "As a decoration embellishing the architectural setting," he concluded, "the mural . . . had to conform both in color treatment and design to the architect's decorative scheme for the room; to make it consistent with the established conditions of the room necessitated a close co-ordination between the mural itself and the general treatment of the surrounding walls and lighting of the room."[34]

Fink also provided a key to understanding the subject matter and the characters in the mural:

> The presentation of my subject depicts the transitional development of the state from its wild and primitive state represented by the Seminole Indian group on the right in a setting of native tropical wilderness to the natural products of sea and soil, fishing and fruit growing, and from there passing toward the left, of my composition, in the foreground I have presented an assembly of units representing the various outstanding phases in the cultural development of the locality. . . . The judge is shown off the bench making this contact less formal and suggests a closer and more intimate relationship between the court and its people.[35]

In his roles as the artistic director of Coral Gables and art professor at the University of Miami, Fink contributed to the emerging visual vocabulary that characterized south Florida—from its built environment to its marketing image. In the mural, Fink presented images familiar to the citizens of Miami—local flora and fauna, bathing beauties, a Pan American Clipper airplane, Seminole Indians, and "above all . . . the tropical sun radiating its light over the entire activities"—all of which were the accepted elements of south Florida promotional materials.[36] The mural reinforces community values that brought Miami into being from a harsh wilderness to a tropical paradise. The evidence of this young community's success were its university, its arts and culture, its productivity in agriculture and fishing, and above all, its sustained ability to attract both new residents and tourists.

What does the mural tell us about contemporary life and social attitudes in Miami in 1941 and about the ideals of the New Deal? In New Deal terms, law and justice are the locus of a progressive society. The judge—a benevolent and protective father—represents the federal government in the actions of the local community. The troubled couple appeals to him for support, and he reaches out to the young woman with a firm hand and a warm smile. This central element affirms the federal government's central role in the life

of the community, and it reinforces paternalistic values through its depiction of the nuclear family. Swirling around this troubled couple are people
engaged in productive activities, including agriculture, fishing, shipping,
tourism, and the arts and sciences. Fink has established a system of contrast-
ing views: Seminole Indians are the "primitive" foils to modern, constructive
activities. Their handmade canoe serves as counterpoint to the machine-age
transportation vehicles. The activities of the hand laborers balance those of
the white-collar scientist, architect, and musicians. This diverse group of
people engaged in fruitful labor—young and old, male and female, black,
white, and Indian—provided a reassuring image of continuity and endurance during the difficult economic period of the Depression. At the center
of the canvas is a round, healthy baby dressed in white, symbolizing purity
and regeneration (see plate 5).

Read as a contemporary event of the 1940s, the relationships indicated
and the narrative suggested are notably inadequate. The mural reinforced
common social stereotypes of the period. Only white people are engaged in
professional pursuits, including education. Fink assured local relevance by
portraying several Miami citizens: the man at the drawing table is Phineas
Paist, the architect of the federal building embellished by Fink's mural; the
young schoolgirl is Miss Enna Barbara Brown, Fink's granddaughter; and
the scientist is Dr. E. V. Hjort, head of the University of Miami's chemistry
department. White females are shown in a variety of roles—wife, mother,
student, and sunbather—either alone or paired with a man. The females
and the Seminoles occupy a marginal realm in Fink's composition. They
are stock images recycled from dime-store novels, postcards, souvenirs, and
Miami promotional materials.

The muscular, healthy, and cooperative working-class laborers belie labor tensions prevalent in the 1930s.[37] Although black and white laborers are
depicted, they are not shown working together. Recent scholarship about
depictions of African Americans in Section murals has asserted that even
though poor whites and blacks often did exactly the same work, "the Section
was given to understand, via feedback from committees, postmasters, and
viewers, that in the ideal world of the post office mural, Southern whites
did not wish to be depicted in this manner."[38] As noted in *Florida: A Guide*

to the Southernmost State, Miami's restricted Negro district represented 30 percent of the city's population.[39] Moreover, the black labor force—an essential element of Miami's booming agricultural and tourist industries—is represented by two male laborers presented as closer to nature than the whites, semiclothed, and one balancing a fruit-filled basket on his head. They are exotic men of African decent, and in this context they may have represented the early black Bahamian settlers in Coconut Grove who were outsiders in this white-dominated society. Rather than record the lives of black hotel workers, field hands, and ordinary citizens (images readily found in 1930s photo journals—see chapter 3), Fink reinforced a black stereotype popular in 1930s travel and tourism publicity.[40] During the review process, the Section wrote to Fink that "it was slightly distressing to have the negro with the basket of fruit on his head on the unbroken vertical supporting the figure of Justice."[41] If the Section was looking for an image of "Florida's progress," they accepted a very limited view. Section administrators did not advocate a rethinking of racial stereotypes in southern communities.[42] If so, Fink might have been asked to portray students from Booker T. Washington Junior/Senior High School, the first public high school in Dade County that offered a twelfth-grade education to black children, or a prominent member of the black community, such as Dana A. Dorsey (1872–1940), believed to be the city's first black millionaire. At the same time that the mural project was being bantered about between Washington and Miami, Miami's power brokers, including Coral Gables founder George Merrick (who would become postmaster in 1940), advocated slum clearance and "negro resettlement," under the guise of New Deal housing reform (see chapter 6).[43]

The mural has remained on view since 1941 and has reappeared periodically in the local press. In 1968 the *Miami Herald* reported that Judge Ritter showed *Herald* staff reporter Cy Berning a preliminary sketch of the mural by Denman Fink in 1935. The sketch included an image of a "monk of the Spanish inquisition, his eyes glaring villainously." Berning, sensing that the "sanguinary monk might cause unnecessary controversy," shared his thoughts with a priest at Gésu Catholic Church, in order to see if there would be real objections to the depiction. "About two weeks later all merry hell broke loose, [and] the mural was withdrawn." The article is significant for two reasons. First, it reveals that Miami's Catholic community in the 1930s was powerful enough to force the mural to be withdrawn. It also reinforces the black community's continued estrangement from the political power base in Miami over forty years after the mural was installed by unequivocally stating that it was "one of the least controversial murals ever placed in a public building."[44]

Episodes from Florida History

The Miami Beach Post Office mural commission was awarded on the "basis of competent designs submitted in the Miami, Florida, competition" to Charles Russell Hardman [c.1912–unknown], a twenty-six-year-old painter from Augusta, Georgia. The correspondence housed in the National Archives reveals the intimate involvement of the Section with the artist regarding choice of subject matter and formal issues of composition, color, and placement. The inexperienced artist, with only "six months of formal training," appreciated Rowan's critiques and dutifully followed his suggestions.[45]

In the initial offer, the Section suggested "subject matter which embodies some idea appropriate to the building or to the particular locale of Miami Beach." Hardman went to Miami Beach to meet with the postmaster and members of the Miami Beach Chamber of Commerce in order to learn about the community where the mural would be placed. Several letters chronicle Hardman's difficulty in finding a suitable theme. Hardman wrote, "The only thing that worries me is the comparative lack of subject matter, except for sports, that a city like Miami Beach can furnish." Rowan assured him that he did not have to limit the subject to Miami Beach, but that he "would regard any subject matter related to the southern part of Florida as appropriate."[46]

In November, Hardman submitted a preliminary sketch that was a "radical departure from my other."

> The left panel symbolizes the truck industry, which is one of south Florida's largest. The sugar cane and vegetables will all be done with great faithfulness

and can be made quite beautiful. The middle panel represents the adaptability of the climate to athletic activities. The Miami Beach Chamber of Commerce was very insistent that sports play the major part in the decoration. The third panel represents the citrus fruit industry.[47]

Rowan's response — "Frankly we were all disappointed in the design" — must have been difficult for the young artist to receive. Rowan continued, "No objection is offered to the subject matter which was suggested by the Miami Beach Chamber of Commerce and by other interested citizens but it will be necessary for you to use this subject matter with some real conviction and authority. One suggestion is that the central panel include the theme of the conquistadors similar to the panel which you submitted in the Miami, Florida, mural competition and which first attracted the members of this office to your work. The side panels might then be given over to some indication of contemporary Florida and particularly Miami Beach." Another suggestion was "to make it completely historical."[48] Hardman responded with great aplomb, requesting that Rowan answer a number of questions, lamenting that he could not afford a trip to Washington, D.C., to meet with Rowan in person. Hardman presented Rowan with some options for new designs and relayed his struggle to reconcile historical and contemporary themes.[49] A month later, Rowan responded that the Section favored a historical theme in the center panel flanked by contemporary scenes. If the artist were unable to achieve the "subtlety of transition from contemporary designs to historical," the Section recommended the completely historical conception.[50]

The correspondence trail leads to some confusion about how the final selection was made. In a letter dated April 26, 1939, Hardman tells Rowan that he developed a new scheme that balanced two contemporary views of the beach and fishing scenes with two historical scenes. Two weeks later, Rowan informs Hardman that "the historical panels, three in number, are regarded as satisfactory at this stage."[51] Finally, on September 15, 1939, the Section executed a contract with Hardman for a three-part mural, *Episodes from the History of Florida*.

The history of the Spanish conquest in Florida is not particularly relevant to Miami or Miami Beach. Depictions of the conquistadors and Indians sig-

FIGURE 49. Hardman's 1939 color sketch for *Episodes from the History of Florida*. Miami Beach Post Office. Courtesy of NARA.

naled the American cultural bias of the 1930s regarding progress, European superiority, and manifest destiny. Although Hardman portrays the Indians with dignity—they stand erect, they are muscular and powerful, and they challenge the European settlers (the Seminole wars lasted most of the nineteenth century)—the incontrovertible conclusion is that the Indians were forced to adapt to white civilization. During the 1930s, the federal government took a paternalistic approach toward the Seminole population, providing funding for land reclamation, medical care, and education. New Deal Indian policy, codified in the Wheeler-Howard Act of 1934, proposed Indian sovereignty, self-government, and the establishment of tribal business corporations. As historian Harry A. Kersey Jr. has noted, despite the government reforms, there was a "thin line between proponents of assimilation and proponents of reservation heritage" because they shared the underlying assumption that the "Indian could achieve a balance between these seemingly contradictory ways of life."[52]

The language used to describe the three historical scenes reflects how the government subtlety fostered the acceptance of their new policies. The annotations on Hardman's preliminary sketches read, "Ponce de León lands and claims in name of Spain, calls the land La Florida, after the nature of it's [*sic*] vegetation and because it was the day of the Feast of Flowers; Scene from de Soto's attempted conquest; and Oceola [*sic*] and chieftains meet with Jessup [*sic*] of United States Army and agree to their removal west of Mississippi." Later, published descriptions of the murals indicate decisive

PLATE 1. Coral Gables Women's Club and Public Library, WPA, 1937. Courtesy of the HMSF.

PLATE 2. Postcard of the Overseas Highway to Key West, PWA, 1939. Courtesy of the HMSF.

PLATE 3. "Negro migratory workers by a juke joint." Belle Glade, February 1941. Marion Post Wolcott. Courtesy of the FSA/OWI.

Florida for me all the Time.

PLATE 4. Postcard from the early twentieth century. Courtesy of the HMSF.

PLATE 5. Detail of central scene in Denman Fink's *Law Guides Florida Progress*, 1941, Miami. Courtesy of the HMSF.

changes, most likely provided by the Section administration.[53] For example, Ponce de León "discovers" Florida, he doesn't "claim" it; de Soto is being "attacked by Indians," not attempting conquest; and army officers are shown "conferring" with Seminole chiefs, not removing them to reservations.[54] Although these choices privilege the white European over the Indian, they also reveal how the Section avoided scenes that might have appeared outright inflammatory. The word *conferring* implies that the U.S. Army was acting in a fraternal way toward the Indians, not in a hostile manner.

Although there are no notes to substantiate where Hardman conducted his pictorial research, he would have consulted historical texts to gather information to convincingly render the horses, flags, and costumes. In an early letter to Rowan, Hardman boasted about his home library.[55] His appropriation of the compositional elements of Paolo Uccello's celebrated Renaissance painting *The Battle of San Romano*, for example, corroborates his use of illustrations. Hardman may have copied the Indians' hairstyles from portrayals in eighteenth-century illustrations, such as John Trumbull's drawing of a Creek Indian chief (1790), in which the man's hair emerges from the top of a wide headband, or the frontispiece of William Bartram's *Travels of William Bartram* (1791), in which the hair is treated in a very ornamental way.[56]

Hardman did not depict the local Seminoles he might have seen at such Miami attractions as Musa Isle, nor did he use George Catlin's famous 1838 portrait of the Indian leader Osceola as a guide for his portrayal. Hardman's Indians are pure Hollywood fantasy—attractive, virile, and scantily clad. Just like a movie, the mural has action, narrative, and sex appeal. During the Depression, movies were America's escape, and Miami Beach served a similar purpose for close to a million tourists each year. The Section cautioned Hardman at one stage during the review process that "the subject matter for a Post Office must be treated in a more dignified way than the requirements of hotel decoration."[57]

The Section rejected all of Hardman's proposals with contemporary scenes, including trucking, citrus groves, and sports. The Miami Beach Chamber of Commerce's insistence on including sports may have influenced Hardman's presentation of this historical scene. Perhaps in the "world

FIGURE 50. "Ponce de León lands and claims in name of Spain, calls the land La Florida, after the nature of it's [*sic*] vegetation and because it was the day of the Feast of Flowers." Hardman's *Episodes from the History of Florida*, 1940, left panel, Miami Beach Post Office. Courtesy of NARA.

FIGURE 51. "Oceola [*sic*] and chieftains meet with Jessup [*sic*] of the U.S. Army and agree to their removal west of Mississippi." Hardman's *Episodes from the History of Florida*, right panel, Miami Beach Post Office. Courtesy of NARA.

of moneyed industrialists, boulevardiers, and stars of stage and screen," as Miami Beach was described in the Federal Writers' Project guide to Florida, Hardman's image would have had celebrity appeal.[58] Historian Barbara Melosh reasoned that the Section confronted the "contradictory conditions" of its work when dealing with issues of leisure and consumption, two important aspects of modernity.[59] I would suggest that the mural affirms the Section's acceptance of modernity disguised as an historical narrative—the American assumption of power represents progress, and the partially nude, muscular bodies symbolize economic health and consumption. Billed as the "largest mural in area," it was well received in the community at the time of its inauguration in January 1941.[60]

Seminole Indians and Two Landscapes

Charles Rosen (1878–1950) received the commission for the Palm Beach Post Office murals based on the work he was completing for the post office in Beacon, New York.[61] Rosen, an easel painter from upstate New York, described his strengths as landscape, paintings of industrial plants, harbors, and portraits.[62] Soon after agreeing to submit sketches for Palm Beach, Rosen contacted the local community (the postmaster, librarian, and chamber of commerce) for information about the town. Since the commission was presented to Rosen during the winter months, it is not surprising that his immediate suggestion was a mural based on "native trees, flowers, sea and sky (and sunshine)."[63] Rosen submitted sketches in June and in July that Rowan found too conventional or not specific enough to the locality. Rowan also suggested that Rosen rethink the layout originally suggested by the Section.[64] Rosen resubmitted sketches "based on the development of modern Palm Beach, from the time Mr. Flagler arrived there in the 'nineties' and saw its possibilities."[65] Included are Henry Flagler's railroad flanked by his two grand hotels, the Royal Poinciana and the Breakers. Why the Section rejected this design is difficult to discern, since it contained themes commonly found in Section murals, including the local landscape and railroads. In a later composition, Rosen incorporated a Seminole Indian group in place of the "old street in the Negro section in the early days of the town." He wrote to Rowan that he "feared that the street scene would not be acceptable to the people of Palm Beach.[66] Although Rosen implies that this was self-censorship, the fact remained that Palm Beach had no "Negro settlement" and Negroes were "not allowed on the streets after dark unless actively employed in the city."[67] Nevertheless, the Negro settlement would have been out of place even if Rosen were depicting the historical period associated with the arrival of Flagler's Florida East Coast Railway. Flagler's workers' settlements were located in West Palm Beach, not Palm Beach.

In January 1938, Rosen and his wife set off to Palm Beach, having just attained preliminary approval for his design: two landscapes, the lakeshore and the seashore, flanking a central panel with three scenes of contemporary Seminole Indian life. In Palm Beach, Rosen met the mayor, city manager, and the postmaster.[68] He undertook extensive research on the Seminole Indians, benefiting from the expertise of Louis Capron, a local historian of Seminole life and culture, whom Rosen reported was "reputed to know more about Seminoles than any one in the state."[69] Rosen wanted to present the Seminoles in a "respectful and sincere manner," so he visited "the Seminoles up and down the East Coast, becoming acquainted with them, taking pictures, sketching, studying their daily life."[70] In addition, both popular postcard images and photographs from the Everglades Federal Art Project and Farm Security Administration provided ample visual material about Seminole art and culture.[71] Despite government efforts on behalf of the Indians, popular discourse about the Seminoles was conflicted. According to an article in the Lake Worth newspaper, the mural "shows redskins" in their palmetto thatched hut.[72] Even in the Florida Writers' Project guide to Florida, which was criticized by conservatives for promoting liberal policies, the Seminoles were discussed in the chapter "Archeology and Indians," and Seminole images taken by FSA photographers appeared in the section "Along the Highway II." The effect was to marginalize the Seminoles as living history and a tourist curiosity.

Rosen's composition suggests a contrast between the modern cultivated landscape of Palm Beach and that of the enduring traditions of the Seminole community living in the Everglades. The mural offers an instructive context for understanding the description of Palm Beach published in

FIGURE 52. Charles Rosen's 1937 sketch for Palm Beach Post Office mural. Courtesy of NARA.

the guide to Florida: "To this slender ribbon of sand almost within sight of the Everglades has been transplanted the luxury of the world. It is a luxury tempered with good taste, and though the city is in many ways artificial, its beauty is genuine."[73] The Seminoles in the post office mural exist outside of the economies of progress that built Palm Beach. Unlike African Americans whom Rosen had earlier depicted in conjunction with the coming of the railroad, the Seminoles did not compete with poor whites for jobs, nor did they interact with the elite of Palm Beach as domestics or hotel workers. Rosen's romantic depictions of industrious and family-oriented Seminoles reassured citizens of Palm Beach that their own traditions were valued and ongoing like those of the Seminoles, despite the fast pace of modern life. The mural and the new post office building itself, built in Mediterranean Revival style, stood as visual reminders that the federal government, too, respected America's cultural heritage even as it promoted economic and so-

FIGURE 53. Rosen's *Seminole Indians and Two Landscapes*, 1938. Palm Beach Post Office. Courtesy of NARA.

cial progress. Through the agency of the federal postal service, citizens were able to conduct the affairs of a modern, productive life. As Christine Bold has suggested, through the action of the federal government, landscapes became "sites of stability and cultural reassurance: comforting in the density of their historical and contemporary sights, in their evidence of progress, in their orderliness."[74]

The Legend of James Edward Hamilton, Mail Carrier

The West Palm Beach Post Office mural cycle provides a noteworthy complement to the Palm Beach mural. Where Rosen depicted nature as a vital part of the Seminoles' living tradition, Dohanos's images underscore the changes that have taken place in south Florida since the 1880s. When the commission was awarded to Stevan Dohanos (1907–1994), a noted commercial artist and illustrator, he was already at work on a Section mural for the post office in Elkins, West Virginia. Bruce's letters to Dohanos are gracious and friendly. Bruce wrote directly to most artists with national reputations, and he took a personal interest in Dohanos, treating him with a degree of professionalism that is often missing from Rowan's letters. Bruce suggested that Dohanos visit Marineland, a new aquarium just outside of St. Augustine, in order to get some ideas for the mural. When Dohanos responded that he already had a theme developed, Bruce replied that the "postmaster down there talked to me about your plan and you certainly made a highly successful impression on him. I don't want to urge anything on you and upset any idea which you have already developed."[75]

The mural cycle recounted the tale of James Edwards Hamilton, whom Dohanos described to Bruce as a "romantic individual that walked the most part of 80 miles through unchartered [sic] trails along the coastline just about fifty years ago. This is a part of the history of West Palm Beach that is spoken of often and there are legends connected with it." Hamilton's story was widely known in the community. Just two years earlier, in 1937, the Lake Worth Pioneer Association had installed a bronze tablet at the Jupiter Lighthouse to commemorate Hamilton's life. In the second half of the nineteenth century, mail was carried from the Jupiter Lighthouse, north of the Palm Beaches, to Miami by U.S. mail carriers who walked along the seashore, the only road then in existence. Dohanos told Bruce that the subject matter was "very appropriate to the town as well as to the Post Office Building" and that he had conducted "comprehensive research" on site, collecting photographs and talking to "old timers."[76] Dohanos contacted Charles Pierce, the postmaster at Boynton Beach in 1939, who provided information about the mail carriers and sent him a photograph of Hamilton. [77] This tangible link to the pioneer families of Palm Beach County provided an avenue for local citizens to connect to the past not only through the historical tale but also through members of their own community.

By November 1939 the murals were taking shape, and Dohanos wrote to the Section: "I have rounded up a lot of good props and information which I am incorporating into my cartoons. . . . It has been fun. . . . In the near

FIGURES 54–59. Stevan Dohanos's 1940 mural, *The Legend of James Edward Hamilton, Mail Carrier*, presented in six panels. West Palm Beach Post Office. Courtesy of NARA.

future I shall apply myself to the thrill of putting color to the designs."[78] The completed mural was described in a federal publication: "In six designs relating to the tragedy of this mail carrier who lost his life in line of duty in 1887, Mr. Dohanos has portrayed a true and dramatic story of the Barefoot Route of the U.S. Postal Service—a strip of eighty miles of lonely beach between the Lake Worth area and Miami, Florida. The panels depict incidents during his journey from the lighthouse to the bayou where he lost his life attempting to retrieve a skiff in water infested with sharks and alligators."[79] Although the tale of James Edward Hamilton was not solely a West Palm Beach story, it made sense for it to be placed in the West Palm Beach Post Office. Hamilton's life reminded citizens about how their community came into existence. By the late 1930s, West Palm Beach had grown into the county's civic and commercial center. The construction of the new federal building and post office signaled that the community had come of age.

Postal service history was the most typical subject suggested by the Section for a post office mural. Presented during the difficult times of the Depression, this historical tale addressed issues of commitment, hard work, and endurance, as well as romantic notions about adventure and freedom. Hamilton's journey began at the Jupiter Lighthouse, a symbol of safety and security, which is reinforced by the depiction of the stoic lighthouse keeper and his wife and the pair of pelicans in the background. In the first three episodes, Hamilton is shown with other people: the lighthouse keeper and his wife, the postal clerk, and two well-dressed travelers. In the last three panels, the postman continues his journey in solitude. In two scenes where the postman is shown alone, birds appear in pairs, perhaps symbolizing fidelity and the community. The fifth episode is the only one in which the postman is shown in the background of the scene, and it is the only time that the postman faces the viewer. The alligators in the foreground are the sole indication of danger. In the final scene Hamilton is alone but unthreatened.

The murals celebrated the barefoot mailman's work; they did not commemorate his death. The knowledge that the mail carrier walked barefoot along the beach, free from the confines of modern society, inspired not only respect for the past but also an appreciation of individual sacrifice for the good of the community. The murals presented an opportunity for the federal government to demonstrate that its expanded role in the life of individual citizens was not a political imposition. Rather, the murals conveyed that the nation's success depended on the contributions of millions of individual citizens. This is what makes the story of the barefoot mailman so compelling. Its strength lies in the fact that this peculiar local story could have significance to a national audience. It is the "stuff" of American lore.

A Living Legacy

The four Section murals under discussion shared a predilection for reinvention. From Ponce de León and the barefoot mail carrier to Seminoles and bathing beauties, these images conveyed complex ideas regarding how the federal government viewed the community, how the community defined itself in the past, and what it looked forward to in the future. Progress and modernity went hand in hand in shaping these images. The nation was in transition, and the murals crystallized the uncertainties of the times. Because federal goals were presented through the lens of the local community, depictions of race, gender, and class were tempered by local custom and didn't always meet the progressive goals of the New Deal. As historian Jerrold Hirsch has pointed out in his recent work on the Federal Writers' Project, one of the inherent problems with the New Dealers' desire to unite Americans in a common understanding of their shared identity was that they ignored the very issues that divided them.[80]

All four murals commissioned for south Florida by the Section are still on view. Dohanos's *Legend of James Edward Hamilton, Mail Carrier* murals have been moved from their original location to a new postal facility in West Palm Beach, while the others remain in their original locations. Nevertheless, do visitors know the events depicted? Do they know why the murals were placed in these federal buildings? Do they understand how they reinvented history in a troubled time? There is no general way to find answers to these questions. Certainly, while some people pride themselves on knowing these stories, others do not. Newspaper clippings confirm that the murals have received some public attention over the years.[81] The murals have often reentered public discourse when they were being restored or relocated. When Dohanos's murals were reinstalled in 1986 after restoration, the Palm Beach postmaster, August Bernola, said, "It really cheers the lobby up. I think it looks a lot better."[82] Whether he intended to or not, Bernola expressed why these murals still exert their charm in their original settings—they were one way that the federal government tried to reinforce positive and progressive aspects of American life during the Depression. Giving work to artists, extending the reach of the federal government beyond politics and the economy into cultural affairs, reinforcing the federal government's interest and concern about the whole country, not just the few closest to Washington, D.C., all made for a better democracy. But as the country quickly moved into the Second World War, and democracy became a touchstone of U.S. policy at home and abroad, the effect would be to end the federal art programs. Examined together, each of the south Florida murals contributes to the growing body of information about how the government interacted with artists and local communities to fashion a national culture through the celebration of regional differences.

Notes

1. Judging from a 1940 photograph, Hardman's mural has been relocated within the post office building at 1300 Washington Avenue, Miami Beach, from the main hall to the rotunda/entry hall. *Miami Daily News*, Dec. 29, 1940, 5. Fink's mural is in its original setting at the Federal Building and Courthouse, 300 Northeast First Avenue, Miami. Rosen's murals are in their original setting at the Palm Beach Post Office, 95 North County Road, Palm Beach, and the Dohanos murals have been relocated to the West Palm Beach Post Office, 3200 Summit Boulevard, West Palm Beach.

2. The records of the Section are held by the National Archives and Records Administration (hereafter NARA) in Washington, D.C., Records of the Public Buildings Service, Records Concerning Federal Art Activities, Textual Records of the Section of Fine Arts, Public Building Administration, and Its Predecessors, Case Files Concerning Embellishments of Federal Buildings, RG 121, entry 133.

3. For a succinct summary of New Deal art programs, see Bruce I. Bustard, *New Deal for the Arts* (Washington, D.C.: National Archives and Records Administration in Association with the University of Washington Press, 1997). I am also indebted to the research provided by Susan Valdes-Dapéna, who collaborated with me on the

exhibition "Public Works" held at The Wolfsonian, Miami Beach, Jan. 11 to Apr. 26, 1998.

4. The Section was established in October 1934 and dissolved in July 1943. It was known by various titles: Treasury Section of Painting and Sculpture (1934–38); Treasury Section of Fine Arts (1938–39); Section of Fine Arts of the Public Buildings Administration of the Federal Works Agency (1939–43).

5. Marlene Park and Gerald E. Markowitz, *Democratic Vistas: Post Offices and Public Art in the New Deal* (Philadelphia: Temple University Press, 1984: 6); Belisario Contreras, *Tradition and Innovation in New Deal Art* (London: Associated University Presses, 1983), 235–37.

6. Valdes-Dapéna, "Black and White: Ethel Magafan's Cotton Pickers," *Journal of Decorative and Propaganda Arts* 24 (2002): 266.

7. Virginia Mecklenberg, *The Public as Patron: A History of the Treasury Department Mural Program Illustrated with Paintings from the Collection of the University of Maryland Art Gallery* (College Park: University of Maryland Art Gallery, 1979): 12, from *Bulletin Section of Painting and Sculpture* 1 (Mar. 1, 1934): 34.

8. Barbara Melosh, *Engendering Culture: Manhood and Womanhood in New Deal Public Art and Theater* (Washington, D.C.: Smithsonian Institution Press, 1991), 1–12.

9. Park and Markowitz, *Democratic Vistas*, 6–9; Valdes-Dapéna, "Black and White," 259–60.

10. *Bulletin Section of Painting and Sculpture* 2 (Apr. 1, 1935): 8, NARA, RG 121/130, box 1.

11. For a brief but detailed assessment of recent scholarship about Section murals, see Valdes-Dapéna, "Black and White," 259–60.

12. Edward Rowan to Charles Hardman, Sept. 21, 1939, NARA, RG 121/133, box 15.

13. Valdes-Dapéna, "Black and White," 265.

14. Karal Ann Marling, *Wall-to-Wall America: A Cultural History of Post-Office Murals in the Great Depression* (Minneapolis: University of Minnesota Press, 1982), 20; Hardman to Rowan, Nov. 17, 1938, NARA, RG 121/133, box 15; Michael Zimny, "New Art, New Deal," *Florida Heritage* 6 (Winter 1998): 15–19.

15. Joel M. Hoffman, "From Augustine to Tangerine: Florida at the U.S. World's Fairs," *Journal of Decorative and Propaganda Arts* 23 (1998): 48–85, quotation on 73.

16. Beth Dunlop, "Inventing Antiquity: The Art and Craft of Mediterranean Revival Architecture," *Journal of Decorative and Propaganda Arts* 23 (1998): 195, 198.

17. Fran Rowin, "New Deal Murals in Florida Post Offices," *Historical Association of South Florida Update* 4 (Feb. 1977): 6–8, 10; Susan Hale Freeman, "Monument to Three Artists," *Historical Association of South Florida Update* 14 (Aug. 1987): 3–5.

18. Rowan to Judge Halsted Ritter, June 14, 1935, NARA, RG 121/133, box 14.

19. Inslee A. Hopper, memorandum to Edward Rowan, Nov. 29, 1935, NARA, RG 121/133, box 14.

20. The competition announcement appeared in *Bulletin* 11 dated Sept. 1936–Feb. 1937. NARA correspondence indicates that the announcement for the competition was approved and an extension was granted to close the competition on Feb. 10, 1937.

21. Rowan to Eve Fuller, Oct. 12, 1936, and Fuller to Rowan, Sept. 29, 1936, NARA, RG 121/133, box 14.

22. Competition announcement in *Bulletin* 11, and the release date was Feb. 2, 1937, NARA, RG 121/130, box 1, Announcement of Competitions.

23. Steward and Paist to Hopper, Mar. 19, 1937, NARA, RG 121/133, box 14.

24. Edward Bruce to Fuller, June 1, 1937, NARA, RG 121/133, box 14.

25. These and others may be found in NARA, RG 121/133, box 15.

26. Steward to Rowan, Aug. 30, 1937, NARA, RG 121/133, box 15.

27. Rowan memo to the competition, Oct. 1, 1937, NARA, RG 121/133, box 15.

28. Rowan to Jack Guthrie, Oct. 12, 1937, NARA, RG 121/133, box 15.

29. Rowan to Bruce, June 15, 1938, NARA, RG 121, Miami Post Office and Courthouse, June 1938–Apr. 1944.

30. Rowan to Fink, June 6, 1938, NARA, RG 121, Miami Post Office and Courthouse, June 1938–Apr. 1944. A draft of a contract with Fink for *Law Guides Florida Progress* had been prepared on May 23, 1938, see NARA, RG 121/133, box 15.

31. Fink to Rowan, June 10, 1938, NARA, Miami Post Office and Courthouse, June 1938–Apr. 1944.

32. Fink to Rowan, n.d., ca. Oct. 17, 1939, NARA, RG 121/133, box 15.

33. Edward Bruce to Maria Ealand, Mar. 20, 1940, NARA, RG 121, Miami Post Office and Courthouse, June 1938–Apr. 1944.

34. Typescript by Fink re: Miami Post Office and Courthouse, NARA, RG 121, Miami Post Office and Courthouse, June 1938–Apr. 1944.

35. Ibid.

36. Ibid.

37. See Erika Doss, "Looking at Labor: Images of Work in 1930s American Art," *Journal of Decorative and Propaganda Arts* 24 (2002): 230–57.

38. Valdes-Dapéna, "Black and White," 272.

39. *Florida: A Guide to the Southernmost State*, American Guide series (New York: Oxford University Press, 1939, 7th ed., 1955), 211.

40. *Fun Map of the Sunshine Zone*, Greyhound Corporation, [1936], Mitchell Wolfson Jr. Collection, Wolfsonian-Florida International University, Miami, XB2002.03.4.

41. Rowan to Fink, Mar. 17, 1939, NARA, Miami Post Office and Courthouse, June 1938–Apr. 1944.

42. Melosh has made this point, as has Sue Bridwell Beckham in *Depression Post Office Murals and Southern Culture: A Gentle Reconstruction* (Baton Rouge: Louisiana State University Press, 1989.

43. Raymond A. Mohl, "Trouble in Paradise: Race and Housing in Miami during the New Deal Era," *Prologue* 19 (1987): 13.

44. Nixon Smiley, "Picture Shown 'in Confidence' Created a Furor, Killed Mural," *Miami Herald*, May 15, 1968.

45. Rowan to Charles Hardman, Aug. 22, 1938, NARA, RG 121/133, box 15. Hardman had one other commission from the Section: the Guntersville, Ala., Post Office, *Indians Receiving Gifts from the Spanish*, 1947.

46. Hardman to Rowan, n.d. [stamped received by Section on Sept. 6, 1938], and Rowan to Hardman, Sept. 14, 1938, both in NARA, RG 121/133, box 15.

47. Hardman to Rowan, Nov. 17, 1938, NARA, RG 121/133, box 15.

48. Rowan to Hardman, Dec. 13, 1938, NARA, RG 121/133, box 15. Hardman's was one of fourteen submissions to the second Miami competition. See the Miami Florida Competition memorandum, NARA RG 121/133, box 15.

49. Hardman to Rowan, Dec. 17, 1938, NARA, RG 121/133, box 15.

50. Rowan to Hardman, Jan. 18, 1939, NARA, RG 121/133, box 15.

51. Hardman to Rowan, Apr. 26, 1939, and Rowan to Hardman, May 10, 1939, both in NARA, RG 121/133, box 15.

52. Harry A. Kersey Jr., *The Florida Seminoles and the New Deal, 1933–1942* (Boca Raton: Florida Atlantic University Press), 49–50, 150.

53. Rowan to Hardman, May 10, 1939, NARA, RG 121/133, box 15.

54. *Miami Beach Tropica*, Dec. 27, 1940. Clipping found in NARA, RG 121/133, box 15.

55. Hardman to Rowan, July 28, 1938, NARA, RG 121/133, box 15.

56. Dorothy Downs, *Art of the Florida Seminole and Miccosukee Indians* (Gainesville: University Press of Florida, 1995), 27, 32.

57. Rowan to Hardman, Jan. 18, 1939, NARA, RG 121/133, box 15.

58. Federal Writers' Project, *Florida*, 210.

59. Melosh, *Engendering Culture*, 201.

60. *Miami Beach Tropics*, Dec. 27, 1940; George E. Merrick to Bruce, Jan. 6, 1941; Merrick to Rowan, Jan. 24, 1941; *Miami Beach Times*, Dec. 27, 1940; *Miami Daily News*, Dec. 29, 1940, NARA, RG 121/133, box 15.

61. Memorandum to the director of procurement inviting Rosen to submit designs for the Palm Beach Post Office, stamped approved on Mar. 1, 1937, NARA, RG 121/133, box 15.

62. Rosen to Rowan, Apr. 16, 1935, Charles Rosen papers, Archives of American Art, DC 40, frame 0217.

63. Rosen to Rowan, Mar. 28, 1937, NARA, RG 121/133, box 15.

64. Rosen to Rowan, June 3, 1937, Rowan to Rosen, June 26, 1937; Rosen to Rowan, July 4, 1937, and Rowan to Rosen, July 15, 1937, NARA, RG 121/133, box 15.

65. Rosen to Rowan, Sept. 1, 1937, NARA, RG 121/133, box 15.

66. Rosen to Rowan, Oct. 6, 1937, NARA, RG 121/133, box 15.

67. Federal Writers' Project, *Florida*, 229.

68. Rosen to Rowan, Jan. 26, 1938, NARA, RG 121/133, box 15.

69. Rosen to Rowan, Apr. 7, 1938, NARA, RG 121/133, box 15.

70. "Mural Paintings Are Placed on Resort Post Office Walls," *Palm Beach Post*, May 26, 1938, 2. From Charles Rosen papers, Archives of American Art, reel 1119, frame 0446. Rosen's papers contain photographs of Seminole Indians including an image of Seminole Indian toy makers that was published by the Works Progress Administration Federal Writers' Project in the *Guide to Miami and Environs* (Northport, N.Y.: Bacon, Percy and Daggett, 1941).

71. Southeast Museum of Photography, *Imag(in)ing the Seminole Photographs and Their Use since 1880* (Daytona Beach: Daytona Beach Community College, 1993); Donald D. Spencer, *Seminole Indians in Old Picture Postcards* (Ormond Beach, Fla.: Camelot, 2002); Florida Writers' Project, *Florida*, 472–73.

72. "Artist Here Paints Murals for Palm Beach Post Office," *Lake Worth Herald*, May 27, 1938, Charles Rosen Papers, Archives of American Art, reel 1119, frame 0445.

73. Florida Writers' Project, *Florida*, 231.

74. Christine Bold, *The WPA Guides: Mapping America* (Jackson: University Press of Mississippi, 1999), 13.

75. Bruce to Dohanos, Apr. 4, 1939, Dohanos to Bruce, Apr. 5, 1939, and Bruce to Dohanos, Apr. 11, 1939, NARA, RG 121/124, Correspondence of Edward Bruce, folder Dohanos Stevan.

76. Dohanos to Bruce, Apr. 5, 1939, NARA, RG 121/124, Correspondence of Edward Bruce.

77. The term *barefoot mailman* was not used in the nineteenth century, but it was coined later by Theodore Pratt as the title of his 1943 book. See Stuart McIver, "The Barefoot Mailman," *Broward Legacy* 2 (July 1977): 24; Barbara Lawless, "Dohanos' Post Office Murals Pay Tribute to Barefoot Mailman," *Palm Beach Daily News*, Aug. 23, 1989, A1, A4.

78. Dohanos to Bruce, Nov. 21, 1939, NARA, RG 121/124, Correspondence of Edward Bruce.

79. "Exhibition of Photographs of Murals and Sculpture" (Washington, D.C.: Section of Fine Arts, Public Buildings Administration, Federal Works Agency), ca. 1940, RG 121/DC 40:1367.

80. Jerrold Hirsch, *Portrait of America: A Cultural History of the Federal Writers' Project* (Chapel Hill: University of North Carolina Press, 2003), 3.

81. Gary Schwan, "Barefoot Mailman Art Gets First-Class Handling," *Palm Beach Post*, Aug. 18, 1984, A13–14; Mary Stapp, "Murals: When the Drawing Is on the Wall," *Sun-Sentinel*, Aug. 14, 1988, 1; and Barbara Lawless, "Dohanos' Post Office Murals."

82. Chris Hunter, "Indians, Palm Trees Return," *Palm Beach Daily News*, Sept. 18, 1986, 5.

FIVE

The Civilian Conservation Corps in South Florida

TED BAKER

This chapter explores the activities of the Civilian Conservation Corps (CCC) in south Florida, one of the longest lasting New Deal programs to be established in the area. The CCC helped to reshape the natural and constructed landscapes of the region and addressed the conflicts between a sometimes difficult natural subtropical environment and the need for viable recreation centers for residents and tourists. South Florida had the distinction of being one of the first in the nation to open a CCC camp and one of the first to exhibit the energetic works of the CCC youth known across the country for their regimented organization and their impact on communities and environments.[1] The CCC projects in south Florida were led locally by landscape architects A. D. "Doug" Barnes and William Lyman Phillips and nationally by Robert Fechner, the head of the CCC, and President Franklin Delano Roosevelt. Each of these men brought to south Florida specific ideas of conservation and land management that created tensions inherent in land stewardship in the region. The idea for a national conservation initiative came from Roosevelt, who made it an imperative of his administration to continue the environmental focus manifest in his early political career. While serving as a New York state senator from the 26th District—a jurisdiction that included his Hyde Park home in Dutchess County—Roosevelt assumed a primary role in administering the New York Senate's Forest, Fish, and Game Committee. His independent ecological zest became apparent in this role as he fought for the passage of bills that would protect New York's forests from fires and enhance its natural landscapes. As senator and later as governor, Roosevelt frequently noted his dissatisfaction and frustration over the absence of a substantive environmental agenda in New York's legislative politics, something he wished to change nationally through policies and objectives that delineated the mission of the CCC.

Over the years, Roosevelt's passion for America's public landscape became almost legendary. He was keenly aware of natural landscape attributes that contributed to a sense of place, and he understood that such natural elements constructed the essential relationship between humans and nature. Roosevelt invested his financial resources and intellectual capital in various environmental projects at his Hyde Park property. Many of these endeavors were precursors of the future activities in which the CCC enterprise would engage. The work of students of New York State's College of Forestry at Syracuse University was one such example: this group commenced a forest-planting program at Roosevelt's Creek Road Farm in Hyde Park in 1931. Likewise, contacts in the early 1930s with Pennsylvania governor Gifford Pinchot reinforced the universality of his commitment to the land. An instrumental figure in the development of the U.S. Forest Service under President Theodore Roosevelt, Pinchot understood the importance of appropriate resource conservation and land management practices. Roosevelt's faith in conservation as a binding egalitarian concept was so complete that it transcended the entirety of his presidency: shortly before his death, Roosevelt proposed a conference on conservation as a basis of permanent peace with Churchill and Stalin. There he noted, "There is no question that the conservation of natural resources, including the rehabilitation of agricultural areas that have been denuded for one reason or another and the planned use of the world's subsoil resources, is of the greatest importance for the future well-being of the world. Also, there is no question that international collaboration in this field is needed."[2] Given the economic crisis and unemployment that plagued America during much of his presidency, Roosevelt's belief in a Civilian Conservation Corps acted as a catalyst for New Deal action.

On the occasion of his inauguration in March 1933, Roosevelt observed that the nation's desire for social, physical, and emotional restoration required not merely philosophical discourse but "action, and action now. Our greatest primary task is to put people to work."[3] A few days later, he asked the secretary of war, the secretary of the interior, the secretary of agriculture, and the secretary of labor to form an informal committee to coordinate plans for the proposed CCC.[4] Roosevelt envisioned that a resurgence of trust in public and private institutions would be combined with full employment: he knew these would be important measures in establishing stability throughout the land. An early legislative package proposed by the executive branch—including the Emergency Conservation Act, the Farm Loan Act, the Bankruptcy Act, and the Home Loan Act—marked the president's resolve. The timely passage of these acts played a vital role in the early restoration of citizens' trust in the government and its policies and in private institutions as well. The Emergency Conservation Act was enacted by Congress on March 31, 1933, just four weeks after Roosevelt's inauguration. Roosevelt's charge to the informal committee of cabinet secretaries was that the CCC should employ young men between the ages of 18 and 25 in a variety of projects designated by the Department of the Interior through its National Park Service and by the Department of Agriculture through its Forest Service. CCC projects were to engage in activities related to the prevention of fires, floods and soil erosion, the control of pests and disease, and the general stewardship of the nation's forests and parks.[5]

By Executive Order 6101, signed April 5, 1933, the president appointed Robert Fechner to be the director of emergency conservation work. Born in the South, Fechner lived much of his adult life in other parts of the United States and resided in Boston. He had a long history with labor, serving as a member of the General Executive Board of the International Association of Machinists, and he was the ideal person to bring together aspects of the Departments of Agriculture, the Interior, War, and Labor to form the new agency.[6] Roosevelt also appointed Fechner to allay fears among the rank and file that the Emergency Conservation Work Act was a threat to organized labor. Concomitant with its primary objective, Executive Order 6101 charged the army with the responsibility of housing, feeding, and clothing enrollees, while the projects to be executed by the CCC came under the jurisdiction of the Departments of Agriculture and the Interior.[7]

Roosevelt directed that the first CCC camp was to be established within a week of the enacting legislation, and on April 17, 1933, Camp Roosevelt,

NF-1, opened in Virginia in George Washington National Forest.[8] Members of Roosevelt's administration strongly believed that early successes would result in positive impacts on the nation's economic recovery, and only a month elapsed between Roosevelt's inauguration and the induction of the first CCC enrollee on April 7, 1933.[9] The CCC became a rallying point for the more than 500,000 young American men enrolled in 2,650 camps by 1935. Central to the CCC was an imperative to protect natural systems and to achieve a positive human condition—and this was more than fifty years before the confluence of such human-nature relationships became the subject of rigorous and specialized academic study in the field of landscape ecology.

Although its initial focus was the engagement of unemployed men in restoring the lands, woodlands, and riparian corridors of the American landscape, the CCC soon provided various modes of formalized education at its camps. The Emergency Conservation Work Act of 1933 did not identify specific education or training objectives, but it became apparent that the CCC could facilitate both formal educational and vocational training components. Roosevelt appointed Clarence S. Marsh as the first director of education for the CCC in the fall of 1933. Subsequently, the position of educational advisor—responsible for organizing vocational and academic educational programs and monitoring their effectiveness—was established in each camp. The submission of monthly educational reports was required from each camp. These provide historical data on the academic and vocational activities of participating CCC men. Courses were offered at both the elementary and high school levels, and vocational training opportunities were also available. Worthy of particular note is that over the course of its existence, the CCC taught more than 40,000 illiterate CCC men to read and write.[10] In the south Florida region, the University of Miami in Coral Gables offered the men of Company 269 (in Miami) free tuition for courses as well as credit for any university or college credits they had completed, provided that they had been enrolled in a university or college before entering the CCC. The university further offered to send its professors and instructors to the various CCC camps to facilitate enrollment and attendance.[11] Yet most of the young men either were still in high school or were recent graduates.

Edward L. Wallace, a senior leader in the CCC in Miami, commented that "the educational program offers to the enrollees all elementary and high school subjects, mechanics, woodworking, bookkeeping, stenography, drafting, and farming," and he noted further that even though participation in the educational programs was "not compulsory," he urged the men to take advantage of the courses and attend night school or a Miami high school. Quick to dispel local suspicions about the CCC camps, Wallace pointed out that "contrary to popular belief, the camps are not composed of hoboes and vagrants, but youths from the farms and the cities who prefer a steady job with board and room furnished by Uncle Sam to being a burden on their families and communities."[12] In this regard and many others, although the Miami CCC camp was among the earliest established, it shared many similarities with other camps across the country. There were, however, moments in the south Florida camps when morale became low and enrollees wanted to go home. In July 1935, for example, rumors of a strike abounded. Phillips, who replaced Prentiss French as the CCC camp superintendent in Miami, handled these uprisings with care by holding discussions, "town-meeting-wise," with all the enrollees, which helped keep the Miami camps productive and relatively quiet.[13]

The Dade County Park System

As the only contiguous subtropical region in the continental United States, Dade County (now Miami-Dade) has been the focus of anthropologic, topologic, and geologic study; the site of a host of military incursions including aspects of three wars fought between the Seminoles and the U.S. government; a place of curious explorations and investigations; and the base of operations for the occasional turn-of-the-century huckster. But most important, Dade County has served as the locus of settlement and development efforts for more than three centuries. By the 1900s, Miami and Dade County were both rapidly expanding in population and physical area. They were desirable destinations for growing numbers of northerners seeking the challenges of new opportunities and a lifestyle in a warmer climate. It was not until 1914, however, that the City of Miami recognized the potential benefit of constructing a park along the bay, to be located near the east terminus of Flagler Street along the west shore of Biscayne Bay. After a long period of discussion and consideration, this park ultimately began to take shape in 1926, after acquisition of lands owned by Henry Flagler's Florida East Coast Railroad, located along the bay front and underwater on the bay bottom.

The planning and design of the park in large part became the responsibility of Doug Barnes, who had worked for the City of Miami since 1925 and was a freshly minted landscape architectural graduate of the Massachusetts Agricultural College in Amherst. When coupled with such early private endeavors as the swimming pool on the property of Flagler's celebrated Royal Palm Hotel, this early bay front park was the seed from which blossomed a public appreciation of diverse recreational experiences that integrated the subtropical climate with the physical landscape. Concurrent with an expanding population was a growing awareness of the need for development of public recreation opportunities within Dade County. This need was given a face and a voice in the newly elected county commissioner, Charles H. Crandon. Upon his election in 1929, Crandon formed and headed the park committee within the county commission, which set out to formulate a vision for a countywide park system along the lines of what the young Robert Moses had been attempting in New York. Crandon immediately enlisted Barnes to be the first county parks director. It was in this role that Barnes became the primary force that brought the CCC to Dade County.

Barnes had been hired by Dade County in 1929 to administer a roadside beautification program within the County Road and Bridge Department. While Barnes was highly effective in moving roadside beautification projects along, he also had a vision to address the recreational needs of a growing population by preserving and developing an accessible park system.[14] A few of the parks Barnes was responsible for creating in the expanding Dade County system during the 1930s included Matheson Hammock (1930), Pelican Harbor (1930), Surfside (1932), Snapper Creek Canal (1932), Greynolds Park (1933), Redland Fruit and Spice Park (1935), Haulover (1935), Coral Gables Canal (1936), Fairchild Tropical Garden (1938), South Miami Wayside (1938), and Homestead Bayfront (1938), several of which were aided by the work of the CCC.[15] Barnes remained consistently interested in the presence of water in the parks, an interest expressed in nearly every park of this period, starting with his design for Miami's original Bayfront Park in the mid-1920s and continuing with Matheson Hammock Park and Greynolds Park a decade later.

Barnes first encountered William Lyman Phillips in 1932. Phillips's philosophical views on garden design grew from the influences of his New England youth and his graduate studies at Harvard in landscape architecture. Under the tutelage of Fredrick Law Olmsted Jr., and influenced by professors James Sturgis Pray and Henry Hubbard, Phillips was schooled in the European Beaux Arts tradition of design. A landscape architecture program had been established at Harvard around the turn of the twentieth century and included a few initial courses offered by Nathaniel S. Shaler, dean of the Lawrence Scientific School of Harvard College, and others. Among these courses was Landscape Architecture I, taught by Olmsted. At the behest of Harvard president Charles W. Eliot, Olmsted structured a formal landscape architecture curriculum with coursework that included horticulture, fine arts, and engineering and that would rely upon studies in the axial formality of the great gardens and public spaces of Europe. This was the intellectual context Harvard offered Phillips. In one of his papers, entitled "What Is the Garden?" Phillips described the garden as an art form that was appropriately an enclosed space or that at least provided the sense of some enclosure. He expressed the opinion that the quality of a garden is determined by its spatial composition and the relationships of objects to defined spaces. He invoked perhaps the modes of thinking of the painter and sculptor, with the utilization of plants and materials that have to be known and understood. He considered the problem of garden design, at this point, to be one of form alone.[16] After his schooling, Phillips went on to be the "Olmsted Representative in Complete Charge" for the exclusionary Mountain Lake Colony, and worked on the Bok Tower Gardens (formerly Mountain Lake Sanctuary) in Lake Wales, Florida.[17] When work in Florida slowed, Phillips was offered a position with the Olmsted Brothers in Houston. In 1932, he returned from Houston to be with his family and established his own landscape architectural practice in West Palm Beach.[18] Economic conditions, however, made it difficult for him to obtain rewarding design commissions, and in 1933 he became a project superintendent for the Civilian Conservation Corps. Their shared New England backgrounds probably contributed to the strong work relationship developed between Barnes and Phillips that served the CCC well in its south Florida projects.

The Civilian Conservation Corps in South Florida

A broad range of CCC projects were managed under the auspices of the National Park Service of the Department of the Interior and the U.S. Forest Service of the Department of Agriculture. One of the most controversial aspects of the CCC to some was that its facilities "looked like the nucleus of a fascist militia."[19] In fact, the army or War Department was completely responsible for the administrative personnel, camp maintenance, and the men's welfare and education. This fact was downplayed slightly in the 1938 handbook, *Your CCC*, which described the CCC as an entity of the U.S. government providing jobs and training for energetic young men seeking to conserve and replenish the public lands of the country.[20] Enrollment for men ages 17–28 was run by the army, who selected CCC men for a twelve-month period and focused first on men from those families that were receiving some form of aid from relief agencies. Each enrollee was provided with military-style uniforms, housing, and meals, and he received an average monthly compensation of thirty dollars. Of the monthly salary, the CCC would forward an allotment of twenty-five dollars to the family of each enrollee, with each CCC man retaining five dollars for incidental expenses. This government policy of allocation was intended to maintain a desirable level of financial equity among all enrollees, while distribution of the re- maining funds to the family of each man was intended to supplement—and sometimes supplant a portion of—various forms of public aid and relief. The absence of this allotment might well have left many of these families unable to provide for even their very basic needs. Generally considered an inflexible policy, men who were known to receive money from their families while in a CCC camp were subject to discharge from the program.

In the early days, the CCC operated like the army and sent new recruits to camps far from home. This policy, however, proved to be too disruptive

FIGURE 60. Hurricane-proof CCC camp at the intersection of North Kendall Drive and South Dixie Highway, 1936. Courtesy of the HMSF.

to community life and to the well-being of the CCC enrollees. In fact, the first camp in Miami, located at Northwest 7th Avenue and 27th Street in the County Fair Building that was later the site of Bobby Maduro Baseball Stadium, was comprised entirely of "Northern boys" from Missoula, Montana. On August 18, 1935, these northerners were moved to a project in Oregon and replaced by 150 southerners, about half of whom were from Miami. It was this southern group of CCC enrollees who helped to clean up after the great Labor Day hurricane of 1935 struck the Florida Keys and whose own camp was destroyed by the hurricane that hit Miami two months later. A new camp for the CCC was constructed to withstand hurricane forces—the first of its kind in the nation—at the intersection of North Kendall Drive and South Dixie Highway, near the current site of the Dadeland Mall. Completed in February 1936, the camp included a working educational farm that provided vegetables for the camp and scientific research facilities for investigating the crop growth in the south Florida environment.[21] It also had an interesting afterlife over the next two decades. It was used to house German prisoners of war and then functioned briefly as Camp Tequesta, a county-operated facility offering recreational opportunities for children. In the 1950s, some of these structures were relocated to Camp Owaissa Bauer, a county park in south Miami-Dade County; none of these structures exist today.[22]

CCC activities commenced in south Florida in October 1933 and extended through March 1941. CCC projects in south Florida were planned, designed, managed, and ultimately constructed with the direct guidance and daily involvement of Barnes and Phillips. These included Greynolds Park, Matheson Hammock Park, and Fairchild Tropical Garden. In addition, Phillips served as landscape architect in the master planning and subsequent development of Royal Palm State Park, constructed exclusively by the men of CCC Camp 262, located southwest of Homestead.

Royal Palm State Park

The Royal Palm State Park may have been the first "public/private" partnership in south Florida that supported recreational activities. It was created by an act of the Florida legislature in 1915, when 960 acres of publicly owned land were designated for park use. One account of further park development suggests that in the same year Mary Lily Kenan Flagler donated an additional 960 acres, and in 1921 the Florida legislature designated an additional 2,080 acres.[23] However, writer and horticulturalist Faith Rehyer Jackson suggests in her account of William Lyman Phillips that May Mann Jennings, wife of the former governor of Florida, dedicated nearly 4,000 acres of Jennings's Paradise Key land to the Federated Women's Clubs of Florida, including 300 acres of unique tropical jungle that botanically belongs to the West Indies and is now called the Prince of Hammocks.[24]

In late 1933, a parcel of land south of the Homestead business area was designated as the site of a temporary CCC camp to house the men working on the Royal Palm Park project. The camp used a vacant restaurant nearby for meal preparation and dining facilities. Florida did not have a statewide park enterprise at the time, and although Royal Palm State Park and its newly constructed Royal Palm Lodge were privately held and administered by the Florida Federation of Women's Clubs, the acquisition of the camp housing site on nearby Krome Avenue assured the Federation that their pe-

FIGURE 61. Royal Palm Lodge at the Royal Palm State Park. Dade County, ca. 1935. Courtesy of the HMSF.

tition to the CCC for a camp to assist with construction activities at Royal Palm State Park had been heard. It is likely that May Jennings played a significant role in obtaining the commitment that would engage the CCC men on what was at the time essentially a privately held project. With the establishment of the Everglades National Park in 1947, the infrastructure of Royal Palm State Park was retained as the Royal Palm Ranger Station. From the outset, the park was immensely popular. The National Park Service designated Jennings to be the local park authority, and Barnes was made the park's procurement officer.[25] It was to this 4,000–acre site that William Lyman Phillips and the CCC men of Company 262 devoted themselves in intense labor from October 1933 through September 1934. As the site was transformed, the rustic Royal Palm Lodge was constructed and opened for public use and enjoyment.[26]

For many of the CCC men, Royal Palm State Park was a hostile environment with bountiful wildlife, unpredictable weather, and the incessant threat of fire, particularly in the winter and spring. Despite their difficulties with the challenging subtropical weather, the enrollees prospered under Phillips's patient guidance. They engaged in controlled burning and brush cutting, clearing and grubbing for road and path construction, and preparing the planting pits for trees and palms in the hard coral rock substrate. They cut and maintained firebreaks and installed fencing. A series of construction projects was also undertaken, including the Lily Pool, a lookout tower, and a visitors shelter with thatched palm roof on the order of a traditional Seminole chickee.[27]

Phillips was sensitive to the natural environment of Royal Palm Park and used a number of native plants including Marlberry, Wild Coffee, Velvet

FIGURE 62. The Lily Pool constructed by the CCC at the Royal Palm State Park. Dade County, ca. 1935. Courtesy of NARA.

FIGURE 63. CCC surveying the Royal Palm State Park. Dade County, 1934. Courtesy of NARA.

Seed, Wax Myrtle, and Groundsel Tree in the park's existing landscape. The dearth of wholesale nurseries in the 1930s—and those that did exist focused primarily on limited species and quantities of native plant materials—necessitated a careful process of selection and root pruning of existing native plants from within the bounds of the park. Phillips also expressed his intention to plant the Royal Palm abundantly and to restore the richly varied hammock growth.[28] More than fifty years before the south Florida wholesale nursery industry began producing native species for ornamental landscapes, Phillips was already using native plants to accomplish ecologically sensitive landscape development. It was a strategy for landscape development that he would soon revisit at Greynolds Park.

Greynolds Park

In October 1933, the first CCC camp in Dade County was employed to develop a park on county-owned property at Camp Greynolds. The arrival of the CCC men was a coup for the county, since the land holdings marked by Doug Barnes for park development in concert with CCC forces were conspicuously small compared with the enormous projects covering thousands of acres that were the norm across the country. It was with some initial reluctance that Harold Weatherwax, a field representative from the CCC Area Four Atlanta office, agreed to consider the roughly 250 acres of Greynolds property. It was located in Ojus, twelve miles north of Miami in mangrove and pine forests, and was once the site of a rock pit dredging operation. Barnes impressed Weatherwax with his broad vision for the entire parks system and urged him to accommodate northern CCC enrollees during the winter in Miami where they could continue their work.[29] Barnes also used his connections with Conrad Wirth, the National Park Service's assistant director and a fellow landscape architectural graduate of the Massachusetts Agricultural College. Weatherwax considered the fairgrounds at Northwest 7th Avenue suitable for the CCC camp. He assigned two hundred CCC men to the Ojus site, which included a combination of the 160–acre donation from the Ojus Rock Company owned by A. O. Greynolds of West Palm Beach and the 60 acres donated by Palm Beach County. The members

FIGURE 64. Aerial view of Greynolds Park under construction. Ojus, northern Dade County, ca. 1935. Courtesy of NARA.

of this CCC camp also contributed their efforts to the small but workable 80–acre Matheson Hammock site.[30]

The CCC men of Camp 269 set to work on Phillips's master plan for Greynolds Park. The abandoned rock pit was littered with derelict and decaying machinery and concrete debris that had been utilized over the years in quarry operations. Lacking a suitable disposal site for this detritus, Barnes and Phillips directed the CCC men to dismantle as much of the machinery as was possible and to deposit the pieces at the site of the proposed observation tower. Excess earth and rock from the shaping and finished grading of land areas, lakes, and lagoons was then used to bury the pieces of machinery and create the mound and observation tower earthwork that were some of the most outstanding features of Phillips's master plan. Phillips's designs for Greynolds Park featured coral rock quarried from the site. This material was used in the construction of many of the park's amenities, including pedestrian and vehicular bridges, a caretaker's residence, and numerous walls.

The mound and observation tower, however, were especially significant for Phillips. He felt they connected south Florida to places he had experienced in his travels around the world. He wrote earnestly to his supervisors in Washington that the newly constructed tower "rules the scene with graceful domination."

> As one moves about, it draws the gaze in much the manner as does Vesuvius or Popoctypetl, from every corner of the countryside. . . . The walls of the rotunda rise sheer and boldly above you; at the foot of the stone ramp on the north the wind is shrewd like a mistral whining around ancient whitened keeps on the hills beyond Avignon. . . . The landscape when viewed from this height—a height that would be insignificant in a hilly region—reveals a scene of interest and charm unsuspected from normal points of view.[31]

The creation of such a mark on the south Florida landscape provided visitors and residents with a new way to appreciate the surrounding area. For the first time, the general public was offered rare views of the south Florida

FIGURE 65. Mound and observation tower at Greynolds Park. Ojus, northern Dade County, 1936. Courtesy of NARA.

FIGURE 66. Pedestrian bridge made from hand-cut coral rock at Greynolds Park. Ojus, northern Dade County, ca. 1935. Courtesy of NARA.

FIGURE 67. Greynolds Park caretaker's home made from the local coral rock. Ojus, northern Dade County, ca. 1935. Courtesy of NARA.

FIGURE 68. Coral rock entrance wall at Greynolds Park. Ojus, northern Dade County, 1936. Courtesy of NARA.

landscape that previously had only been available to those who could afford to occupy the highest floors of buildings or a ride in an airplane.

Phillips sent weekly reports to the CCC regional office. He commented on the two miles of roads to provide access to picnic areas with tables and benches and noted the appearance of the boathouse, refectory, and a remarkable stone entrance marker that had been constructed from native rock quarried from within the boundaries of the park. Cypress logs, which were once common in Florida and southern Georgia, were split into shakes to form the covering for many of the roofs on the property.[32]

The master plan for Greynolds Park responded to the existing borrow pits and stone quarries that had become a series of lagoons and lakes. Within some of these lakes and lagoons, Phillips directed his CCC men to use dynamite and a small dragline to create islands from exposed limerock.[33] He also created a sandy beach along the shores of the larger lagoon. As he had done at Royal Palm Park, he had the understory selectively thinned, and he designed winding paths and bridle trails to meander through the park site.

The park was opened to great fanfare on Sunday, March 29, 1936, a date selected to correspond to the centennial anniversary of Dade County. The connection between the two events was strengthened by a pageant entitled "Coral Heritage," directed by George Storm and carried out on the sandy edges of the lagoon near the boathouse. Storm served as the narrator of the pageant, which, according to the *Miami Herald*, included "Seminole Indians in native costume landing at the beach followed by Indian dances and music . . . landing of the first survey party of white men, a covered wagon with early settlers, typical music of pioneer days, and a climax picturing civilian conservation corps workers landing from barges to begin modern improvements."[34]

A dedication address by Robert Fechner capped the celebrations. To the gathered crowd of several hundred city and county officials, candidates for public office, and members of the public, Fechner pronounced:

Today we are witnessing a dream come true, for Greynolds park is suitable for recreation and the enjoyment of its physical beauties. This is typical of what has been done and is being done through the country. . . . We have beauty spots unequaled by any other nation, but have had no opportunity to enjoy them. Now the government has been glad to make these recreation places. Through the leadership of the federal government we have had the stimulation to create such parks as we have here.[35]

Greynolds Park showcased the confluence of Barnes's vision, Phillips's planning and design, and the commitment of the CCC to enhance communities through projects that engaged their nature environments. The park is one of the earliest examples in south Florida of what some consider the "fundamental aspects" of Phillips's design sensibility, namely, the conception of landscape architecture as a means to achieve the "use, convenience, and pleasure of people that gave identity to native landscapes."[36] This involved transforming Greynolds Park's largely inhospitable mangrove and pine forests and its quarries and junk piles into a sanitized environment with hills and sandy beaches. Greynolds Park immediately became a popular place to enjoy a picnic and the water. It might be argued, however, that a negative consequence of its successful transformation was that it helped to lull future generations of south Floridians into the expectation that acceptable subtropical environments were docile and comforting rather than simply those best for supporting natural habitats. However, nowhere were these issues more important than in the design and construction of Phillips's next project.

Matheson Hammock Park

In January 1930, before the New Deal was established, Matheson Hammock became the first public park in Dade County with the execution of the deed transferring title from Commodore W. J. Matheson to the county. The park opened for public use in the summer of 1930, with a number of caveats stipulating that the property would be forever kept in its original condition and used as a botanical park with the least possible intrusion on the natural landscape.[37] The actual development of significant infrastructure at Matheson, however, did not commence until the arrival of the CCC and Phillips in 1935, following the purchase of an adjacent 420 acres of land by Dade County.

CCC Company 1421 first started work on Matheson Hammock Park in 1935, while they were still engaged in Greynolds Park, and continued there until 1942. As Phillips noted to his supervisors in Washington, the two parks required very different strategies from the outset. At Greynolds Park, he wrote, "the points of attack presented a wide open front," which, he commented, contrasted greatly with the initial work at Matheson Hammock to open a relatively small access road from Old Cutler Road to the waterfront, where most of the CCC activities would take place.[38] Among these activities were the clearing and development of nature trails throughout the park; construction of the dock master's residence and a combination park office and picnic pavilion, all of native limestone quarried, cut, and shaped by hand on-site; dredging of channels and a boat harbor and construction of docks; the production of plant materials in a nursery; the installation of large quantities of trees and shrubs; construction of two swimming atolls

FIGURE 69. Aerial view of swimming atolls nearing completion at Matheson Hammock. Dade County, ca. 1938. Courtesy of HMSF.

at either end of the park; and the construction of picnic "chickees" from cypress logs with palm thatched roofs in the Seminole tradition. Also in the plans were a series of observation towers, which, if constructed, would have brought Matheson Hammock closely in line with the recreational facilities already found at Greynolds Park.[39] Barnes, Phillips, and the CCC men implemented the road system and paths of the park that largely preserved undisturbed concentrations of tropical hardwood hammock and shoreline mangrove. The entry road was one of the first and most difficult aspects of Matheson Hammock for the CCC enrollees to build and reflected one of Phillips's most profound statements about the local environment that harkened back to schooling in the creation of spaces within the landscape. He wrote that these errors generated profound experiences:

> The qualities here are the properties of a foil, of a contrasting element . . . the
> hammock through which the road enters the area, and the mangrove swamp is

FIGURE 70. Steps to roof-level dance floor of the picnic pavilion at Matheson Hammock Park made from coral rock quarried on the site. Dade County, ca. 1938. Courtesy of the Miami-Dade Public Library/Romer Collection.

FIGURE 71. CCC men working on the boat harbor at Matheson Hammock Park, ca. 1938. Courtesy of HMSF.

FIGURE 72. CCC men working the Matheson Hammock Park nursery, ca. 1938. Courtesy of HMSF.

FIGURE 73. Picnic "chickee" made of cypress logs with thatched roofs at Matheson Hammock Park, ca. 1938. Courtesy of HMSF.

wide enough and the cover high enough to shut one off completely from what
was left behind and what is coming before. The swamp is silent, windless,
monotonous. Suddenly one comes out into the open of a quiet cove where low
dark forest walls are reflected in still water, and the illimitable Bay is seen past
a headland of high wind-molded trees. It is as if one has passed through a dim
chamber into a bright and splendid hall.[40]

As at Greynolds Park, native on-site limestone was quarried and carefully
cut by hand by the CCC men. It was a durable and economically viable
material to use in the construction of a number of park elements. The picnic shelters designed in the Seminole vernacular were relatively simple and
inexpensive and shielded visitors from the unrelenting south Florida sun.
Some were designed to be large enough to accommodate gatherings of forty
or fifty picnickers.

From its opening in April 1938, the swimming atolls at Matheson
Hammock were the top attractions, offering free access to the shores of
Biscayne Bay within protected marine environments.[41] The enclosure of
the more southerly swimming atoll with an earth and rock promenade
was popular with strolling park visitors. Along with swimming and strolling, the other popular events were the Sunday afternoon performances of
the Miami Federal Symphony Orchestra, sponsored by the Dade County
Commission.[42] In 1940, Matheson Hammock also opened as part of a statewide "Stay Thru May" campaign coordinated with hotels in Miami and
Miami Beach to retain winter visitors for longer periods of time and reduce
the seasonal economic disparity in the region.[43]

Conclusion

In addition to Royal Palm State Park, Greynolds Park, and Matheson
Hammock, several other CCC projects were of equal importance to the
growth of the south Florida region, but they involved less CCC energy and
input. Primary among these was Fairchild Tropical Garden.[44] The garden
began with the acquisition by Colonel Robert Montgomery of lands adjacent to Matheson Hammock Park. It was Montgomery's intention to honor

the legacy of his friend Dr. David Fairchild, the internationally recognized botanist and plant collector. Incorporated in 1936 and dedicated in 1938, the garden was designed by Phillips, and parts were constructed by CCC enrollees, including the Old Cutler Road limestone boundary walls, the vine pergola that parallels Old Cutler Road, the two-story gatekeeper's lodge, the Overlook, the Amphitheater, and much of the original terracing within the garden.[45]

Another New Deal project that had a great impact on the region was the Overseas Highway to Key West. In August 1938, enrollees in Company 1418 on Ramrod Key undertook mosquito eradication and the construction of various facilities that would provide a well-structured road system with enhanced recreational opportunities for residents and tourists alike. These included the construction of parking facilities and other amenities along the entire stretch of the highway and in close proximity to the parkway corridor. The highway and recreational opportunities along it constructed by the CCC remain to this day an important component of the economy of the region.[46]

On January 1, 1940, Robert Fechner died at the age of 63, just two weeks before the official opening of Matheson Hammock, where he was scheduled to speak.[47] Born in Tennessee, Fechner had been one of the guiding forces in securing a large number of CCC camps in the South in general and in south Florida, in particular. One particularly difficult aspect of his position as director was to deal with questions of regional identity, race, and the CCC. During the New Deal, segregation continued to be a way of life for most Americans. CCC men from the North, such as those initially in Miami, did not always feel welcome in the South. Likewise, the public rejected early experiments with racially mixed CCC camps, and the idea of providing similar camps for young women was never seriously considered. Despite these inequities in the system, under Fechner's leadership, Crandon, Barnes, and Phillips were able to undertake projects that profoundly influenced how residents and visitors alike viewed the natural environment in south Florida. With the help of the CCC, they founded a park system for south Florida that incorporated the use and reuse of local plant species and building materials and that also emphasized orchestrated vistas and paths and manmade recreational facilities. Of all those involved in the CCC, no one was more aware than Phillips of the potential incompatibility of these goals. Phillips sought in all the CCC parks to strike a balance between the "wild" south Florida landscape and one tamed for human consumption and appreciation. This remains one of the most important legacies of the CCC in the region.

Notes

1. While there are many published sources on the New Deal, Franklin Delano Roosevelt, the CCC, and conservation, the study of the activities of the CCC in south Florida has only recently been explored. An article of particular relevance in this regard is Joanna Lombard, "The Memorable Landscapes of William Lyman Phillips," *Journal of Decorative and Propaganda Arts* 23 (1998): 261–87. A few of the recent studies of the national impact of the CCC include David B. Woolner and Henry L. Henderson, *Roosevelt and the Environment* (New York: Palgrave Macmillan, 2005); Louise I. Gerdes, ed., *The 1930s* (San Diego: Greenhaven Press, 2000); Bernard Sternsher, ed., *Hope Restored: How the New Deal Worked in Town and Country* (Chicago: Ivan R. Dee, 1999); Edwin G. Hill, *In the Shadow of the Mountain: The Spirit of the CCC* (Pullman: Washington State University Press, 1990); and John A. Salmond, *The Civilian Conservation Corps, 1933–1942* (Durham, N.C.: Duke University Press, 1967).

2. Edgar B. Nixon, ed., *Franklin D. Roosevelt and Conservation, 1911–1945* (Hyde Park, N.Y.: General Services Administration, National Archives and Records Service, Franklin D. Roosevelt Library, 1957), 635.

3. John Gabriel Hunt, ed., *The Essential Franklin Delano Roosevelt* (New York: Gammercy Books, 1995), 30.

4. For questions regarding the precise influences that resulted in Roosevelt's establishment of the CCC, see Nixon, *Roosevelt*, 209–10, and Richard St. Barbe Baker, *Green Glory: The Forests of the World* (New York: A. A. Wyn, 1949), 66–67.

5. Nixon, *Roosevelt*, vol. 1 (1911–1937): 62, 147.

6. The story of Fechner's history with labor appeared in "Robert Fechner, Head of CCC, Dies," *New York Times*, Jan. 1, 1940, 29.

7. A. D. Barnes, *History of the Dade County Park System: The First Forty Years, 1929–1969* (Miami: Metro-Dade County Parks and Recreation Dept., 1986), 19.

8. Ray Hoyt, *"We Can Take It": A Short Story of the C.C.C.* (New York: American Book Co., 1935), 12.

9. Ray S. Carter and Fred E. Leake, *Roosevelt's Tree Army: A Brief History of the Civilian Conservation Corps* (Arlington, Va.: National Association of Civilian Conservation Corps Alumni, 1983), 1.

10. Ibid., 3.

11. *Miami News*, Dec. 22, 1934, n.p.

12. Edward L. Wallace, "CCC Camp Located near Kendall Is Thrown Open to the Public Today," *Miami Herald*, Dec. 20, 1936. 6E.

13. W. L. Phillips, "Narrative Report for the Months of June and July 1935," National Archives and Records Administration, RG 79, Records of the National Parks Service; Barnes, *History*, 21; Faith Rehyer Jackson, *Pioneer of Tropical Landscape Architecture: William Lyman Phillips in Florida* (Gainesville: University Press of Florida, 1997), 147.

14. Jack McCormack, preface to Barnes, *History*.

15. Barnes, *History*, 67.

16. Jackson, *Pioneer*, 112–13.

17. Ibid., 70.

18. Lombard, "Phillips," 271–72.

19. Raymond Gram Swing, "Take the Army out of the CCC," *The Nation* 141 (Oct. 23, 1935), 459.

20. *Your CCC: A Handbook for Enrollees* (Washington, D.C.: Happy Days, 1938). Reprinted in 2000.

21. Wallace, "CCC Camp Located near Kendall."

22. Howard Kleinberg, *Miami: The Way We Were* (Surfside, Fla.: Surfside, 1989), 170.

23. "Visitors Confess Royal Palm State Park Holds Myriads of Wild Charm," *Miami News*, Mar. 8, 1942, n.p.

24. Jackson, *Pioneer*, 127.

25. Barnes, *History*, 20–21.

26. Jackson, *Pioneer*, 127.

27. Ibid., 129, 134.

28. Ibid., 130.

29. Barnes, *History*, 19.

30. *Designation Report* (Miami, Fla.: Miami-Dade County Historic Preservation Board, 1983). Greynolds Park also obtained another thirty acres on the east side of

Federal Highway in 1934. See "Formal Ceremony to Open Dade County's Newest Park," *Miami Herald*, Mar. 22, 1936, 11–A.

31. "Formal Ceremony to Open Dade County's Newest Park."

32. Barnes, *History*, 25.

33. Jackson, *Pioneer*, 149.

34. "Formal Ceremony to Open Dade County's Newest Park."

35. "Ceremonies Mark Dedication of Park," *Miami Herald*, Mar. 30, 1936, 1–A, 10–A.

36. Lombard, "Phillips," 286.

37. Barnes, *History*, 6.

38. Phillips, "Narrative Report"; also Barnes, History, 26.

39. Wallace, "CCC Camp Located near Kendall," 11E.

40. Phillips, "Narrative Report."

41. "South Miami CCC Camp Today Invites Public for Open House Celebration on Fifth Anniversary and Founding of Company," *Miami Herald*, Apr. 3, 1935, n.p.

42. "Open House at CCC Camp," *Miami Herald*, Apr. 9, 1939, 6–H.

43. "A Florida Campaign," *New York Times*, Apr. 20, 1941, XX4.

44. Lombard, "Phillips," 276–87.

45. Barnes, *History*, 22.

46. "Master Plan, Overseas Road and Toll Bridge. Commission of the United States," Plan No. FLA-SP-11 in four sheets. Sept. 16, 1940 and Sept. 20, 1940. Montgomery Library, Fairchild Tropical Botanic Garden Collection, Fairchild Tropical Botanic Garden, prepared by William Lynar Phillips.

47. "Robert Fechner, Head of CCC, Dies."

SIX

Liberty Square

Florida's First Public Housing Project

JOHN A. STUART

On February 6, 1937, Liberty Square in Miami became one of the first of seventeen federally sponsored housing projects to open its doors to black residents during the New Deal. The project was constructed in little over a year on a vacant twenty-acre site located at what was then outside the city of Miami at Northwest 62nd Street and Northwest 14th Avenue.[1] Its land was the least expensive of any purchased for housing by the federal government, and at only twelve dwellings per acre, it had the lowest density of any project completed by the Public Works Administration's Housing Division.[2]

One of the primary challenges for its architects was negotiating the relationship between architecture and race. They sited the project just outside of, instead of within an existing black neighborhood, thereby altering the highly contentious racial geography in Miami and opening up vast territories for the expansion of the black community. The project's planning and design, however, reinforced notions of racial segregation and isolation. This chapter explores the extent to which Liberty Square modified long-standing community expectations in the relatively young city of Miami. Like all of the fifty-one projects completed by the Housing Division during Roosevelt's administration, Liberty Square was a living experiment in innovative standards for housing materials and new methods of construction and a contestation between federal ideals for housing and local conditions and expectations.

Previous accounts of Liberty Square have focused on the impassioned conflicts between the white citizens of Miami and the federal government over the project's location. These were fiercely fought battles over nothing

FIGURE 74. Aerial view of the recently completed Liberty Square, ca. 1937. Courtesy of the HMSF.

less than the future racial and economic geography of the city. Michael Straus and Talbott Wegg (the first of whom was an assistant to Secretary of the Interior Harold Ickes and the second, a member of the editorial section of the Branch of Research in the Housing Division) included the first detailed summary of the story within *Housing Comes of Age*, their history of the PWA Housing Division. Lavishing more pages on Liberty Square than on any other project in the nation, Straus and Wegg concluded that while its problems were exceptional for the "controversial detail and warmth of feeling aroused," they also contained general lessons about housing, since no detail of the story was "unique to the city or project in question."[3] Wegg knew the story intimately. He had been personally involved with Liberty Square and spent much time in Miami working on it in the mid-1930s. During World War II, Liberty Square's first black housing manager, James E. Scott, produced a substantial insider's account of Liberty Square for an issue of the *Crisis* dedicated to Miami. Scott provides a glowing assessment of the project, even though the number of residents had tripled in number without similar increases in funding or communal amenities. He wrote that tenants "of Liberty Square have excellent environmental conditions for their children and wonderful opportunities for developing genuine cooperative spirit and community pride."[4] After World War II, Robert C. Weaver, who had been the brilliant young Advisor on Negro Affairs to Secretary Ickes, returned Miami to the national spotlight in his 1948 book, *The Negro Ghetto*. Weaver noted that "few cities in America have worse living conditions for the vast majority of their Negro residents than Miami." He felt that Miami, following other young southern cities like Durham and Tulsa, had more "spatial separation" between black and white communities than older southern cities. He noted that Liberty Square had broken the established traditions of inhabitation in the city's "Black Belt," since it allowed the black community to expand into new areas of the city.[5]

In the late 1980s, upon the fiftieth anniversary of its dedication, Liberty Square again became the focus of study. Paul S. George and Raymond Mohl were among the first scholars to explore the wealth of materials on Liberty Square preserved in the National Archives in Washington, D.C. Paul George explored the early history of the project and made oral histories of some of its first tenants. George found that morale at Liberty Square began to slip after 1965 when income requirements were relaxed. The carefully structured income ceilings designed to encourage residents to find housing on their own were lifted, and the minimum income requirements were dropped, allowing some families with little or no means to pay rent to move into the project. George noted, "There are no policies or procedures evident in the files which prepare or encourage tenants to aspire to a future outside of the project."[6] Mohl's work looks specifically at the racist struggles for territory involved in the planning of Liberty Square and at the broader effects that New Deal policies had on urban communities.

Within his evaluation of the New Deal's Home Owner's Loan Corporation, Mohl considers the "devastating and long-term consequences for Miami" from federal redlining of neighborhoods, which effectively restricted vast numbers of people from receiving critical forms of financial assistance.[7] My research for this chapter is, of course, indebted to all who have written on this subject before me and particularly to the work of Raymond Mohl and Paul George.

The story of Liberty Square began on July 8, 1933, when Franklin Delano Roosevelt appointed Harold Ickes to lead the Federal Emergency Administration of Public Works, otherwise known as the Public Works Administration (PWA). Shortly after assuming the position, Ickes established the semi-autonomous "Housing Division" within the PWA. The division was intended to provide relief by stimulating employment in the building industries to create much-needed federally subsidized housing for low-income Americans. Led by the New York architect Robert D. Kohn, the division initially solicited applications for loans to private and public "limited dividend" corporations, so called for their expectation of limited, rather than maximum, profits on projects intended for lower-income individuals. More than five hundred applications poured in from newly minted limited dividend corporations across the country. Architects within the Housing Division favored proposals that cleared areas of what they deemed substandard housing from urban environments. By and large, applications sought loans for what most Americans understood housing to be—modest projects of a few houses on small plots of vacant land that provided the greatest financial benefit to the local developer.[8] Of the initial five hundred, only seven limited dividend projects were approved, and these were considered insufficient to stimulate broader areas of the economy.

Four limited dividend corporations from Miami sent applications for consideration by the Housing Division. Architect Arthur B. Gallion (1902–78) found that three of these were for "moderately priced real estate developments," intended for white people, and "obviously not related to slum clearance."[9] One application stood out. Miami's Southern Housing Corporation's application of December 1933 proposed to resettle thousands of Miami's black residents from the notorious "slum" area then called "colored town." Far from the government's ideal, the SHC proposal, however, came the closest to meeting the government's specifications because of its potential to provide black residents a way out of the substandard conditions in Overtown.

The SHC applied for $1.1 million to house 5,000 black Miamians in 800 houses spread over 120 vacant acres between 62nd and 71st Streets and 12th and 14th Avenues. Although the site included the ground on which Liberty Square would eventually be built, the proposal called for a suburb of six or seven individual single-family homes per acre and with an average household of more than six residents each. The SHC application stressed the advantages of the site: the land was dry, it was near (but not inside) the city limits of Miami, and it had transportation lines along nearby avenues. Most important, the site was "within one or two blocks of the present colored school and churches and adjoins a colored section, and was the only land contiguous to Miami available for a colored section."[10] The SHC application claimed that work on the project could start with four weeks notice and would take just six months to complete, employing 1,432 men. The members of the SHC included Miami City recreation manager and lawyer Dr. George Henry Bradford as president; Judge John C. Gramling, secretary; Floyd L. Knight, project attorney; Walter C. DeGarmo, project architect; M. B. Garris, project consulting engineer; D. L. Bosworth, project vice president; Vincent R. Brice, project treasurer; and Paul R. G. Sjostrom, executive secretary. Although all the members of the SHC were white, leaders from Miami's black community supported the application.

By November 1933, President Roosevelt shifted the government's focus from loans to direct government construction and signed an executive order creating the Public Works Emergency Housing Corporation with an appropriation of $100 million. By June 1934, architect, builder, and West Point graduate Horatio B. Hackett was appointed head of the new Housing Division. Its focus was to design and construct housing in urban areas across the country that would lead to "slum clearance."

The application, however, was misplaced for several months in the chaos of the Housing Division's transition to direct construction projects. It did not resurface until June 1934, when housing official Arthur Gallion reviewed it and announced, "The low land prices and the particular location, coupled with the desire of the Negroes themselves to work for the success of the project, indicate that this presents an opportunity to do an excellent job of planning to meet an obvious need. I believe this project offers excellent possibilities and deserves serious and immediate consideration."[11]

The project was largely the work of the SHC secretary, Judge Gramling, who was by far its most persistent advocate and who was in frequent contact with members of the Housing Division. As noted by Mohl and George, Gramling's motives for supporting a black housing project in Miami were not simply altruistic. He sought clean public housing for Miami's black population that would relieve the dilapidated and overpopulated areas of "Colored Town" where epidemics of Dengue Fever and other illnesses were thought to originate. These and similar concerns over the health of middle-class white people who brought black people into their homes helped to initiate broader discussions of black health.[12] Gramling felt that the high rate of disease among the black servant population in Miami would have a negative impact on the permanent white population of the city and on the tourist economy. His response was to clean up and isolate the black community even further from its white neighbors. He informed Hackett that the "city will have you to thank for the saving of many lives in consequence of this project making it possible to segregate the negroes and clean up colored town."[13]

Gramling had also played a role in selecting a site for the project owned by his client, the white developer Floyd W. Davis, and he stood to gain financially as well as politically from the project.[14] Members of the Housing Division depended on Gramling as a local leader and even shared some of his paternalistic attitudes toward the black population. Their differences were most notable when Housing Division officials insisted that they were constructing not just clean buildings but an entire community planned around public amenities and support previously unheard of for the black residents in Miami.

From the outset, Miami's black leaders also played critical roles. In October 1933, Richard E. S. Toomey, a black lawyer, led a group of Miami's prominent black residents to write two position papers. The first,

FIGURE 75. Richard
E. S. Toomey, ca. 1920.
Courtesy of the Black
Archives, History and
Research Foundation of
South Florida, Miami.

a short statement entitled "Statement of Congested Conditions of Colored
Section of Miami, Dade County Florida" delineated the boundaries of
"Colored Town" and its deplorable conditions of overcrowding. The signers included Dr. W. B. Sawyer, founder of Christian Hospital and owner
of the Mary Elizabeth Hotel, H. S. Bragg, a contractor and builder, Julius
Lane, Ellis Lindsey, H. B. Barkley, Chas S. Thompson, W. B. Thomas,
and J. W. Drake.[15]

The second paper, however, was longer and more substantive. It included
a letter of support for the SHC project addressed to Federal Housing Director
Robert Kohn. It was signed by "a committee of colored men selected by the
representative business and colored men of Miami." The letter opened with
the observation that since the original 343 acres had been set aside for "col-

ored town" in the early part of the twentieth century, the population had risen to 25,000 and the area left to live in had been greatly reduced by the addition of "warehouses, commission houses, business districts, churches and schools." This, the authors pointed out, left only enough territory on which "10,000 people could live and enjoy proper light, air and sanitation, in one-story houses." The committee stated further that the "environment in which our children are growing up is revolting to the educated, well-bred colored people of Miami." To create a better situation in the city, the committee suggested that "it is necessary to obtain a territory contiguous to Miami where we may segregate some of the best families from the classes of undesirable elements." It was argued that with the lower-income families re-moved from Overtown, wealthier black families and their businesses could continue to thrive near downtown.[16]

The black leaders expressed the desire that the "colony" would offer a permanent suburban alternative to life in "Colored Town." They envisioned a community of houses, with "a civic center, parks, and play grounds." Each of the well-built homes would be "provided with bath, toilet, electric lights," and be separated from its neighbors with "only one dwelling to each lot." Toomey and his colleagues expected that "the houses may be leased for a long term of years and eventually owned by the tenant, who improves the property and lives a decent and law-abiding life in accordance with the rules and regulations of the State Housing Board." In the new project as envisioned by the black committee members, community facilities would enrich both the bodies and minds of its inhabitants, and residents would have access to a health clinic and attend lectures by distinguished national speakers. The black leaders, however, echoed the sentiments of their white counterparts and wrote that the clinic was needed "in order that we may send out to the white people of Miami cooks, washwomen, maids, chauf-feurs, yard-men, and other servants free from disease."[17] They believed that this federal housing project would maintain the delicate "status quo" of racial relations in Miami by creating a model of decent living conditions that would be acceptable to both black and white citizens. Those drafting this initial document were sympathetic to the federal government's initiative to create projects that supported the black working classes and essentially ignored the plight of the very poor. This stance became one of the most common critiques leveled against the Housing Division over the course of its existence and yet was key to its initial success.[18]

For the black leaders, the issue of location was clearly tied to the potential of future flexibility and growth. As Toomey wrote, "All our programs will have to be abandoned unless the model city is placed in the location where we can expand.[19] He and J. Harvey Smith, president of the Miami Colored Chamber of Commerce, concurred that the 62nd Street area was ideal because it offered thousands of acres for future expansion.[20]

For many white Miamians, the prospect of unrestricted black expansion was unacceptable. As one enraged citizen wrote, "Negro settlements are like bonfires during dry season. They spread like fury."[21] In addition to "Colored Town," there were three other established black communities in Miami. These included what was called Black Coconut Grove, Brownsville, and the Davis Subdivision commonly known as Liberty City. "Colored Town" was home to Miami's black doctors, lawyers, dentists, and other professionals and offered the only truly urban black experience in Miami. The site proposed for Liberty Square was just a few blocks east of Liberty City and did not technically lie within any recognized territory designated for black habitation. This matter was so critical that the Dade County Commission attempted to veto the project on the basis of boundaries alone. In July 1935 the county commissioners resolved that

> the existence of such established recognized boundaries [between black and white communities] has to a large extent been responsible for the harmony which has existed between the whites and Negroes in this county . . . the location of said proposed negro colony . . . is separated from all existing negro settlements, is surrounded on three sides by densely populated white residential district, and is so located as to lower the assessed value of the property of several thousands of white home-owners . . . and realizing that ultimate development and expansion of the city of Miami, to the North, would be definitely be retarded, this board registers its objection to the plan as outlined.[22]

The initial plans were to set the project on a twenty-acre piece of land located between northwest 12th and 13th Avenues and 62nd and 67th Streets.

The plan located the project in unincorporated Dade County, outside the boundaries of the city of Miami. This not only satisfied those interested in moving the poor black population out of Miami but also eliminated opposing forces in Miami's municipal government from being critical to the process of acquiring land and building permits. The site was problematic for two reasons: It was not immediately adjacent to the existing black community of Liberty City, and it would make NW 12th Avenue a convenient north-south artery for black workers to get to their jobs in downtown Miami and Miami Beach. NW 12th Avenue, however, was key to the northward expansion of the downtown businesses, and critics claimed that allowing black people on the "white avenue" could cause "infinite racial strife and bloodshed."[23] Others claimed that the introduction of black residents on NW 12th Avenue would create "attendant hardship" on the white popula-

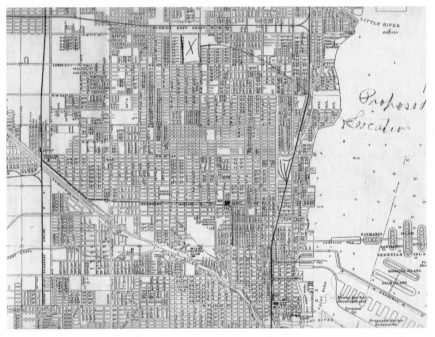

FIGURE 76. Map of Dade County used by members of the Housing Division to indicate the future location of Liberty Square, ca. 1935. Courtesy of the National Archives and Records Administration (NARA).

tion.[24] Architects in the Housing Division had anticipated this resistance and designed a "buffer strip facing on the NW 12th Avenue frontage, at least four hundred feet wide."[25] This, however, did not satisfy critics. A petition to the federal government signed by 3,000 Miami residents claimed that each signer would have considerably diminished property values if the project were constructed. Officials in the Housing Division carefully studied the petition, which included an address with each signature, and found that only 5 percent of the signers who claimed they would be ruined by the project lived within a mile of the proposed site (see fig. 77).[26] Even if the critics did not sway the federal government, they were able to persuade the county commission to vote against the project on its original site. To save the project, Secretary Ickes approved the purchase of forty acres of land immediately to the west of the original site between NW 13th and NW 15th Avenues. The project was shifted to the westernmost twenty-acre block—that closest to the existing Liberty City—with the forty acres to the east set aside as a buffer against black expansion. In this location, the county commission finally approved the plan, and the outcry against the project almost immediately subsided. Although no one knew it at the time, the dreaded expansion of the project would occur almost immediately. In 1939, just two years after the federal project for Liberty Square was completed, its impact on the community was determined to be inadequate because of its small size. Local housing authorities expanded it from 243 to 730 residents by filling in the "buffer" and pushing Liberty Square next to NW 12th Avenue with two full blocks of housing similar in appearance to the original project. To maintain a separation between the black residents and the "white" avenue, the city built what had been planned by the federal government as a buffer. This included a new fifty-foot-wide avenue for whites, a fifty-foot-wide parkway with a "high woven wire fence" (which was constructed as a tall concrete wall), and a second fifty-foot-wide street for black residents that ran parallel to 12th Avenue, effectively restricting access from Liberty Square to this important north-south thoroughfare.[27] The parallel street and parts of the wall are both still in existence today (see fig. 78).

After the site was finalized and the project approved for construction, federal officials were still hesitant to include members of the black commu-

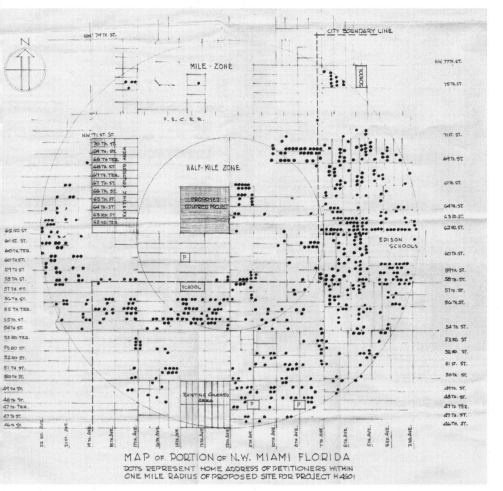

FIGURE 77. Map centered on the future location of Liberty Square that pinpoints the addresses of those who signed a petition against the construction of Liberty Square on that site, July 29, 1935. R. Moore. Courtesy of NARA.

FIGURE 78. View north of "black" 12th Avenue on the left, the buffer wall and zone to the east of Liberty Square, and "white" 12th Avenue on the right, 2006. Photo by author.

nity in the process in significant ways. They made a halfhearted attempt to establish a black advisory committee "with some impressive title so that they might feel personal interest and responsibility in the project." In a somewhat patronizing tone, Wegg commented that from "my observation of their reactions, I believe that such an invitation would mean more to these men than any consideration they might ever receive."[28] Government officials asked Gramling to suggest names for the black advisory board. He provided the names of the prominent doctor Sawyer, businessman Kelsey L. Pharr, the owner of Lincoln Memorial Park Cemetery, and Toomey. These men selected four others to join them on the black advisory board: John R. Scott, John R. Michael, Henry Reeves, and Ellis Lindsey.[29] The black advisory board was asked to weigh in on the naming of the project. Even in this task, their opinions seem to have been blatantly disregarded.

In 1935, Angelo R. Clas, director of the Housing Division, asked Toomey to suggest a name for the project. Clas wrote that "we would prefer a name that was either distinctive of the location or in memory of some outstanding citizen. We do not favor names which suggest promotional real estate subdivisions."[30] Toomey organized a committee including the Reverend J. E. Culmer of St. Agnes Episcopal Church, Dr. H. H. Green, Dr. Sawyer, Dr. F. D. Mazoun, and Sergeant-Major A. C. Goggins. The committee met and recommended calling the project either "Utopia" or "Toomeyville." Clas rejected both options. He replied that while "Utopia" implied a "new and vastly improved community," he felt it seemed "too general" for a "specific project in Northwest Miami." As for Toomeyville, Clas noted that it was the Housing Division policy that individuals for whom housing projects were to be named had to be "not only distinguished but deceased," adding "under the circumstances, I could not wish to see you qualified for this distinction." The committee put forth "Liberty City Gardens."[31] Toomey and his colleagues had little choice but to consent to Clas's suggestion.[32]

The committee's work, however, sparked some degree of controversy in the black community. An anonymous writer accused Toomey and Culmer of being "foreigners" and unqualified to name the project. This writer suggested naming the project "Roosevelt Hill," "Franklin's Hill," "Solomon's Grove," or "Solomon's Hill," with "Farr's City" and "Abyssinia City" provided as alternatives.[33] The president of the Miami Colored Chamber of Commerce, J. Harvey Smith, along with Executive Secretary M. B. Williams and Recording Secretary H. G. Dargan, were also critical of both the process and the name. They suggested naming the project "East Liberty City" or "Washington Park" after Booker T. Washington. Not realizing that the government had rejected the name, they expressed their concern that Toomey did not have the stature to have the project named after him, noting that "if it is named after any living person, we would like some person who has made some outstanding success."[34] If anything may be drawn from the list of names presented by the black community leaders, it is perhaps the clear sense of dedication the black community had to Roosevelt himself and the immense amount of hope they placed in a community of modern housing they wished to call "Utopia."

Nearly a year later, the white advisory board was asked to reexamine the naming of the project. Their names included various combinations of parks, squares, and the names *Booker T. Washington, Lincoln,* and *Liberty.* The board decided on "Liberty Square," citing their impressions that "Liberty City was a well-known name in Miami," and the project was "within the limits of Liberty City." They accurately predicted that black residences would "completely surround" Liberty Square, and that the project would be expanded, if not into a perfect square with twenty acres buffering it from the white community to the east as they hoped, then as a long rectangle extending to 12th Avenue.

Members of the black advisory board, however, further delayed the naming. They expressed their desire that the project be known forever as a product of the New Deal and not simply as an outgrowth of the southern city of which it was a part, and they offered the name *Roosevelt Square.*[35] Discontent again arose on the part of the Miami Colored Chamber of Commerce, that included Reeves, who was vice president of the *Miami Times,* Bragg, millionaire D. A. Dorsey, J. Harvey Smith, president, and M. B. Williams, executive secretary of the Miami Colored Chamber of Commerce, Inc. These prominent black leaders accused those on the black advisory board, now called the Advisory Board to the Housing Manager, as having misrepresented their educational credentials and claimed that members of the Miami Colored Chamber of Commerce had actually been the first to bring the housing conditions for black people in Miami to the attention of officials in Washington. They suggested that the Advisory Board to the Housing Manager be expanded to include members of the Miami Colored Chamber of Commerce, a request that Washington did not fulfill.[36] In addition to a committee on the name, a black advisory committee was formed to persuade black residents to apply for residency in the project. Members of this committee included Pharr, Sawyer, Charles E. Thompson, Culmer, and Toomey.[37]

Although federal architects designed Liberty Square, Housing Division authorities selected a team of local architects to create an external appearance for the project and the drawings required for its construction. In December

1934, the Housing Division sent Arthur B. Gallion, a member of Housing Division's Branch of Initiation and Recommendation, to Miami.[38] Passing through on his way to Puerto Rico, Gallion had little more than a day to size up the architectural scene in Miami and was remarkably self-assured given his youth and experience. Gallion, however, was one of the died-in-the-wool "housers" with strong beliefs in the future of housing. A native of Chicago, he had graduated from the University of Illinois at Urbana-Champaign. In 1933, he took a job paying $30 per week with the federally funded Housing Study Guild in New York. His colleagues included the guild's prominent founders, Henry Wright, Catherine Bauer, Lewis Mumford, and Clarence Stein, who were some of the nation's leading experts in housing, planning, and architectural criticism. Supported by the Civilian Works Administration, members of the guild studied all aspects of modern housing and had constant access to consultants in technical fields to assess aspects of engineering, cost analysis, and management. The Housing Study Guild turned out to be something of a training ground for the Housing Division. In the spring of 1934, Robert Kohn offered Gallion a job. Gallion traveled across the country to spread the message of federal housing to local municipalities and encourage them to form regional housing and planning departments. He also selected projects worthy of federal funding and interviewed local architects who were interested in working with the federal government on the design and construction of housing in their areas.[39]

Gallion arrived in December 1934 to select architects for the Miami housing project. He was most impressed by Vladimir Virrick, a Russian architect who had studied at Columbia University and had experience with housing in Russia. Writing to his superiors in Washington, Gallion observed that Virrick had "submitted [a] paper on Industry and Housing in this country . . . So in my opinion, very capable and warrants definite consideration."[40] He was, however, also very supportive of the firm of Paist and Steward, noting the years they had been in practice, their origins and experience in the north (Pennsylvania and New Jersey, respectively), their work on the Miami Federal Building (1931/32), and their role as the supervising architects for the City of Coral Gables. Gallion commented that he could "well see Mr. Paist as logical coordinator." Gallion also wished to include the twenty-nine-year-old architect C. Sheldon Tucker, who had worked for the Chicago firm of Holabird and Root before coming to Miami, and E. L. Robertson of Robertson and Patterson. Without college training, Robertson had fifteen years of work experience and was president of the Florida South chapter of the American Institute of Architects. August Geiger was already the architect of the PWA–sponsored Miami Beach Senior High School, and George L. Pfeiffer had been hired by the PWA to design additions to Jackson Memorial Hospital. For these reasons, Gallion did not interview them.[41] Russell Pancoast was rejected as "a wealthy arch't with considerable large residential work now. A very good man, however." Gallion also rejected Walter DeGarmo, noting that he "did not have much confidence in his ability," but later intended to include him based upon his "association with the project from its inception." Kiehnell and Elliot were considered "good architects," but were not able to arrange interviews.

In summary, Gallion advised his colleagues in Washington that his "first choice would be Vladimir Virrick, Paist and Steward, with C. Sheldon Tucker; including Walter C. DeGarmo, if necessary because of his previous contact with the project and Robertson if there are not sufficient men already."[42] Within five days of Gallion's recommendation, Phineas Paist was invited to Washington to discuss the leadership of his architectural team, which was to include Virrick, Tucker, and DeGarmo. Virrick did not seem to work well on the team, and in the final organization, the "senior group" consisted of coordinators Paist and Steward with Robertson, while the "associate group" comprised DeGarmo, Virrick, and Tucker.[43] Paist proposed to work with Virrick on the landscape architecture for the project, but Virrick was relieved of that responsibility when landscape architect Frank Button was placed on the project. Black architects were never considered for the Miami project, although they were selected to participate in the design of similar black housing projects in Chicago, New York, Nashville, and Washington, D.C.[44]

In February 1935, just two months after the Miami team had been selected, Horatio Hackett instructed the architects of Liberty Square to "prepare sketches of a site plan and houses."[45] These, however, had already been prepared by architects in the Housing Division and would be published within a month in the PWA Housing Division's *Unit Plans: Typical Room Arrangements, Site Plans, and Details*. Considered for several years the definitive text on modern housing created by architects in the Housing Division, the book offered a glossary of terms and a series of "housing standards" with rules of thumb. The site and unit plans presented were the federal "ideals," the best examples of projects designed by government architects. They were ostensibly generalized to be modifiable for any site and made an enormous impact on housing in America. The plan of Liberty Square presented in the *Unit Plans* differed from that presented in Miami only by proposing that the community center "and shops" be located on the south rather than the east side of the project and by presenting a bandstand, which was never proposed. In the remarks below the plan, it is noted that this "method of grouping housing is economical and efficient. Charm and domesticity emphasized."[46] (See figs. 79, 80.)

Memoranda internal to the Housing Division revealed that the program for the housing project was initially quite different than that expressed by local black leaders who had been interested in improving conditions in Overtown by moving poorer black residents to Liberty Square. According to government documents, however, Liberty Square was to be designed for "Negroes of all income status," with certain more desirable units set aside to attract "leaders of the Negro community." These special units were to be distinguished by "preferential location or within reason difference of architectural treatment."[47] While there is no evidence that such special apartments were ever designed, and none of the original promoters of Liberty Square moved into the project, in most respects the program given to the architects by the government was followed closely. The Miami architectural team was given the design of the project's appearance, fleshing out the exterior elevations, as well as construction details related to the materials used. Taking their cue from Catherine Bauer's 1934 book, *Modern Housing*, members of the Housing Division considered Modernism to be a matter of functional planning, not simply a question of style.

The Housing Division plans for Liberty Square were formed around a swimming pool, community center and stores, and playgrounds. A pool was

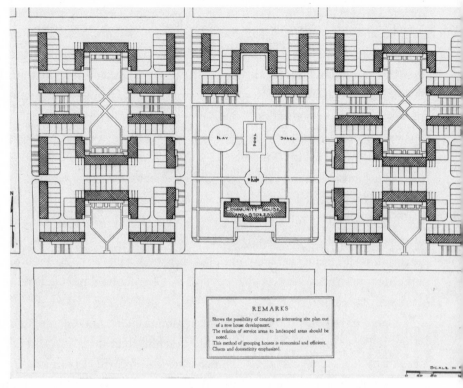

FIGURE 79. Site plan of an unidentified project that provided the basis for the design of Liberty Square. Published in *Unit Plans*, 1935.

an unusual feature among low-cost housing projects, and only one other example in the *Unit Plans* included one.[48] In Miami, the idea of a pool for black residents funded by taxpayers' dollars stirred up debates on hygiene and leisure that separated the black and white communities. Access to pools and beaches formed the experiential core for Miami visitors and its white citizens. The identity of south Florida was largely inseparable from recreational activities related to water. One white Miamian went so far as to claim that it is "ridiculous" that in a city with so many ocean and bay fronts citizens should pay for pool maintenance and lifeguards at Liberty Square. Showing great restraint, a member of the Housing Division reminded the resident that "the ocean and bay fronts . . . are not available for the use of

Negroes" and that "in the whole of Dade County there are no recreational facilities of any description for the use of Negroes."[49]

Although Dade County sported more than twenty pools for white people, the largest number of any county in the state, it had no public bathing facilities or accessible beaches for black people. A privately run pool had existed in Liberty City and was briefly closed in the mid-1930s. The only two public pools for black residents in Florida during the 1930s were at schools for black children in St. Augustine and Marianna, Florida.[50] A prominent member of the white advisory board, Dr. Marvin Smith, strongly disapproved of a pool at Liberty Square, fearing it would facilitate the spread of venereal disease. This point of view was prevalent and represented strong racist stigmas surrounding venereal disease and black health in the South at this time. Dr. Smith's stance greatly surprised Dr. Von Derlehr of the Public Health Service in Washington, who sent word to the Miami doctor through the architects and project manager that he had "never yet heard of a syphilitic infection from a swimming pool."[51]

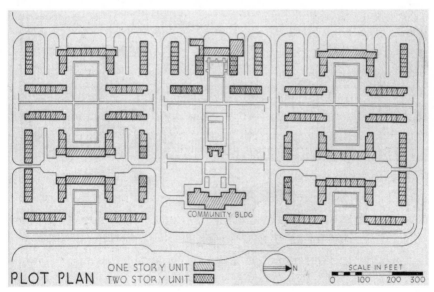

FIGURE 80. Paist and Steward's plot plan for Liberty Square. *Architectural Forum* (May 1937).

Yet for many white citizens, the pool was simply too much of an improvement in the condition of the black residents and threatened to open up too many new opportunities for parities in leisure between black and white residents of the city. While this argument was difficult to make, it was easier to suggest that the inclusion of the pool would make the project difficult to define as "low cost." By October 1935, with the project nearly fully designed, federal officials made the swimming facility an "alternate" (i.e., disposable) item in the project specifications, dependent upon "the securing of funds to operate and maintain it."[52]

Distressed by the idea that the swimming pool was in jeopardy, Harold Steward presented several arguments for keeping it. He contended that the pool was always a "focal point of interest" in the project and had been positively reviewed by Hackett. Likewise, he pointed out that each white subdivision in Miami had its own pool, as did the cities of Coral Gables, Tampa, and St. Petersburg, and that more generally pools are "very popular here in the South." Finally, he appealed to the paternalistic side of the government's housing program, stating that it should "have its influence on the better class of Negro families that we hope to attract to our village," and "if properly managed, would be a great benefit to the negros [sic] and help to educate them in sanitary living conditions."[53] Even with a divided white advisory board (the black advisory board was not consulted), the pool remained a possibility until the end of 1936, when it was finally excluded.

Despite the elimination of the pool, Liberty Square was running over budget. The unusually high costs of sewer and water lines from the city of Miami to the site outside the city limits were primarily to blame. In order to reduce costs, the community building, the first public edifice of its kind for the black populations in Miami, was considered for omission.[54] Like the pool, the building was physically and conceptually critical to the project. It was designed with a large gathering hall, kitchen facility, administration offices, and spaces for stores. Its inclusion elevated the project from a collection of buildings to a community. The community building remained when the City of Miami promised—but did not always come through on—$2,500 per year in operating expenses.[55] To save more money, architects eliminated some modern conveniences and construction details in the dwellings.

Wood floors were replaced with asbestos tile on raw concrete. Electric refrigerators were replaced with old-fashioned ice boxes. Communal laundries were eliminated, and clothes were to be washed in enlarged kitchen sinks. Finally, fences around each individual yard were eliminated, and plant materials in the public areas were greatly reduced.[56]

The dwellings in Liberty Square ranged from two- to five-room one- and two-story row houses. The plans are simple, elegant, and efficient, reflecting the result of research on spatial organizations from the best European and American examples. Living spaces were kept as large as possible, enabling the inhabitants to experience "frictionless living," a term coined by the Berlin architect and planner Alexander Klein and introduced to architects in the United States by Catherine Bauer (see fig. 81).[57]

Each apartment offered exposures through the dwelling from front to back, emphasizing good ventilation and a high quality of light in each room. Bedrooms and kitchens were kept as compact as possible. The bathrooms were standardized throughout the variously sized units. Liberty Square also exhibits the Housing Division rule that in multi-bedroom dwellings, one should never have to pass through the living room to get from a bedroom to the bathroom.[58] The disadvantage of this arrangement was the necessity of a tight, windowless pocket of space outside most bathrooms. Contemporary critiques, however, stressed the living room free from traffic. As Walter R. McCornack, chief architect of the Cedar-Central PWA project in Cleveland and a major proponent of this arrangement, pointed out, the

question arises as to who is to make . . . use of the living-room. It is quite obvious that children of school-age should not be the ones as their sleeping time is longer than that of adults and they should retire earlier. It seems equally inadvisable for the parents, who carry all the responsibility for the family income, not to have a sleeping-room where one may retire before the other, or where rest and quiet may be possible in case of sickness. The living-room might be used as a sleeping-room when the apartment is occupied by several adults not of one family, but it would seem reasonable to protest against constructing low-cost housing by government subsidy for such a group. It is also argued that a lodger might use the living-room. Since the lodger is one of the most

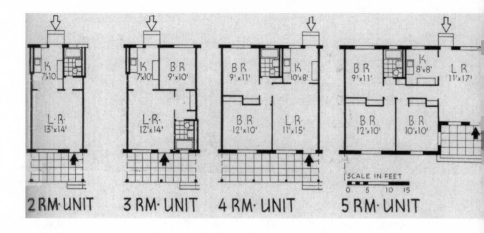

K 7'x10 | L·R· 13'x14' — **2 RM·UNIT**

K 7'x10 | B R 9'x10' | L·R· 12'x14' — **3 RM· UNIT**

B R 9'x11' | K 10'x8' | B R 12'x10' | L·R· 11'x15' — **4 RM· UNIT**

B R 9'x11' | K 8'x8' | L R 11'x17' | B R 12'x10' | B R 10'x10' — **5 RM· UNIT**

SCALE IN FEET
0   5   10   15

unsocial elements in family life, this also should be prohibited. As a matter of fact, a living-room should never be used for sleeping purposes except in an emergency, and rather than permit it, an alternative plan of small, well-aired sleeping compartments is much preferred, as ample ventilation and a comfortable bed are the chief requirements for rest.[59]

The Miami architects led by Phineas Paist and Harold Steward altered the Housing Division row house plans only in minor ways. Most notably, they added a small closet between the living room and the bath in the two-room plan and placed a door to the backyard through the kitchen in the four-room plan. Otherwise, Liberty Square followed the federal model in almost every detail. Units were outfitted with the most basic of appliances including a kerosene stove, an icebox, a kitchen sink/laundry sink, a bath with toilet, sink, and tub, and only cold running water. The dwellings were highly efficient, and despite the loss of the pool and other amenities, they were among the finest examples of low-cost housing completed anywhere in the country.

The image or look of the housing and the rental rates were also critical to the success of the project. Architects in the Housing Division left decisions of style largely to the local design teams, and prided themselves on the diversity of appearances that this policy produced among the various PWA

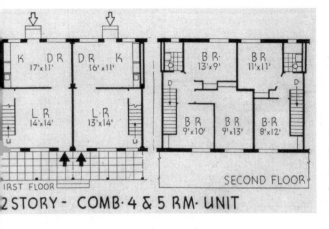

K DR   DR K
17'x11'   16'x11'

L R   L·R
14'x14'   13'x14'

FIRST FLOOR

2STORY - COMB·4 & 5 RM· UNIT

B R·   B R
13'x9'   11'x11'

B R   B R   B·R
9'x10'   9'x13'   8'x12'

SECOND FLOOR

FIGURE 81. Paist and Steward's floor plans for Liberty Square apartment types. *Architectural Forum* (May 1937).

housing projects. Liberty Square and Durkeville in Jacksonville were considered to have "tropical" designs.[60] Phineas Paist had a reputation for creating successful images for architecture. He brought to Liberty Square years of working with private houses in George Merrick's city of Coral Gables. Working with Denman Fink, Walter DeGarmo, and others, Paist designed a Spanish-Mediterranean image of tropical living that made Coral Gables enormously successful during the boom years. For Liberty Square, he and Steward designed one- and two-story row houses with white stucco walls, white asbestos tile roofs, front porches, and casement windows with hinged screens and wooden shutters. The image consisted of a sleek whiteness that had much in common with middle-class housing at the time.[61]

Promotional brochures emphasized continuities between traditional housing for southern white Americans and the low-cost housing project.[62] The cover featured the main element of the project. This was a courtyard created by two-story buildings with deep porches terminating in a stately two-story colonnade topped by a pediment with a small circular opening. The image is striking when one considers the stated preference of members of the black community for single-story dwellings, which are not depicted. Moreover, the two-story colonnade, centered with a Georgian-style symmetry, is clearly reminiscent of some of the most prominent plantation houses of the South.

FIGURE 82. View from the street of one- and two-story apartments in Liberty Square. Photo by Theodore Wood Jr. *Architectural Forum* (May 1937).

FIGURE 83. Central courtyard of Liberty Square. *Architectural Forum* (May 1937).

The brochure described the project as a work in progress for which "co-operative effort should result in a completely new and model community" that was part of the "PWA's slum clearance and low-rent housing program," located "outside of but adjoining the city limits adjacent to Liberty City." It was intended only for "self-sustaining families of limited income," with rental rates ranging from $2.85 to $5.25 per week depending on the size of the apartment. The authors noted that there are four churches and a school under construction nearby. Special emphasis was placed on amenities provided for working residents with children. These included a "day nursery" for young children and an indoor recreational facility for older children. Noting that "only one-fourth of the area is covered by buildings," the authors emphasized the presence of "lawns, play yards and walks" and "front and back yards" for each living unit. Although the project started with only cold water and iceboxes, the brochure deceptively stated that all dwellings have "modern plumbing for both hot and cold water . . . built-in refrigerators," and stoves that could be utilized for heating "in the event of any sudden chilly weather." The project, with its modern appointments and promise, was not only an immediate success among black tenants, with nearly 100 percent occupancy by December 1937, but it was one of the most popular tourist destinations in Dade County for visitors from across the nation during the winter season of 1936/37.[63]

Several scholars have noted that New Deal housing expanded upon existing patterns of urban segregation in cities across the United States, and Liberty Square was no exception.[64] A "Negro Resettlement Plan," proposed and approved by the Dade County Planning Board led by George Merrick, developer of Coral Gables, attempted to block any future expansion of existing black neighborhoods within the city in an effort to promote "logical white development."[65] The plan called for housing 300,000 black residents of Dade County in three settlements spread over 3,000–5,000 acres each. One "model new negro community" was to be "gradually developed" west of what is currently Route 826 along SW 8th Street near what is now Florida International University. Two others were proposed on enormous tracts of land west of Perrine and northwest of Opa Loca. Each would be completely encircled by buffer zones of "green belt park area[s]," that would insulate the white community from black residents while providing "many pools; bathing, fishing and other recreational features." The county proposed individual subsistence farms on lots "no less than 100 feet by 100 feet," with deplorably cheap house construction at as little as $500 per house—far less than the $4,100 per unit spent on Liberty Square. The plan would "tie them [black residents] to the soil in a more happy manner than they have ever been used to in Florida and will gradually build them into more loyal, capable and self-respecting citizens."[66]

The most likely model for this "tropical community" for black residents in Dade County was Grants Town, on the outskirts of Nassau on New Providence. Members of Merrick's Dade County Planning Council held romanticized notions of homes in "Bahamian Negro towns" as having "sound proportions" and "attractive tropical appearance."[67] Late nineteenth-century guidebooks to the Bahamas reinforced the desirability of Grants Town by describing it as "thoroughly tropical in every respect, the people live out of doors, cook their little breakfast over a few embers in the front year, and everywhere may be seen women washing their clothes under the shade of orange or almond trees."[68]

The Dade county resettlement plan was also considered to have potentially large financial benefits for real estate investors. Merrick states this most forcefully in 1937 to an audience of real estate developers:

Personally I have handled several negro towns and know there is money in it! . . . I would not want any better monopoly than for me to be given the job of working this out in just one State of the Southeast. Let the Government give me a unit-loan facility on sound long-time basis and I can show any real estate Board the millions that are available in this! And in doing this kind of a job we can not only make Woolworth-Ford-type volume money, but will make of this kind of population housing, a blessing to our Southeast instead of the curse that its present housing is.[69]

Although Merrick was eager to "remove every Negro family from the city limits," which was one of the immediate achievements of Liberty Square, the project was not to his tastes.[70] He was critical of the "standardized northern thought controlling architects and planners" on the project and considered the architecture of Liberty Square as being "barracks style, as would befit New England or Novia [sic] Scotia," but not subtropical Miami.[71] Merrick promoted the use of native materials in construction and the propagation of native vegetation, both of which were used in abundance on most New Deal projects in the region, but not on housing, which was one of the most "modern" projects to be developed in the region. In 1937, Merrick argued against proposals to expand Liberty Square and attempted to zone the area to the east of the community center on NW 14th Avenue for whites only to curtail the expansion of the black population beyond the initial edge of the project.[72]

While Merrick was raising local and regional criticisms against the project, the national architectural press was lavishing it with fairly significant praise. Liberty Square was featured in articles in the *Architectural Record* and the *Architectural Forum*, two of the most influential architecture journals in the country. The articles prominently listed the names of the architects, provided lists of building details, and the *Forum* professed that in "many respects these houses are most attractive, and they present an incomparable better appearance than the average real estate subdivision."[73] In the *Forum* Liberty Square was presented with Paterson Courts, a black housing project in Montgomery, Alabama, designed by Moreland Griffith Smith. The two projects reveal how building materials impact fairly standardized plans and lead to vastly differing living environments.

One of the best views of early life inside Liberty Square comes from its first black building manager, James E. Scott. For years, Scott was the assistant to the manager, since the white advisory board refused to promote a black man to manage the property. An editor of *Tropical Dispatch* and a graduate of the Housing Division's manager training program, Scott wrote that the project's first tenants "were taught" that "better homes and environment should make healthier, thriftier and happier people." He described Liberty Square in collective terms focused on a "central Community Building with a large social and recreational hall, nursery school, with kitchen and doctor's office and other facilities is the main feature of the project. A Consumers' Cooperative Store, a federal Credit Union, study classes of many kinds are being conducted for the tenants.

The brand of community spirit which would have been impossible and unknown under the old conditions gives tenants additional values they never have enjoyed before."[74]

Relatively little public housing was completed in Miami between 1937 and 1949. Most notable of these were three projects with a total of 1,515 units, two for whites and another for black residents adjoining Liberty Square.[75] By 1951 and the beginning of the cold war, strong resentment arose in Miami and elsewhere against public housing. It was accused of being the product of "socialism" or "communism" and for offering "a free ride for a selected few people."[76] To counter this, private apartment buildings for black residence arose near Liberty Square, as the neighborhood expanded to the east and south. These profitable multi-family and multi-story dwellings, set on individual lots, ignored the New Deal initiatives to design entire communities with public amenities, rather than individual buildings.

When Liberty Square and other New Deal housing projects across the country were handed over to local governmental agencies after completion,

FIGURE 84. Central courtyard of Paterson Courts, Montgomery, Alabama. *Architectural Forum* (May 1937).

FIGURE 85. James E. Scott, ca. 1940.
Courtesy of the HMSF.

they were frequently undermined by a lack of continued financial support
and a constant political opposition that had been present from the start.
Historians Mowry and Brownell claimed that Roosevelt's New Deal "failed
to develop an effective and comprehensive urban policy" and was "short-
sighted" and lacked coordination with other efforts.[77] While this was certainly the case to some degree in south Florida, it was also clear that many
white Miami residents protested even the limited housing proposed by the
federal government. When viewed from this perspective, it seems to be a
huge accomplishment that Liberty Square was ever constructed at all.

Liberty Square reveals that the problems architects were attempting to
solve through changes in the built environment were much larger than
housing. When combined with an inadequate commitment from regional
officials, federal housing could be accused of simply creating new zones
of substandard housing from which it was even more difficult for its residents to escape. These fears were expressed even as the first public housing
projects were being constructed across the nation. In 1935, early civil rights
leader John Preston Davis expressed his opinion that with New Deal federal

housing initiatives, "the new administration seeks in its program of social planning to perpetuate ghettoes of Negroes for fifty years to come."[78] Other critics, like John G. Van Deusen, in a chapter entitled "The Forgotten Man of the New Deal," claimed Roosevelt's housing efforts to be "just 'another' New Deal measure which, like the others, goes 'round and around' and comes out nowhere."[79]

Perhaps most important, however, was the fact that by being designed as complete communities, Liberty Square and other housing projects across the country built for black residents could not successfully challenge racial segregation in the city. In south Florida, it institutionalized segregation within larger boundaries and opened up larger areas in which black residents might reside. In hindsight, it raised the question as to whether European models for collective housing were viable for working black Americans. In Europe, collective projects had been designed to create homogeneous communities for working and middle-class families in need of housing after World War I. For black working-class American populations, however, who were already stigmatized and marginalized by a culture of racism, the separation provided by Liberty Square and similar housing projects across the country offered little hope for a future of racial equality.

The resentment caused by this continued culture of separation is fully evident in the short piece written in 1943 by Mercedes H. Byron, a twelfth grade student at Booker T. Washington High School in Miami. Published in the *Crisis*, the piece offers a view of the city divided clearly along lines of race. Far from the conciliatory tone assumed by Toomey at the beginning of the century, or the hope expressed by Scott, Byron articulated with forceful confidence the unacceptable dichotomy of her existence in Miami. She wrote:

> I am a Miamian—young, free, intelligent, personable—but BLACK. And so for me there are two of them—("Amis," I mean)—*Mi*-ami and *Their*-ami. *Their*-ami is the 'ami' that I and hundreds, yes, thousands of other boys and girls whose faces, too, are black may see in news reels and colorful advertisements, or as maids, chauffeurs or other servants of men and women who represent any race except Negro Americans—Germans, Japs, Jews, Chinese,

Dutchmen, Cubans, Indians, Spaniards—but definitely no American Negro. *Their*-ami is the 'ami' that the vacationist dreams about—miles and miles of beautiful Atlantic Beach with a background of towering coconut and royal palms, majestic hotels and apartments, attractively furnished and finished. For *Their*-Amians there is beautiful Biscayne Bay, ideal for yachting, fishing sailing, beautiful moonlight rides. It is the 'ami' of wide thoroughfares and avenues, of the renown Orange Bowl Stadium. Yes, *Their*-ami is the 'ami' I can only imagine and dream of.[80]

Byron presented a new black voice in Miami, one that would call for the end of segregation in the city and a reconfiguration of south Florida's racial geography during the twentieth century.

Notes

1. For the beginning of construction on Liberty Square, see Federal Emergency Administration, *Urban Housing: The Story of the PWA Housing Division, 1933–1936* (Washington, D.C., 1936), 42.

2. Twelve dwellings per acre were considered ideal by most New Deal architects. See Walter R. McCornack, "Elements in Housing Design," *Housing Officials' Yearbook 1936* (Chicago: National Association of Housing Officials, 1936), 135. For the price of the land, see Michael W. Straus and Talbott Wegg, *Housing Comes of Age* (New York: Oxford University Press, 1938), 96. For the site coverage, see James E. Scott, "Miami's Liberty Square," *Crisis: A Record of the Dark Races* 49 (Mar. 1942): 87.

3. Straus and Wegg, *Housing Comes of Age*, 102.

4. Scott, "Liberty Square," 87. Brief accounts of Liberty Square may be found in Federal Writers' Project, *Florida: A Guide to the Southernmost State* (New York: Oxford University Press, 1939). For Scott's personal history, see Marvin Dunn, *Black Miami in the Twentieth Century* (Gainesville: University Press of Florida, 1997), 167–68.

5. Robert C. Weaver, *The Negro Ghetto* (New York: Harcourt, Brace, 1948), 154.

6. Paul S. George, "Liberty Square, 1933–1987: The Origins and Evolution of a Public Housing Project," *Tequesta: Journal of the Historical Association of Southern Florida* 48 (1988): 53–68.

7. Raymond Mohl, "Trouble in Paradise: Race and Housing in Miami during the New Deal Era," *Prologue: Journal of the National Archives* 19 (Spring 1987): 7–21.

8. Straus and Wegg, *Housing Comes of Age*, 36–37.

9. I have found no other record of these three projects. Since they were rejected, their applications were not kept by the Housing Division. See Arthur B. Gallion to Robert B. Mitchell, June 27, 1934, National Archives and Records Administration (NARA), RG 196, box 297, Records of the Public Housing Administration.

10. "Application of the Southern Housing Corporation, Miami, Florida, to the Administration of Public Works, Division of Housing, Washington, D.C., for Financing Low Cost Housing Project at Miami, Florida," Dec. 19, 1933, NARA, RG 196, box 301, 8.

11. Gallion to Mitchell, June 27, 1934, NARA, RG 196, box 297.

12. See William F. Brunner, "The Negro Health Problem in Southern Cities," *American Journal of Public Health* 5 (Mar. 1915): 190; and James H. Jones, *Bad Blood: The Tuskegee Syphilis Experiment* (New York: Free Press, 1981).

13. Gramling to Horatio B. Hackett, Sept. 29, 1934, NARA, RG 196, box 297.

14. Raymond Mohl, "Trouble in Paradise," 9–10. For more on Gramling's segregationist attitudes, see Paul S. George, "'Colored Town': Miami's Black Community, 1896–1930," *Florida Historical Quarterly* 56 (Apr. 1978): 444.

15. R. E. S. Toomey, "Statement on Congested Conditions of Colored Section of Miami, Dade County, Florida," Dec. 12, 1933, NARA, RG 196, box 301.

16. The signatories of this letter included all from the first letter plus Willie Slater, A. E. Flowers, H. H. Green, and Luseiana Evans. See Toomey to Robert D. Kohn, Jan. 15, 1934, NARA, RG 196, box 301.

17. Toomey, "Statement."

18. Straus and Wegg, *Housing Comes of Age*, 166.

19. Toomey to Hackett, May 1, 1935, NARA, RG 196, box 298.

20. J. Harvey Smith to Angelo R. Clas, May 17, 1935, NARA, RG 196, box 298.

21. Isabelle Sanderson to Clas, May 17, 1935, NARA, RG 196, box 298.

22. Dade County Commission Resolution of July 9, 1935, NARA, RG 196, box 298.

23. Sanderson to Clas, May 17, 1935, NARA, RG 196, box 298.

24. M. J. Orr to Clas, July 10, 1935, NARA, RG 196, box 298.

25. Clas to Adele Cobb Kerrigan, June 27, 1935, NARA, RG 196, box 298.

26. Straus and Wegg, *Housing Comes of Age*, 106, NARA, RG 196.

27. Floyd Davis to J. O. Preston, Nov. 29, 1937, Historical Museum of Southern Florida, George Merrick Archives, box 1.

28. Talbot Wegg to M. Drew Carrel, Sept. 12, 1934, NARA, RG 196, box 297. See Gramling to Hackett, Sept. 17, 1934, PHA, RG 196, NARA, box 298. Although the white advisory board was created immediately, a black advisory board was first created two years later.

29. Gramling to Hackett, Sept. 17, 1934, NARA, RG 196, box 298.

30. Clas to Toomey, Oct. 25, 1935, NARA, RG 196, box 298.

31. Toomey to Clas, Nov. 20, 1935, NARA, RG 196, box 298.

32. A handwritten note by a government official stated, "When acknowledging this fact [the native], please specify his recommendations as being given consideration." Toomey to Clas, Nov. 20, 1935, NARA, RG 196, box 298.

33. Anonymous to Director of Housing Administration, Nov. 3, 1935, NARA, RG 196, box 297.

34. J. Harvey Smith, M . B. Williams, and H. G. Dargan to Clas, Nov. 9, 1935, NARA, RG 196, box 298.

35. Clarence S. Coe to Clas, June 11, 1936, NARA, RG 196, box 299.

36. See J. Harvey Smith and M. S. Williams to Coe Oct. 5, 1936, NARA, RG 196, box 297. For the response from Washington, see H. A. Gray to Coe, Oct. 9, 1936, NARA, RG 196, box 297.

37. "Minutes of the Advisory Committee Meeting," May 14, 1936, NARA, RG 196, box 298.

38. Information below taken from Arthur Gallion's unpublished memoirs, provided to me by his daughter-in-law, Judith Gallion.

39. Straus and Wegg, *Housing Comes of Age*, 53.

40. Gallion to Mitchell, Dec. 5, 1934, NARA, RG 196, box 289. For Talbot Wegg's support of Virrick, see Mitchell to Hackett, Dec. 10, 1934, NARA, RG 196, box 301.

41. Gramling had suggested DeGarmo, Pfeiffer, and Geiger as those with the firms in Miami most familiar with "low cost housing." See Gramling's responses in the "Public Works Emergency Housing Corporation, Washington, D.C., Preliminary Questionnaire—Housing Project," July 5, 1934, p. 3, NARA, RG 196, box 297.

42. Gallion to Mitchell, Dec. 5, 1934, NARA, RG 196, box 298. For DeGarmo, see Margot Ammidown, "Walter DeGarmo: Fantasies in Concrete," *Update* 11 (1984): 3–6.

43. Mitchell to Hackett (handwritten draft), Feb. 14, 1935, NARA, RG 196, box 301.

44. The Public Housing Administration, "The Dream and the Substance: A Short History of Public Housing for Negroes" (unpublished manuscript, c.1954), 17, NARA, RG 196, box "Short History of Public Housing."

45. Hackett to Paist, Feb. 14, 1935, NARA, RG 196, box 301.

46. United States, Public Works Administration Housing Division, *Unit Plans: Typical Room Arrangements Site Plans and Details for Low Rent Housing* (Washington, D.C.: Government Printing Office, 1935). A brief account of the production of this book is told in Straus and Wegg, *Housing Comes of Age*, 67–68.

47. Mitchell to Hackett, Feb. 14, 1935, NARA, RG 196, box 301.

48. The pool had been a feature that drew tenants to the 1935 limited dividend Carl Mackley Houses in Philadelphia. See Gail Radford, *Modern Housing for America: Policy Struggles in the New Deal Era* (Chicago: University of Chicago Press, 1996), 130–35. See also Jeff Wiltse, *Contested Waters: A Social History of Swimming Pools in America.* (Chapel Hill: University of North Carolina Press, 2007), 121–54.

49. Clas to S. Hildegarde Young, Aug. 21, 1935, NARA, RG 196, box 299.

50. See the Florida State Planning Board, *Florida Park, Parkway and Recreational-Area Study Prepared in Cooperation with Florida Board of Forestry and the National Park Service. Official WPA Project 665–35–3–6* (Tallahassee, 1940), 39. The new Dixie Pool opened in Liberty Square in early 1937. See cutting from Stanley Sweeting's column in the *Tropical Dispatch* (1937) in the clipping files, Florida Room, Miami-Dade Public Library microfilm collection. The first public beach for black bathers in south Florida did not open until August 1945 at Virginia Key. See Dunn, *Black Miami*, 160.

51. Clas to Coe, Jan. 10, 1936, NARA, RG 196, box 303.

52. "Chief of Branch II Plans and Specifications" to "Chief of Branch V Management," Oct. 4, 1935, NARA, RG 196, box 303.

53. Steward to Clas, Oct. 4, 1935, NARA, RG 196, box 303.

54. Steward to Clas, Jan. 15, 1936, NARA, RG 196, box 303.

55. "Agreement between the City of Miami and the United States of America," Dec. 23, 1936, NARA, RG 196, box 297; James E. Scott to Gray, July 13, 1937, NARA, RG 196, box 303.

56. "Minutes of the Advisory Board," Apr. 2, 1936, NARA, RG 196, box 299; Gray to Coe, Oct. 24, 1936, NARA, RG 196, box 299.

57. Catherine Bauer, *Modern Housing* (Boston: Houghton Mifflin, 1934), 203.

58. Housing Division, *Unit Plans*, HD-41, HD-60, 3.

59. McCornack, "Elements in Housing Design," 137–38.

60. Straus and Wegg, *Housing Comes of Age*, 68.

61. See Paist and Steward's A. T. Mossman house (1935) in *American Architect* 140 (May 1935): 42–43.

62. The only known reproduction of this brochure exists on microfilm in the "Miami Housing-Negro" clipping files found in the Florida Room, Miami-Dade Public Library.

63. Scott to Nathan Straus, Dec. 19, 1937, NARA, RG 196, box 303.

64. See, e.g., Robert E. Forman, *Black Ghettos, White Ghettos, and Slums* (Englewood Cliffs, N.J.: Prentice-Hall, 1971), 151.

65. The National Urban League Department of Research, *A Review of Economic and Cultural Problems in Dade County, Florida, as They Relate to Conditions in the Negro Population: A Study Conducted for the Council of Social Agencies of Dade County Florida* (New York, 1943), 26, 29. See also Mohl, "Trouble in Paradise," 13.

66. *Review of Economic and Cultural Problems*, 27.

67. Ibid., 28.

68. James H. Stark, *Stark's History and Guide to the Bahama Islands* (Boston: Photo-Electrotype Company, 1891), 122.

69. George Merrick, "Real Estate Development Past and Future," transcript of address to the Southeastern Convention of Realty Boards, Nov. 29, 1937, NARA, RG 196, box 298.

70. George Merrick, "Planning the Greater Miami for Tomorrow," transcript of address to the Miami Realty Board, May 27, 1937, NARA, RG 196, box 298.

71. George Merrick, "Developing Realty Value from Native Resources," transcript of address to the State Convention of Realty Boards, Nov. 27, 1937, NARA RG 196, box 298.

72. Merrick to J. O. Preston, Dec. 2, 1937, Historical Museum of Southern Florida, George Merrick papers, box 1.

73. "Liberty Square," *Architectural Record* 82 (May 1937): 20–21; "Liberty Square," *Architectural Forum* 66 (May 1937): 422–23.

74. Scott, "Liberty Square," 87. See also Coe to Members of the Liberty Square Advisory Committee, Jan. 16, 1936, NARA, RG 196, box 299.

75. Mohl, "Trouble in Paradise," 14.

76. Department of Housing Relations, *Negro Housing in Greater Miami and Dade County: A Pictorial Presentation* (Miami, 1951), Florida Collection, Rare Books Section, Richter Library, University of Miami.

77. George E. Mowry and Blaine A. Brownell, *The Urban Nation, 1920–1980* (New York: Hill and Wang, 1981), 107–8.

78. John P. Davis, "A Black Inventory of the New Deal," *Crisis* 42 (May 1935): 142.

79. John G. Van Deusen, *The Black Man in White America* (Washington, D.C.: Associated, 1938), 122.

80. Mercedes H. Byron, "Negro Youth Looks at Miami," *Crisis* 49 (Mar. 1942): 84.

Bibliography

Adam, Lisa Kay. "Terrebonne Farms, Louisiana: An Anthropogeographic Study of a New Deal Resettlement." PhD diss., Louisiana State University Agricultural and Mechanical College, 2000.

Allman, T. D. *Miami: City of the Future. New York: Atlantic Monthly Press,* 1987.

Arsenault, Raymond. "The End of the Long Hot Summer: The Air Conditioner and Southern Culture." In *Searching for the Sunbelt*, edited by Raymond Mohl. Knoxville: University of Tennessee Press, 1990.

Ballinger, Kenneth J. *Miami Millions: The Dance of the Dollars in the Great Florida Land Boom of 1925*. Miami: The Franklin Press, 1936.

Barnes, A. D. *History of the Dade County Park System: The First Forty Years, 1929–1969*. Miami: Metro-Dade County Parks and Recreation Department, 1986.

Beckham, Sue Bridwell. *Depression Post Office Murals and Southern Culture: A Gentle Reconstruction*. Baton Rouge: Louisiana State University Press, 1989.

Berkowitz, Michael. "A 'New Deal' for Leisure: Making Mass Tourism during the Great Depression." In *Being Elsewhere: Tourism, Consumer Culture, and Identity in Modern Europe and North America*, edited by Shelley Baranowski and Ellen Furlough. Ann Arbor: University of Michigan Press, 2001.

Berman, Marshall. *All That Is Solid Melts into Air: The Experience of Modernity*. New York: Simon and Schuster, 1982.

Biles, Roger. *The South and the New Deal*. Lexington: University Press of Kentucky, 1994.

Bold, Christine. *The WPA Guides: Mapping America*. Jackson: University Press of Mississippi, 1999.

Breyer, Stephen G. *Administrative Law and Regulatory Policy: Problems, Text, and Cases*. 6th ed. New York: Aspen Publishers, 2006.

Bush, Gregory W. "Playground of the USA: Miami and the Promotion of Spectacle." *Pacific Historical Review* 68 (May 1999): 153–72.

Bush, Gregory W., and Arva Moore Parks. *Miami, the American Crossroad: A Centennial Journey, 1896–1996. New York: Simon and Schuster, 1996.*

Bustard, Bruce I. *New Deal for the Arts*. Washington, D.C.: National Archives and Records Administration in Association with the University of Washington Press, 1997.

Capitman, Barbara. *Deco Delights: Preserving the Beauty and Joy of Miami Beach Architecture*. New York: E. P. Dutton, 1988.

Carlebach, Michael, and Eugene F. Provenzo. *Farm Security Administration Photographs of Florida*. Gainesville: University Press of Florida, 1993.

Cartier-Bresson, Henri. *The Decisive Moment*. New York: Simon and Schuster, 1952.

Ceo, Rocco J., and Joanna Lombard. *Historic Landscapes of Florida*. Miami: Deering Foundation and the University of Miami School of Architecture, 2001.

Colburn, David R., and Lance deHaven-Smith. *Government in the Sunshine State: Florida since Statehood*. Gainesville: University Press of Florida, 1999.

——. *Florida's Megatrends: Critical Issues in Florida*. Gainesville: University Press of Florida, 2002.

Cole, Jeffrey Scott. "The Impact of the Great Depression and New Deal on the Urban South: Lynchburg, Virginia as a Case Study, 1929–1941." PhD diss., Bowling Green State University, 1998.

Conkin, Paul K. *FDR and the Origins of the Welfare State*. New York: Thomas Y. Crowell, 1967.

Contreras, Belisario. *Tradition and Innovation in New Deal Art*. Lewisburg: Bucknell University Press and London: Associated University Presses, 1983.

Croucher, Sheila L. *Imagining Miami: Ethnic Politics in a Postmodern World*. Charlottesville: University Press of Virginia, 1997.

Curtis, James. *Mind's Eye, Mind's Truth: FSA Photography Reconsidered*. Philadelphia: Temple University Press, 1989.

Danese, Tracy E. *Claude Pepper and Ed Ball: Politics, Purpose, and Power*. Gainesville: University Press of Florida, 2000.

Daniel, Pete. "New Deal, Southern Agriculture, and Economic Change." In *The New Deal and the South*, edited by Frank Burt Freidel, James C. Cobb, and Michael V. Namorato . Jackson: University Press of Mississippi, 1984.

Doner, Michele Oka, and Mitchell Wolfson, Jr. *Miami Beach: Blueprint of an Eden: Lives Seen Through the Prism of Family and Place*. New York: Regan, 2007.

Dos Passos, John. *U.S.A..* New York: Modern Library, 1937.

Doss, Erika. "Looking at Labor: Images of Work in 1930s American Art." *Journal of Decorative and Propaganda Arts* 24 (2002): 230–57.

Downs, Dorothy. *Art of the Florida Seminole and Miccosukee Indians*. Gainesville: University Press of Florida, 1995.

Dunlop, Beth. "Inventing Antiquity: The Art and Craft of Mediterranean Revival Architecture." *Journal of Decorative and Propaganda Arts* 23 (1998): 190–207.

Dunn, Marvin. *Black Miami in the Twentieth Century*. Gainesville: University Press of Florida, 1997.

Durward, Long. "Key West and the New Deal, 1934–1936." *Florida Historical Quarterly* 46 (Jan. 1968): 209–18.

Federal Writers' Project of the Work Projects Administration for the State of Florida. *Florida: A Guide to the Southern-most State*. New York: Oxford University Press, 1939.

Fields, Dorothy Jenkins. "Tracing Overtown's Vernacular Architecture." *Journal of Decorative and Propaganda Arts* 23 (1998): 323–33.

Fleischhauer, Carl, Beverly W. Brannan, Lawrence W. Levine, and Alan Trachtenberg, eds. *Documenting America, 1935–1943*. Berkeley: University of California Press in association with the Library of Congress, 1988.

Forman, Richard T.T., and Michel Godron. *Landscape Ecology*. New York: Wiley, 1986.

Forman, Robert E. *Black Ghettos, White Ghettos, and Slums*. Englewood Cliffs, N.J.: Prentice-Hall, 1971.

Gannon, Michael, ed. *The New History of Florida*. Gainesville: University Press of Florida, 1996.

George, Paul S. "Colored Town: Miami's Black Community, 1896–1930." *Florida Historical Quarterly* 56 (Apr. 1978): 432–47.

George, Paul S., and Thomas K. Peterson. "Liberty Square, 1933–1987: The Origin and Evolution of a Public Housing Project." *Tequesta: Journal of the Historical Association of Southern Florida*. 48 (1988): 53–68.

Gerdes, Louise I., ed. *The 1930s*. San Diego: Greenhaven Press, 2000.

Ghirardo, Diane. *Building New Communities: New Deal America and Fascist Italy*. Princeton: Princeton University Press, 1989.

Green, Elna. *The New Deal and Beyond: Social Welfare in the South since 1930.* Athens: University of Georgia Press, 2003.

Greer, Thomas H. *What Roosevelt Thought: The Social and Political Ideas of Franklin D. Roosevelt.* East Lansing: Michigan State University Press, 1958.

Grenier, Guillermo J., and Alex Stepick, eds. *Miami Now! Immigration, Ethnicity, and Social Change.* Gainesville: University Press of Florida, 1992.

Haaften, Julia Van. *Berenice Abbott, Photographer: A Modern Vision: A Selection of Photographs and Essays.* New York: New York Public Library, 1989.

Hayes, Jack Irby, Jr. *South Carolina and the New Deal.* Columbia: University of South Carolina Press, 2001.

Hendrickson, Paul. *Looking for the Light: The Hidden Life and Art of Marion Post Wolcott.* New York: Knopf, 1992.

Hill, Edwin G. *In the Shadow of the Mountain: The Spirit of the CCC.* Pullman: Washington State University Press, 1990.

Himes, Joseph S., ed. *The South Moves into Its Future: Studies in the Analysis and Prediction of Social Change.* Tuscaloosa: University of Alabama Press, 1991.

Hirsch, Jerrold. *Portrait of America: A Cultural History of the Federal Writers' Project.* Chapel Hill: University of North Carolina Press, 2003.

Hoffman, Joel M. "From Augustine to Tangerine: Florida at the U.S. World's Fairs." *Journal of Decorative and Propaganda Arts* 23 (1998): 48–85.

How the Farm Security Administration Is Helping Needy Farm Families. Washington, D.C.: United States Farm Security Administration, 1940.

Hoyt, Roy. *We Can Take It: A Short Story of the C.C.C.* New York: American Book Co., 1935.

Hurston, Zora Neale. *Their Eyes Were Watching God.* Philadelphia: J. B. Lippincott Co., 1937.

Jackson, Faith Rehyer. *Pioneer of Tropical Landscape Architecture: William Lyman Phillips in Florida.* Gainesville: University Press of Florida, 1997.

Kersey, Harry A. *The Florida Seminoles and the New Deal, 1933–1942.* Boca Raton: Florida Atlantic University Press, 1989.

Kleinberg, Howard. *Miami: The Way We Were.* Surfside, Fla.: Surfside Publishing, 1985.

———. *Miami Beach: A History.* Miami: Centennial Press, 1994.

Laas, Virginia. "Reward for Party Service: Emily Newell Blair and Political Patronage in the New Deal." In *The Southern Elite and Social Change: Essays in Honor of Willard B. Gatewood Jr.*, edited by Randy Finley and Thomas A. Deblack. Fayetteville: University of Arkansas Press, 2002.

Lange, Dorothea, and Paul Taylor. *An American Exodus: A Record of Human Erosion*. New York: Reynal and Hitchcock, 1939.

Lavender, Abraham D. *Miami Beach in 1920: The Making of a Winter Resort*. Charleston: Arcadia Publishing, 2002.

LeJeune, Jean-François, Allan T. Shulman, and Sonia R. Chao. *The Making of Miami Beach, 1933–1942: The Architecture of Lawrence Murray Dixon*. New York: Rizzoli, 2000.

Leuchtenburg, William E. *Franklin D. Roosevelt and the New Deal*. New York: Harper and Row, 1963.

Lombard, Joanna. "The Memorable Landscapes of William Lyman Phillips." *Journal of Decorative and Propaganda Arts* 23 (1998): 261–87.

Lummus, John Newton. *The Miracle of Miami Beach*. Miami: Miami Post Publishing Co., 1940.

Marling, Karal Ann. *Wall-to-Wall America: The Cultural History of Post Office Murals in the Great Depression*. Minneapolis: University of Minnesota Press, 1982.

Mazzari, Louis. *Southern Modernist: Arthur Raper from the New Deal to the Cold War*. Baton Rouge: Louisiana State University Press, 2006.

McDonogh, Gary W., ed. *The Florida Negro: A Federal Writers' Project Legacy*. Jackson: University Press of Mississippi, 1993.

McEuen, Melissa. *Seeing America: Women Photographers between the Wars*. Lexington: University Press of Kentucky, 2000.

McIver, Stuart. *The Greatest Sale on Earth: The Story of the Miami Board of Realtors, 1920–1980*. Miami: E. A. Seemann, 1980.

McNally, Michael J. *Catholicism in South Florida, 1868–1968*. Gainesville: University Presses of Florida, 1982.

Mecklenberg, Virginia. *The Public as Patron: A History of the Treasury Department Mural Program: Illustrated with Paintings from the Collection of the University of Maryland Art Gallery*. College Park: University of Maryland Art Gallery, 1979.

Melosh, Barbara. *Engendering Culture: Manhood and Womanhood in New Deal Public Art and Theater*. Washington, D.C.: Smithsonian Institution Press, 1991.

Metropolitan Dade County Office of Community and Economic Development, Historic Preservation Division, *From Wilderness to Metropolis: The History and*

Architecture of Dade County, Florida, 1825–1940. Miami: Metropolitan Dade County, 1982.

Millas Aristides J., and Ellen J. Uguccioni. *Coral Gables, Miami Riviera: An Architectural Guide*. Miami: Dade Heritage Trust, 2003.

Miller, Randall M., and George E. Pozzetta, ed. *Shades of the Sunbelt: Essays on Ethnicity, Race, and the Urban South*. Westport, Conn.: Greenwood Press, 1988.

Mohl, Raymond A. "Black Immigrants: Bahamians in Early Twentieth-Century Miami." *Florida Historical Quarterly* 65 (Jan. 1987): 271–97.

———. "The Pattern of Race Relations in Miami since the 1920s." *The African American Heritage of Florida*, edited by David R. Colburn and Jane L. Landers. Gainesville: University Press of Florida, 1995.

———. "Trouble in Paradise: Race and Housing in Miami during the New Deal Era." *Prologue*. Journal of the National Archives. 19, no. 1 (Spring 1987): 7–21.

———. "Whitening Miami: Race, Housing, and Government Policy in Twentieth-Century Dade County." *Florida Historical Quarterly* 79 (Winter 2001): 319–45.

Moore, Deborah Dash. *To the Golden Cities: Pursuing the American Jewish Dream in Miami and L.A.* New York: Free Press, 1994.

Mormino, Gary R. *Land of Sunshine, State of Dreams: A Social History of Modern Florida*. Gainesville: University Press of Florida, 2005.

Mowry, George E., and Blaine A. Brownell. *The Urban Nation, 1920–1980*. New York: Hill and Wang, 1965.

Natanson, Nicholas. *The Black Image in the New Deal: The Politics of FSA Photography*. Knoxville: University of Tennessee Press, 1992.

Neumann, Dietrich, and Kermit Swiler Champa, eds. *Architecture of the Night:The Illuminated Building*. Munich and New York: Prestel, 2002.

Page, Max. *The Creative Destruction of Manhattan, 1900–1940*. Chicago: University of Chicago Press, 1999.

Park, Marlene, and Gerald E. Markowitz. *Democratic Vistas: Post Offices and Public Art in the New Deal*. Philadelphia: Temple University Press, 1984.

Parks, Arva Moore. *Miami, The Magic City*. Tulsa: Continental Heritage Press, 1981.

Porter, Bruce, and Marvin Dunn. *The Miami Riot of 1980: Crossing the Bounds*. Lexington: Mass.: Lexington Books, 1984.

Portes, Alejandro, and Alex Stepick III. *City on the Edge: The Transformation of Miami*. Berkeley: University of California Press, 1993.

Redford, Polly. *Billion-Dollar Sandbar: A Biography of Miami Beach*. New York: Dutton, 1970.

Rowin, Fran. "New Deal Murals in Florida Post Offices." *Historical Association of Southern Florida Update* 4 (Feb. 1977): 6–10.

Salmond, John A. *The Civilian Conservation Corps, 1933–1942: A New Deal Case Study*. Durham, N.C.: Duke University Press, 1967.

Schlesinger, Arthur M., Jr. *The Coming of the New Deal*. Boston: Houghton Mifflin, 1958.

Schulman, Bruce J. *From Cotton Belt to Sunbelt: Federal Policy, Economic Development, and the Transformation of the South, 1938–1980*. New York: Oxford University Press, 1991.

Schwarz, Jordan A. *The Interregnum of Despair: Hoover, Congress, and the Depression*. Urbana: University of Illinois Press, 1970.

———. *The New Dealers: Power Politics in the Age of Roosevelt*. New York: Alfred A. Knopf, 1993.

Scott, James E. "Miami's Liberty Square." *The Crisis: A Record of the Dark Races* 49 (Mar. 1942): 87–89.

Shulman, Allan. "Igor Polevitzky's Architectural Vision for a Modern Miami." *Journal of Decorative and Propaganda Arts* 23 (1998): 334–59.

Smith, Douglas L.. *The New Deal in the Urban South*. Baton Rouge: Louisiana State University Press, 1988.

Smith, Jason Scott. *Building New Deal Liberalism: The Political Economy of Public Works, 1933–56*. New York: Cambridge University Press, 2006.

Snyder, Robert. "Marion Post Wolcott and the FSA in Florida." *Florida Historical Quarterly* 65 (Apr. 1987): 458–79.

Spencer, Donald D. *Seminole Indians In Old Picture Postcards*. Ormond Beach, Fla.: Camelot Publishers, 2002.

Standiford, Les, and Henry Morrison Flagler. *Last Train to Paradise: Henry Flagler and the Spectacular Rise and Fall of the Railroad That Crossed an Ocean*. New York: Crown Publishers, 2002.

Stange, Maren. *Symbols of an Ideal Life: Social Documentary Photography in America, 1890–1940*. New York: Cambridge University Press, 1989.

Stein, Sally. "Chronology and Correspondence." In *Marion Post Wolcott, FSA Photographs*. Carmel, Calif.: Friends of Photography, 1983.

Sternsher, Bernard, ed. *Hope Restored: How the New Deal Worked in Town and Country*. Chicago: Ivan R. Dee, 1999.

Stott, William. *Documentary Expression and Thirties America*. New York: Oxford University Press, 1973.

Straus, Michael W., and Talbot Wegg. *Housing Comes of Age*. New York: Oxford University Press, 1938.

Stryker, Roy. "The FSA Collection of Photographs." In *In This Proud Land: America 1935–1943 as Seen in the FSA Photographs*, edited by Roy Stryker and Nancy Wood. Greenwich, Conn.: New York Graphic Society, 1973.

Tebeau, Charlton. *A History of Florida*. Coral Gables: University of Miami Press, 1971.

Valdes-Dapéna, Susan. "'Painting Section' in Black and White: Ethel Magafan's *Cotton Pickers*." *Journal of Decorative and Propaganda Arts* 24 (2002): 258–83.

Van Deusen, John G. *The Black Man in White America*. Washington, D.C.: Associated Publishers, 1938.

Von Briesen, Hans. *Why Not Know Florida? An Informal Guide for the Motorist*. Jacksonville: Drew Press, 1936.

Weaver, Robert C. *The Negro Ghetto*. New York: Harcourt, Brace, 1948.

Wiltse, Jeff. *Contested Waters: A Social History of Swimming Pools in America*. Chapel Hill: University of North Carolina Press, 2007.

Wisser, Bill. *South Beach: America's Riviera, Miami Beach, Florida*. New York: Arcade Publishers, 1995.

Wolff, Reinhold P. *Miami: Economic Patterns of a Resort Area*. Coral Gables: University of Miami, 1945.

Woolner, David B., and Henry L. Henderson. *FDR and the Environment*. New York: Palgrave Macmillan, 2005.

Wurster, Catherine Bauer. *Modern Housing*. Boston: Houghton Mifflin Company, 1934.

Yochelson, Bonnie. *Berenice Abbott: Changing New York*. New York: New Press and the Museum of the City of New York, 1997.

Zimny, Michael. "New Art, New Deal." *Florida Heritage* 6 (Winter 1998): 14–19.

Zuckerman, Bertram. *The Dream Lives On: A History of Fairchild Tropical Gardens, 1938–1966*. Miami: Fairchild Tropical Garden, 1988.

Contributors

Ted Baker is a landscape architect and a former associate professor in the School of Architecture at Florida International University.

Marianne Lamonaca is the associate director for curatorial affairs and education at The Wolfsonian–Florida International University.

John F. Stack Jr. is a professor of political science and law and director of the Jack D. Gordon Institute for Public Policy and Citizenship Studies at Florida International University.

John A. Stuart is an associate professor in the School of Architecture at Florida International University.

Mary N. Woods is a professor in the Department of Architecture at Cornell University.

Index

Civil Works Administration. *See* CWA

Class, 24, 111–12; and luxury hotels, 107–10; and millionaires, 99–110. *See also* Migrant worker; Tourism

Clergy, 6–20

Clubs, 55, 56. *See also* Tourism

Colburn, David R., 4, 26n2, 27n12

Cole, Jeffrey Scott, 26n1

Collier, John, 72

Colored. *See* African-American

Colored Chamber of Commerce, 194, 200

"Colored Town," 189–90, 192, 193

Community: and alcohol consumption, 13–14; black, 40, 190–92, 199–200; black migrant, 91; building, 14–16, 50–54; Catholic, 137–38; Jewish, 18, 103, 105, 118n61; life, migrant worker, 84; prosperity, New Deal and, 25–26; and redlining, 188–89; and regional identity, 23–24, 31–32; values, 135–37. *See also* Migrant worker

Conklin, Paul K., 28n28

Conservation, 15, 16; Emergency Conservation Act, 160, 161; and environmental cleanup, 175–76; and Overseas Highway, 58–61

Construction, 2, 32, 41; building communities, 13–16; in Fairchild Tropical Garden, 182; in FERA and PWA, 39–44; of Liberty Square, 186–87, 201; in Miami, 3–4; in Miami Beach, 40–41, 106; and New Deal legislation, 189; projects, 34–35, 55–56, 62–64; and regional identity, 43; in Royal Palm park, 168–69; of schools, 48–50; of sports centers, 43–46; and unemployment, 39; and WPA projects, 31–32. *See also* Building program

Contreras, Belisario, 153n5

Coral Gables, 33, 54–55, 128, 163, 209; Library and Community House, 51–52; Police and Fire Station, 62, 64; racetrack, 66n5

Crandon, Charles H., 163, 182–83

Cuba, 33–34, 36–37

Cumming, Pastor William C., 8–9, 15

Curtis, James, 114n4, 115nn11,12

CWA, 2, 36

Cypress Logging, 127

Dade County, 32, 84, 162–63, 194, 196; and black schools, 137; and black swimming pools, 204–5; and Greynolds Park, 171–77; Matheson Hammock, 177–81; park system, 162–65; Planning Board, 54–55; resettlement plan, 212. *See also* Liberty Square; Miami

Daniel, Pete, 115n16, 116n22

Danse, Tracy E., 27n8

Dargan, H. G., 199

Davis, Floyd W., 191

Davis, John Preston, 215–16

Deering, Charles, 32

Deering, James, 32

DeGarmo, Walter C., 190, 202, 209

deHaven-Smith, Lance, 4, 26n2, 27n12

Denney, Rev. Oscar, 7–8

Dimmick, Rev. Arthur, 8, 12–13, 15

Dinner Key, 34, 35, 41

Discrimination. *See* Racism

Dixon, L. Murray, 68n34, 106, 110

Dohanos, Stevan, 120, 127, 146–51

Doherty, Edward, 106

Dorsey, Dana A., 137, 200

Dos Passos, John, 110, 119n71

Doss, Erika, 155n37

Downs, Dorothy, 156n56

Drake, J. W., 192

Dunlop, Beth, 68n49, 115n15, 127, 154n16

budgets, 111; and Jewish community, 18, 118n61; millionaires, *100*, *102–3*; mural art, 138–43; New York Giants Stadium, 45; Pinecrest Apartments, 78; Post Office, 62, *63*, 120; and Post Wolcott, 76; Roney Plaza, 74; school, 50; tourism, 10, 99–110

Miami Fruit and Spice, 55

Michael, John R., 198

Migrant worker, 21, 73, *81*, 82–83, 85, 88, 89; attitude of, 92–94; black and white, 79; black migrant community, 91; camp, 82–83, 90; *The Grapes of Wrath*, 83; housing, 91–92, 93, 94; and New Deal conservatism, 94; as photography subject, 72, 79–99; and tourism, 90–91, *105*

Migration, 53

Miller, Randall M., 29n30

Millionaires, 99–110

Mizner, Addison, 127

Modern Housing, 203

Mohl, Raymond A., 29n44, 116n26, 117n40, 118n53, 155n43, 188, 189, 218nn7,14, 221n75

Montgomery, Robert, 181–82

Moore, Deborah Dash, 18, 29n43, 118n58, 119n74

Moore Haven, 76, 87

Morgenthau, Henry, Jr., 62

Mormino, Gary R., 4, 27nn11,19

Moses, Robert, 163

Mowry, George E., 215, 222n77

Mumford, Lewis, 201

Mural art, 22; and community, 123–27, 135–37; competition and selection, 129–32, 154nn20,22; cultural bias in, 139–40; current location of, 152n1; Stevan Dohanos, 120, 127, 146–51; Easel Group of artists, 53–54; *Episodes from the History of Florida*, 22–23, 120, *121*, 138–43, 152n1; Denman Fink, 127–38; Charles

Russell Hardman, 138–43; *Law Guides Florida Progress*, 125, 127–38; *Legend of James Edward Hamilton*, 146–51; racial stereotypes in, 53–54, 136–37; Charles Rosen, 120, 126, 143–46; selection process of, 130–33; *Seminole Indians and Two Landscapes*, 120, 143–46; Dewing Woodard, 53

Mydans, Carl, 72

Natanson, Nicholas, 92, 94, 117nn35,37–39,42, 119n78

National Endowment for the Arts, 122

National Industrial Recovery Act. *See* NIRA

Native American, 22–23, 140, 144–46. *See also* Racism; Seminole

Negro Ghetto, The, 188

Neumann, Dietrich, 118n64

New Deal, 2–3, 6–7, 13–14, 21, 25–26; and arts, 122–25; policies of, 5, 9–10, 22–23, 140, 190; policy, lack of urban, 215

New South, 27n10, 79

New Yorker, 31

New York Giants Stadium, 45

New York Times, 31, 34, 36

NIRA, 28n28, 36

Nixon, Edgar B., 183nn2,4

North Miami Recreation House, 50–51

Ockman, Joan, 117n44

Okeechobee, Lake, 16

Old South, 79, 84–87, 97–98

Olmstead, Fredrick Law, Jr., 164

Orange Bowl, 45, 46

Orr, Alexander, Jr., 132

Osceola, 88

Overseas Highway, 2, 23, 34–36, 57–64, *59*–*60*, 182; environmental impact of, 24, 58

Overtown, 17, 19, 22, 24–25, 189–90, 203

Vermeule, Adrian, 28n28

Vilet, C. K., 9

Villard, Oswald Garrison, 41, 68nn33,37

Virrick, Vladimir, 201, 202

Vivona, Alycia J., 27n18

Volstead Amendment, 9, 12

von Briesen, Hans, 66n5

Wagner, S. Peter, 129

Waldman, Max, 21, 22

Walker, Rev. S. D., 13–14

Wallace, Edward L., 162, 184nn12,21, 185n39

Wall Street Journal, 31

Watson, Forbes, 123

Weatherwax, Harold, 171

Weaver, Dumain, 53

Weaver, Robert C., 41, 68n38, 188, 217n5

Wegg, Talbott, 187–88, 198, 217nn2,3, 218nn8,18, 219nn26,39, 221n60

Welfare, 7–10, 110

West Palm Beach, 120, 146–51

Wetmore, James A., 128

Wheeler-Howard Act, 22–23, 140

Wilcox, J. Mark, 130

William, Beatrice Beyer, 129

Williams, M. B., 199, 200

Wirth, Conrad, 171

Wisser, Bill, 118n61

Walcott, Marion Post. *See* Post Walcott, Marion

Woodward, Dewing, 53

Woolner, David B., 183n1

Work. *See* Labor

Works Progress Administration (WPA), 2, 3, 31, 47–55, 71, 122

Wright, Henry, 201

WWFWPA, 31, 47

Wynwood Park Community Center, 51, 53

Yochelson, Bonnie, 114n1

You Have Seen Their Faces, 83

Youst, Al, 56

Zangara, Giuseppe, 35

Zimmy, Michael, 127, 153n14

The Florida History and Culture series

EDITED BY RAYMOND ARSENAULT AND GARY R. MORMINO

Al Burt's Florida: Snowbirds, Sand Castles, and Self-Rising Crackers, by Al Burt (1997)

Black Miami in the Twentieth Century, by Marvin Dunn (1997)

Gladesmen: Gator Hunters, Moonshiners, and Skiffers, by Glen Simmons and Laura Ogden (1998)

"Come to My Sunland": Letters of Julia Daniels Moseley from the Florida Frontier, 1882–1886, by Julia Winifred Moseley and Betty Powers Crislip (1998)

The Enduring Seminoles: From Alligator Wrestling to Ecotourism, by Patsy West (1998)

Government in the Sunshine State: Florida since Statehood, by David R. Colburn and Lance deHaven-Smith (1999)

The Everglades: An Environmental History, by David McCally (1999), first paperback edition, 2001

Beechers, Stowes, and Yankee Strangers: The Transformation of Florida, by John T. Foster Jr. and Sarah Whitmer Foster (1999)

The Tropic of Cracker, by Al Burt (1999)

Balancing Evils Judiciously: The Proslavery Writings of Zephaniah Kingsley, edited and annotated by Daniel W. Stowell (1999)

Hitler's Soldiers in the Sunshine State: German POWs in Florida, by Robert D. Billinger Jr. (2000)

Cassadaga: The South's Oldest Spiritualist Community, edited by John J. Guthrie, Phillip Charles Lucas, and Gary Monroe (2000)

Claude Pepper and Ed Ball: Politics, Purpose, and Power, by Tracy E. Danese (2000)

Pensacola during the Civil War: A Thorn in the Side of the Confederacy, by George F. Pearce (2000)

Castles in the Sand: The Life and Times of Carl Graham Fisher, by Mark S. Foster (2000)

Miami, U.S.A., by Helen Muir (2000)

Politics and Growth in Twentieth-Century Tampa, by Robert Kerstein (2001)

The Invisible Empire: The Ku Klux Klan in Florida, by Michael Newton (2001)

The Wide Brim: Early Poems and Ponderings of Marjory Stoneman Douglas, edited by Jack E. Davis (2002)

The Architecture of Leisure: The Florida Resort Hotels of Henry Flagler and Henry Plant, by Susan R. Braden (2002)

Florida's Space Coast: The Impact of NASA on the Sunshine State, by William Barnaby Faherty, S.J. (2002)

In the Eye of Hurricane Andrew, by Eugene F. Provenzo Jr. and Asterie Baker Provenzo (2002)

Florida's Farmworkers in the Twenty-first Century, text by Nano Riley and photographs by
Davida Johns (2003)

Making Waves: Female Activists in Twentieth-Century Florida, edited by Jack E. Davis and
Kari Frederickson (2003)

Orange Journalism: Voices from Florida Newspapers, by Julian M. Pleasants (2003)

The Stranahans of Ft. Lauderdale: A Pioneer Family of New River, by Harry A. Kersey Jr.
(2003)

*Death in the Everglades: The Murder of Guy Bradley, America's First Martyr to
Environmentalism*, by Stuart B. McIver (2003)

Jacksonville: The Consolidation Story, from Civil Rights to the Jaguars, by James B. Crooks
(2004)

The Seminole Wars: The Nation's Longest Indian Conflict, by John and Mary Lou Missall
(2004)

The Mosquito Wars: A History of Mosquito Control in Florida, by Gordon Patterson (2004)

The Seasons of Real Florida, by Jeff Klinkenberg (2004)

Land of Sunshine, State of Dreams: A Social History of Modern Florida, by Gary Mormino
(2005)

Paradise Lost? The Environmental History of Florida, edited by Jack E. Davis and Raymond
Arsenault (2005)

*Frolicking Bears, Wet Vultures, and Other Oddities: A New York City Journalist in
Nineteenth-Century Florida*, edited by Jerald T. Milanich (2005)

Waters Less Traveled: Exploring Florida's Big Bend Coast, by Doug Alderson (2005)

Saving South Beach, by M. Barron Stofik (2005)

Losing It All to Sprawl: How Progress Ate My Cracker Landscape, by Bill Belleville (2006)

Voices of the Apalachicola, edited by Faith Eidse (2006)

Floridian of His Century: The Courage of Governor LeRoy Collins, by Martin A. Dyckman
(2006)

America's Fortress: A History of Fort Jefferson, Dry Tortugas, Florida, by Thomas Reid (2006)

Weeki Wachee, City of Mermaids: A History of One of Florida's Oldest Roadside Attractions,
text by Lu Vickers and photograph compilation by Sara Dionne (2007)

*City of Intrigue, Nest of Revolution: A Documentary History of Key West in the Nineteenth
Century*, by Consuelo E. Stebbins (2007)

The New Deal in South Florida: Design, Policy, and Community Building, 1933–1940, edited
by John A. Stuart and John F. Stack Jr. (2008)